# Learning Informatica PowerCenter 10.x

## *Second Edition*

Enterprise data warehousing and intelligent data centers

**Rahul Malewar**

BIRMINGHAM - MUMBAI

# Learning Informatica PowerCenter 10.x

## *Second Edition*

First published: December 2014

Second edition: August 2017

Production reference: 1090817

Published by Packt Publishing Ltd.
Livery Place
35 Livery Street
Birmingham
B3 2PB, UK.
ISBN 978-1-78847-122-0

www.packtpub.com

# Credits

**Authors**
Rahul Malewar

**Reviewers**
Umamaheswaran

**Commissioning Editor**
Sunith Shetty

**Acquisition Editor**
Vinay Argekar

**Content Development Editor**
Jagruti Babaria

**Technical Editor**
Danish Shaikh

**Copy Editor**
Manisha Sinha

**Project Coordinator**
Manthan Patel

**Proofreader**
Safis Editing

**Indexer**
Tejal Daruwale Soni

**Graphics**
Tania Dutta

**Production Coordinator**
Deepika Naik

# About the Author

**Rahul Malewar** is a data warehouse consultant, providing Business Intelligence and Data Analytical solutions to customers. He has worked on various Data Warehousing tools for 10 years, majorly on Informatica Power Center--various versions of Informatica Power Center, from version 8.1 to the latest 10.1.0. He has experience of working on multiple real-time projects in a couple of MNCs, utilizing the skills acquired from which, he has written this book. He has been running his own training center named Learn Well Technocraft (www.dw-learnwell.com) for seven years now, wherein training on more than 25 Data warehousing, Cloud Computing, and Data Analytical technologies is provided over classroom, corporate, and online means. He has also written a blog on data warehousing concepts. As of today, he has provided training to more than 1,700 candidates, ranging from freshers to professionals with 20 years of experience in Informatica.

Rahul has also worked on Informatica cloud and has implemented projects on it. Apart from this, he has also provided training on Informatica cloud to big organizations such as monster.com (US).

He is the Director of a software development firm named Gut Lernen Technocraft Pvt. Ltd., where they work on data warehousing and mobile-related projects.

He provides free assistance on Informatica installation-related and other technical issues, for which he can be contacted at `info@dw-learnwell.com`.

# Acknowledgement

With the release of $2^{nd}$ book, I would like to dedicate the book to my 3 year young kid Swara for giving all the happiness and bringing lot of good charm to our family.

With this I also dedicate the book to my parents who took the pain of my childhood and helped me and understood all decision in my life.

Last but not the least, special thanks to my wife Swati, for understanding and standing along even when I am able to give her enough time.

Also a special Thanks to Packt publications for giving me opportunity to write the 2nd book and also to the reviewers and other members I worked while release of book.

And a big thanks to the readers of the Learning Informatica Power Center 9.x book for purchasing and liking the book. I hope you will like the latest release of book as well.

Wish you all the luck for future. Keep smiling and make others smile and make our mother earth a better place to live.

# About the Reviewer

**Umamaheswaran (Uma)** is the Founder & CEO of Ulagellam Pvt Ltd, a lecturer turned software engineer turned entrepreneur, Uma has 17+ years of experience in the Industry, served clients from Japan, United States & Middle East.

Uma worked as a software engineer in Citi Japan, Kaiser, Wells Fargo and with the mighty Yahoo at their headquarters in Sunnyvale, California.

Uma is a regular bootcamper, speaks less, listens more, loves to spend most of his time with his laptop, exploring new things and fighting with them :-)

Uma has also reviewed books on Drools Cookbook, Learning Informatica PowerCenter 9.x, Java Hibernate Cookbook reviewed latest video course on Getting started with Informatic from Packt publishing. For further details visit `http://ulagellam.com`

*Uma would like to thank his wife Chitra, his two kids Sivasweatha & Sivayogeith for their support and cooperation during the review.*

# www.PacktPub.com

For support files and downloads related to your book, please visit www.PacktPub.com.

Did you know that Packt offers eBook versions of every book published, with PDF and ePub files available? You can upgrade to the eBook version at www.PacktPub.com and as a print book customer, you are entitled to a discount on the eBook copy. Get in touch with us at service@packtpub.com for more details.

At www.PacktPub.com, you can also read a collection of free technical articles, sign up for a range of free newsletters and receive exclusive discounts and offers on Packt books and eBooks.

https://www.packtpub.com/mapt

Get the most in-demand software skills with Mapt. Mapt gives you full access to all Packt books and video courses, as well as industry-leading tools to help you plan your personal development and advance your career.

## Why subscribe?

- Fully searchable across every book published by Packt
- Copy and paste, print, and bookmark content
- On demand and accessible via a web browser

# Customer Feedback

Thanks for purchasing this Packt book. At Packt, quality is at the heart of our editorial process. To help us improve, please leave us an honest review on this book's Amazon page at https://www.amazon.com/dp/1788471229.

If you'd like to join our team of regular reviewers, you can e-mail us at customerreviews@packtpub.com. We award our regular reviewers with free eBooks and videos in exchange for their valuable feedback. Help us be relentless in improving our products!

# Table of Contents

# Preface

In lines with the release of book Learning Informatica PowerCenter 10.1.0, we have tried to present a technology in its most simple form to the readers. We have tried to explain every aspect for new learners of Informatica. Also, we have covered everything for the users of the older version to upgrade to the latest version. This book covers everything, from basics, such as downloading, extraction, and installation, to working on the client tools and then high-level aspects such as scheduling, migration, performance optimization, and so on in simple words. The use of this book will eliminate the need to browse multiple blogs available on the internet that talk about Informatica tool. What you get in this book is everything from start to end; using this book, you can develop and deploy end-to-end projects on Informatica. In this book, you will get the step-by-step procedure for every aspect of Informatica Power Center Tool. Informatica Corporation (Informatica), a multimillion dollar company incorporated in February 1993, is an independent provider of enterprise data integration and data quality software and services. The company enables a variety of complex enterprise data integration products, which include Power Center, Power Exchange, enterprise data integration, data quality, master data management, business-to-business (B2B) data exchange, application information life cycle management, complex event processing, ultra messaging, and cloud data integration. You are going to learn the latest version of Power Center tool of Informatica in this book. Power Center is the most widely used tool of Informatica across the globe for various data integration processes. Informatica Power Center tool helps integration of data from almost any business system in almost any format. This flexibility of Power Center to handle almost any data makes it the most widely used tool in the data integration world. While writing this book, we kept in mind the importance of live practical exposure of the graphical interface of the tool to the audience, and hence, you will notice a lot of screenshots illustrating the steps to help you understand and follow the process. We have added images depicting every step that you can follow and practice on your own in your machine. You will also get all the screenshots of the installation procedure, which is totally changed from its previous version. We have also provided a lot of real-life examples to help you understand the development aspects in detail. Each concept in the book is self-explanatory, with the precise screenshot of each step. The arrangement of chapters is such that by the end of the book, you will have complete knowledge--from installation to development skills. Let's take small gist of the contents of the book.

# What this book covers

Chapter 1, *Downloading and Extracting Informatica PowerCenter Software*, describes the detailed steps for the installation process starting from the steps of downloading the software, extracting the software, installing the software and configuring the latest version of software.

Chapter 2, *Understanding Admin Console*, this chapter we will learn the Administrator console of Power Center tool and learn about different services. This chapter talks about creating and configuring various services and also talks about the creation of user for working on Informatica client tool.

Chapter 3, *Understanding Designer Screen and its Components*, talks about the basics of the Informatica Power Center Designer client tool. You will learn you use most widely used components available on the screen. The chapter also talks about working of the Source files and Source tables and similarly talks about working on targets. We have covered the steps which will help you understand how you can import/create flat files and Relational Databases tables. Also the most important aspect of Informatica Power Center tool, Mappings has been covered in the chapter. We have described in details the steps required to create a mapping. By the end of this chapter you will have clear idea about the look and feel of the Power Center Designer Screen.

Chapter 4, *The Lifeline of Informatica - The Transformations* is meant for the most important aspect of Informatica Power Center tool, the transformations. We will talk about various types of transformations in this chapter. Every transformation performs a specific functionality and these are the most important aspect of ETL tools. We will implement the mapping using each transformation so that you get to understand each and every transformation in details. Also we will end this chapter with the classifications of the transformation, different types of cache memories available in Informatica and different tracing levels.

Chapter 5, *Using the Designer Screen – Advanced Features*, talks about the advanced topics of the Designer screen. This chapter is an extension of the Chapter 3. When you work on mappings you usually will need to Debug the process to find the error in your code. Debugger helps you achieve that in very easy manner. We have added a section which will completely help you understand the process to setup the Debugger and steps to use Debugger. The next topic in this chapter talks about the reusable transformation which allows you to reuse the transformations across multiple mapping. On similar lines is Mapplet which is group of reusable transformations. Then we will talk about the Target Load plan, a functionality which allows you to load data in multiple targets in a same mapping maintaining their constraints. It's a very high level concept which you may not need regularly. Also we have touch based on the Compare Objects functionality of the Designer Screen, this allows you to compare objects across the repository.

Chapter 6, *Implementing SCD – Using Designer Screen Wizards,* covers a single but very important aspect of Data Warehousing, i.e. SCD. We have made a separate chapter for this because this is most important aspect and frequently used concept in Data Warehousing. In this chapter we have outlined the steps required to create a SCD mapping using the wizards in Power Center. We will see the implementation of SCD1, SCD2 and SCD3 using wizards. You should be clear with the Data Warehousing concepts to understand this implementation.

Chapter 7, *Using the Workflow Manager Screen,* describes the basics of the Workflow Manager screen. This is the second and last phase of our development work. We will get to learn the different option present on the Workflow Manager screen. We will learn to create session task and workflows. We will also see various connections like Relations, FTP etc. which can be created in Workflow Manager screen. We will also learn to execute the workflow. Last topic of the chapter describes about the connections which can be created for database purpose.

Chapter 8, *Learning various tasks in Workflow Manager Screen*, will teach you the advanced concepts of the Workflow Manager screen. This chapter describes various tasks present in the workflow manager screen. Tasks are the basic building blocks of the workflow as we have transformations in Designer screen. We will also see to make the reusable tasks and Mapplets.

Chapter 9, *Advanced features of Workflow Manager Screen,* We will see some very important concepts called as Scheduling, Parameter Files, File List and Incremental Aggregation.

Chapter 10, *Working with Workflow Monitor Screen*, Monitoring the code describes the Workflow Manager screen of Power Center. This screen allows the monitoring of the process we execute in the Workflow Manager. We will see different log files, status and statistics in the Monitor screen.

Chapter 11, *The Deployment Phase - Using the Repository Manager* is going to teach you about the fourth client screen Repository Manager. Repository Manager is basically used for Migration (Deployment) purpose. We will see various options to migrate the code from one environment to other. Also we will see how to create the folder in client screen.

Chapter 12, *Optimization - The Performance Tuning*, has the contents for the optimizations of various components of Informatica Power Center tool like Source, targets, Mappings, Sessions, Systems. Performance tuning at high level involves 2 stages, finding the issues called as Bottleneck and resolving them.

# What you need for this book

Before you make your mind to learn Informatica, it is always recommended that you have basic understanding of SQL and Unix. Though these are not mandatory and without knowledge of those you can easily 90% of Informatica Power Center tool, to have confidence to work in real time project SQL and Unix is must to have in your kitty. The people who know SQL will easily understand that ETL tools are nothing but the graphical representation of SQL. Unix is utilized in Informatica Power Center with the scripting aspect which makes your life easy at some scenarios.

# Who this book is for

Anybody who can read English can use this book…hahahah!!! Jokes apart anyone who wishes to make career in Data Warehousing or Informatica must go for this book. If you are College graduate, IT professional working in other technologies, university professors – This is for you.

# Conventions

In this book, you will find a number of text styles that distinguish between different kinds of information. Here are some examples of these styles and an explanation of their meaning.

Code words in text, database table names, folder names, filenames, file extensions, path names, dummy URLs, user input, and Twitter handles are shown as follows: "We are using `EMP_SRC_FILE` as reference to import the fixed width file".

**New terms** and **important** words are shown in bold. Words that you see on the screen, for example, in menus or dialog boxes, appear in the text like this: "Clicking the **Next** button moves you to the next screen."

Warnings or important notes appear in a box like this.

Tips and tricks appear like this.

# Reader feedback

Feedback from our readers is always welcome. Let us know what you think about this book—what you liked or disliked. Reader feedback is important for us as it helps us develop titles that you will really get the most out of.

To send us general feedback, simply e-mail feedback@packtpub.com, and mention the book's title in the subject of your message.

If there is a topic that you have expertise in and you are interested in either writing or contributing to a book, see our author guide at www.packtpub.com/authors.

# Errata

Although we have taken every care to ensure the accuracy of our content, mistakes do happen. If you find a mistake in one of our books—maybe a mistake in the text or the code—we would be grateful if you could report this to us. By doing so, you can save other readers from frustration and help us improve subsequent versions of this book. If you find any errata, please report them by visiting http://www.packtpub.com/submit-errata, selecting your book, clicking on the Errata Submission Form link, and entering the details of your errata. Once your errata are verified, your submission will be accepted and the errata will be uploaded to our website or added to any list of existing errata under the Errata section of that title.

To view the previously submitted errata, go to `https://www.packtpub.com/books/content/support` and enter the name of the book in the search field. The required information will appear under the Errata section.

# Piracy

Piracy of copyrighted material on the Internet is an ongoing problem across all media. At Packt, we take the protection of our copyright and licenses very seriously. If you come across any illegal copies of our works in any form on the Internet, please provide us with the location address or website name immediately so that we can pursue a remedy.

Please contact us at `copyright@packtpub.com` with a link to the suspected pirated material.

We appreciate your help in protecting our authors and our ability to bring you valuable content.

# Questions

If you have a problem with any aspect of this book, you can contact us at `questions@packtpub.com`, and we will do our best to address the problem.

# 1
# Downloading and Extracting Informatica PowerCenter Software

In this chapter, you will learn about the various aspects of Informatica's installation, including server and client configuration. You will also learn about the various steps for downloading the correct and latest version of Informatica PowerCenter 10.1.0. This chapter will also teach you how to properly extract the downloaded `.zip` files.

Let's kick-start learning about the latest offering of Informatica.

# Downloading the latest version of Informatica PowerCenter - 10.1.0

To initiate the installation, we will first need to acquire the correct version of the software. The best place to download the Informatica software from for training purposes is the eDelivery website of Oracle. Please perform the following steps to download the latest version (10.1.0) of Informatica PowerCenter:

1. Visit `https://edelivery.oracle.com`:

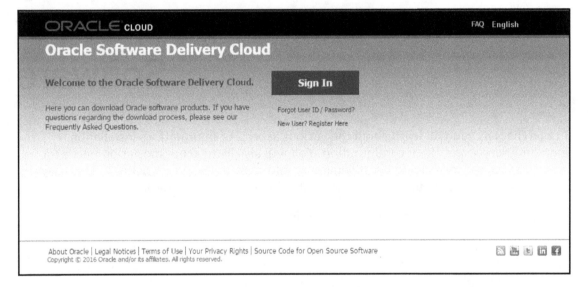

2. Click on **Sign In** to get access to a wide range of software, including Informatica PowerCenter. Log in with valid credentials. If you do not have an account, register for free and create an account with Oracle:

3. Once you have logged in with valid credentials, accept the Oracle terms and conditions, and click on **Continue**. This will take you to the next screen, shown in the following screenshot:

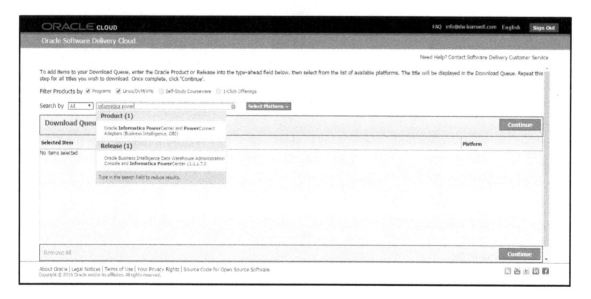

4. To download the Informatica PowerCenter software, start typing **informatica powerCenter** in the search box as shown in the previous screenshot. The matching results will start appearing.

5. Select the option called **Oracle Business Intelligence Data Warehouse Administration Console and Informatica PowerCenter 11.1.1.7.0**.

6. After you have selected the previous option, select platform based on your operating system. We are selecting Microsoft Windows x64 (64-bit). After you have selected the appropriate platform from the drop-down menu, click on **Select**:

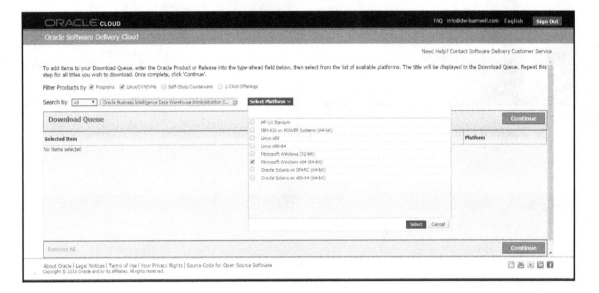

 Please note that Informatica PowerCenter 10.1 is only available for the 64-bit operating system. You will not be able to use 32-bit machines to install version 10.1.

7. The next screen will allow you to confirm your selection as shown in the following screenshot. Make sure the option selected is correct, and click on **Continue**:

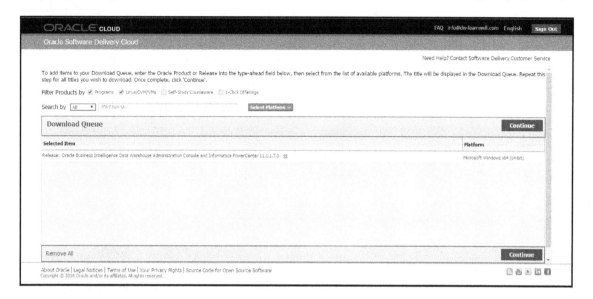

8. The next screen will present you with details about the option you selected for download as shown in the following screenshot. Click on **Continue** to go to the next screen:

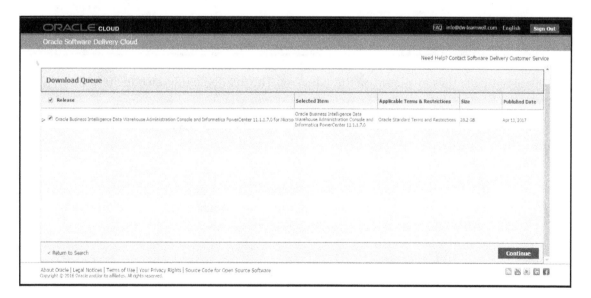

9. You will see the terms and conditions and license agreement details. Please read the details carefully as shown in following screenshot, and tick the **I have reviewed and accept the terms and commercial License, Special Program License, and/or Trial License** option, and click on **Continue**.

10. On the next screen, you will see list of compressed `.zip` files, which you need to download for Informatica PowerCenter:

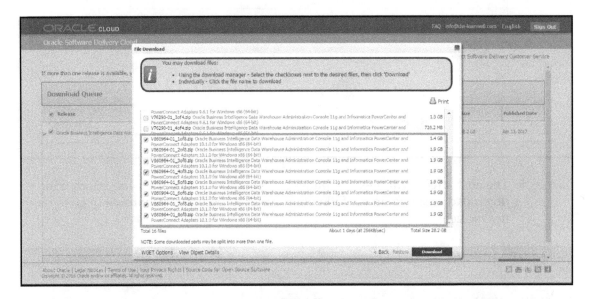

There are multiple files available on the window. The available files also include the compressed files for **Informatica PowerCenter version 9.6.1**.

Select the files as shown in the previous screenshot download the latest version of **Informatica PowerCenter: 10.1.0**. A total of eight files needs to be downloaded to get the complete software.

 Please note that you can select individual files or all eight files together for download. Oracle frequently changes the names of the files. Please make sure you read the description of the files properly before you download.

Once you have selected the eight files properly, as shown in the previous screenshot, click on the **Download** button. Once you have clicked on **Download**, the website will ask you to download and install the download manager.

Since the size of the files is more, depending on your internet connection speed the files may take some time to download. To avoid issues such as an error in downloading the file because of internet connectivity issues, it is recommended to download the files using the download manager.

After the download manager has been downloaded and installed, it will ask you to select the folder where you want your Informatica PowerCenter 10.1.0 files to be saved. Select the folder of your choice.

With this, our download process is complete, and we have acquired a valid license and software for the latest version of Informatica PowerCenter 10.1.0.

# Extracting the downloaded files - preparing the installable

Once the download process is over, you will have eight `.zip` files available for Informatica PowerCenter 10.1.0 as shown in the following screenshot:

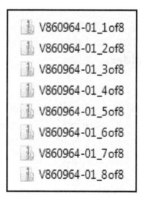

To avoid any confusion with the files later in the installation process, create a separate folder for the Informatica downloaded files. We are using `D:\` as the folder for reference. Also, make sure you have sufficient space available (approximately 35 GB).

We will now start extracting the files. Extracting the files in the correct way is important for proper installation. If the files are not extracted correctly, the installation will fail at a later stage. It is recommended that you use the WinRAR software for extraction.

Right-click on the first file V860964-01_1of8, and extract the file in the same folder D:\. Similarly, right-click on other files from V860964-01_2of8 to V860964-01_8 individually, and extract the files in the D:\ folder. The extracted files will look as shown in the following screenshot:

After you finish extracting all the eight downloaded .zip files, right-click on dac_win_11g_infa_win_64bit_101, and extract the file in the same folder D:\. You will get multiple files extracted in the folder.

The next step is to extract the 1010_Server_Installer_wimem-64t and 1010_Client_Installer_wimem-64t files. Right-click on 1010_Server_Installer_wimem-64t, and extract to the D:\1010_Server_Installer_wimem-64t folder. Similarly, right-click on the 1010_Client_Installer_wimem-64t file, and extract to the D:\1010_Client_Installer_wimem-64t folder. This gives you the final folder structure required for installation, as shown in the following screenshot:

This completes the download and extraction process, and we can proceed with the installation process.

The `Oracle_America_Inc-OEM-V101-Prod_0115939_136933.key` license key required for the installation is present in the extracted folder.

# Informatica installation - the prerequisites

Please be careful while you are doing the installation as any issues with the minimum system requirements might hamper the Informatica PowerCenter installation process and you might have to re-initiate the complete installation.

The following points show some prechecks that you need to do before initiating the installation:

- **Operating system**: Informatica PowerCenter can be installed on Windows-based operating systems or UNIX-based operating systems. Informatica releases different versions of software for different UNIX-based operating systems. For all Windows operating systems, we have a common installable. In this book, we will refer to the Windows operating system.
- **Database**: Informatica PowerCenter requires a database for configuration. Make sure you have installed a database (Oracle, Microsoft SQL Server, or DB2). In this book, we will refer to Oracle the a database. The installation process requires two different database users. Please make sure you create two database users with all admin privileges. In this book, we are using **SYSTEM** as one user and **HR** as the other user.
- **System requirements**: We need to check the system capabilities before we proceed with the installation. Informatica recommends 6 GB of RAM for the installation, but practically even 2 GB of RAM works well. The difference shows up in the processing, but it won't hamper the installation process.

Also, approximately 35 GB of hard disk space will be required for the downloaded, extracted, and installed files and folders.

Before downloading the Informatica software, please check whether your machine is a 32-bit or 64-bit one. Informatica 10.1.0 version can be installed only on a 64-bit machine as against previous versions of Informatica, which can be installed on 32-bit and 64-bit machines.

Once you have checked the minimum system requirements, we are all set to take the next step towards installation.

# Beginning the installation - installing the server

The Informatica installation requires the installation of the server and the client separately. It is always recommended that you install the server first and then the client.

The installable file for the server can be located by navigating to the folder where you extracted the files. We are using the D:\1010_Server_Installer_winem-64t\Server folder . Navigate to D:\1010_Server_Installer_winem-64t\Server | **Server** | **install** as shown in the following screenshot:

Perform the following steps to complete the installation process:

1. Double-click on **install** to start the installation. In some cases, the file can be present as install.exe. This will initiate the installation process for Informatica PowerCenter.

2. Choose the installation type. If you are installing the Informatica software for the first time, select **Install Informatica 10.1.0**. To upgrade to the latest version from previous versions, select **Upgrade to Informatica 10.1.0**. Also accept the terms and conditions. After you have selected the appropriate option, click on **Next**, as indicated in the following screenshot:

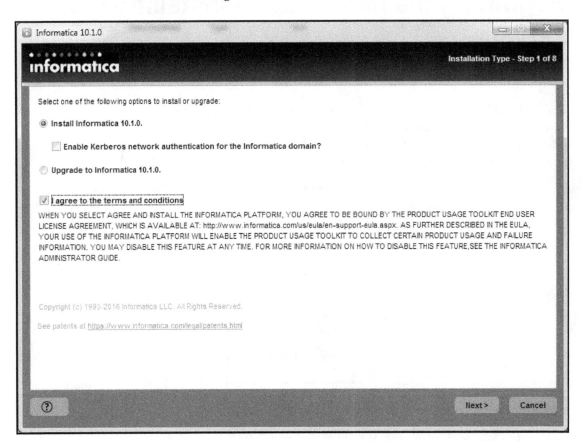

3. On the next screen, verify the prerequisites for installation as shown in following screenshot. Please make sure your machine satisfies all the prerequisites for installation. Click on **Next**:

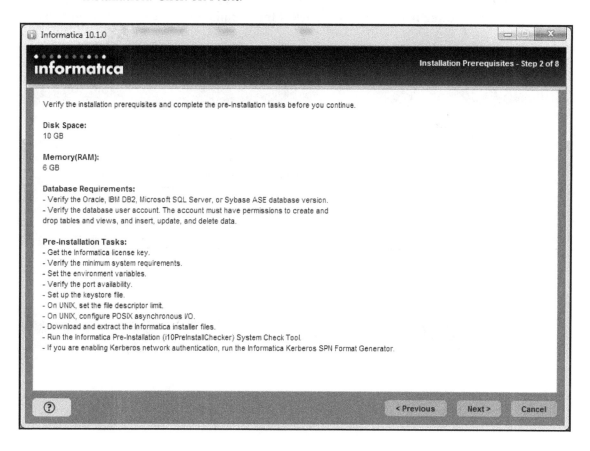

4. The next step, as shown in the following screenshot, is to enter the license key. The license key can be located in the `D:\ Oracle_America_Inc-OEM-V101-Prod_0115939_136933.key` extraction folder. If you are not able to navigate to the path, directly paste the path. Select the installation directory. Click on **Next**:

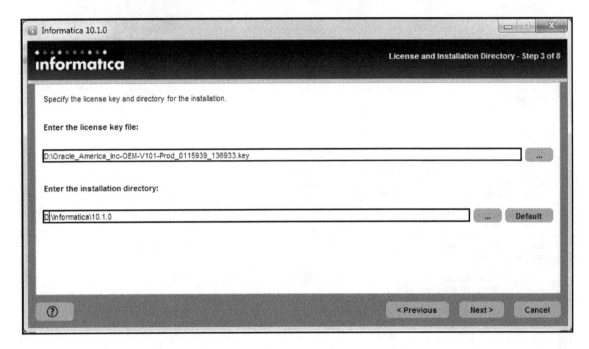

5. The next screen will show a pre-installation summary as shown in the following screenshot:

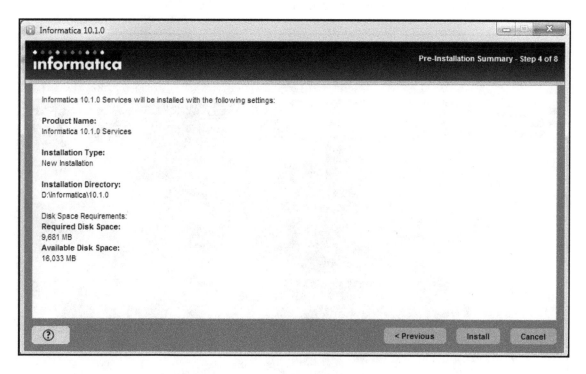

6. Please check the details, and click on **Install**.

7. The installation process will begin as shown in the following screenshot. It will take a few minutes before your installation finishes. The installation time depends on your system configuration:

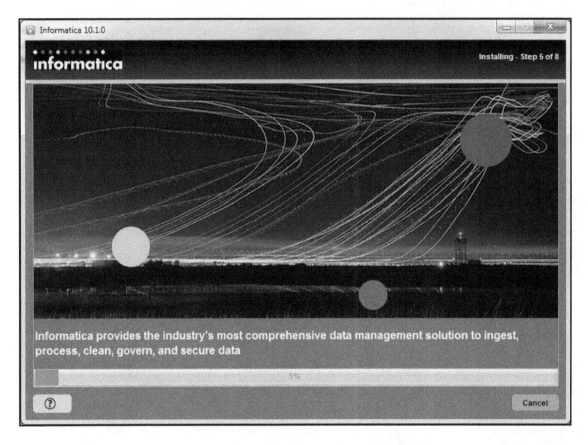

8. When the installation finishes, we will proceed to the next process: configuring the domain and node.

# Configuring the domain and node

Once the server installation has been completed, the next screen will allow you to configure the domain and node. The domain and nodes are very important components of the Informatica PowerCenter architecture. We will be learning about the architecture and related components in the next chapter.

Perform the following steps to configure the domain and node:

1. If you are doing a fresh installation, select **Create a domain** as shown in the following screenshot. This will initiate the process to create a new domain. If you are upgrading, you can select the **Join a domain** option.

2. Also check the **Enable HTTPS for Informatica Administrator** option. Make sure port 8443 is not utilized by any other process. In most cases, port 8443 will be used as the default, so you need not worry about the port number. Check the option Use a keystore file generated by the installer. Please refer to the following screenshot:

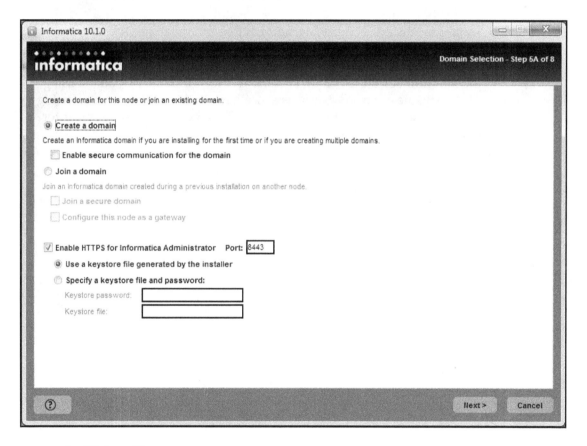

3. Click on **Next**.

4. In the next step, we will configure the domain with the database. Please select the appropriate option:

- **Database type**: Depending on what database (Oracle, SQL, or DB2) you are using, please select the appropriate option. In this book, we are using Oracle as our database.
- **Database user ID**: Mention the database user that you created for the domain configuration. In this book, we are using SYSTEM as the Oracle user.
- **Password**: Specify the password for the database. We are using oracle as our password in this book.
- **Database address**: Mention the address for your database. The address consists of the hostname and the port number, that is, `hostname:portnumber`, where the hostname is your computer name, and the port number is the default port number for the database you are using. The hostname can also be used as a localhost. In this book, we are referring to the database address as localhost:1522. 1522 is the default port number for Oracle 11g.
- **Database service name**: Specify the service name for your database connection; in this book, we are using it as orcl.

Leave the rest of the properties as they are not mandatory. Please refer to the following screenshot for reference:

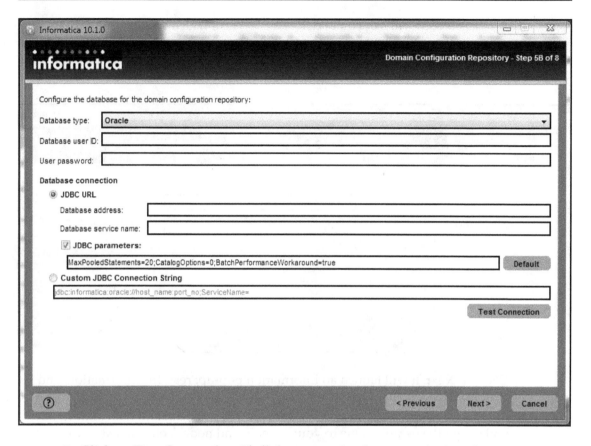

5. Click on **Test Connection**. If all the properties that you mentioned are correct, the database connection will be successful, and we can proceed with the next step. If the connection fails, please recheck your database configuration details, and test them again. After the connection check is successful, click on **Next**.

6. The next screen will ask you to define a keyword, which will be used for the purpose of encryption. Specify the keyword and path you want to set. By default, you can use the default path mentioned by Informatica as shown in the following following screenshot:

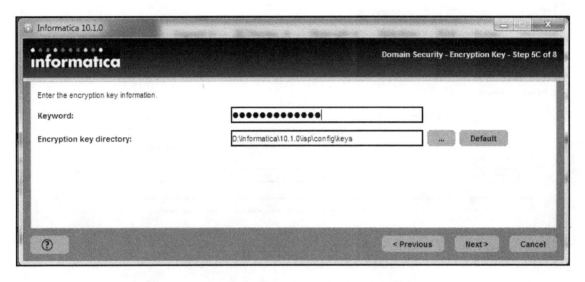

7. Click on **Next**. It will launch an information pop-up; read the information, and click on **OK**.

8. In the next screen, you can assign a name to your domain and node. Informatica will assign the default name to your domain and node. You can leave those unchanged. If you wish to change the name, please do so. Also specify the password of your choice in the domain password and confirm password field.

 Informatica 10.1.0 has added a new feature called Model Repository Service in the architecture of Informatica. You can create the service while defining the domain name in this option; alternatively, it can be configured later from the Administration console of Informatica.

9. As of now, uncheck Configure Model Repository Service and Data Integration Service as shown in the following screenshot:

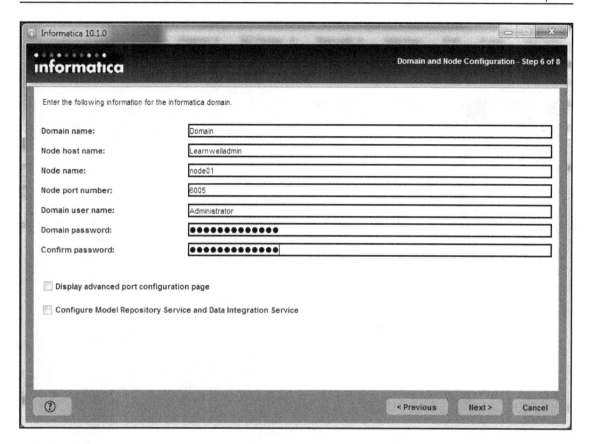

 Please note this domain user name and password will be used to log in into the Informatica Administration console.

10. Click on the **Next** button.

11. On the next screen, uncheck the **Run Informatica under a different user account** option, and click on **Next** as indicated in the following screenshot:

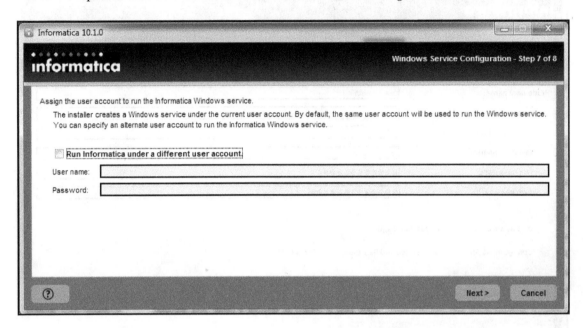

12. The next screen indicates that the installation is complete. Please check the post-installation summary. You can keep those details for your future reference. Please check the following screenshot for reference:

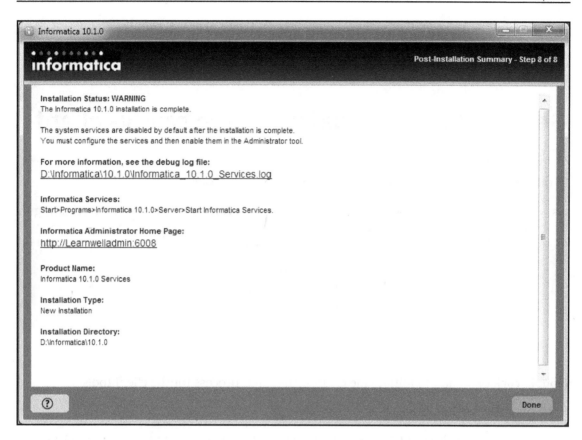

Please note that, if you see the installation status as WARNING, there is nothing to worry about. The status is showing as WARNING because some services that are configured may not be running, and we have not configured one of the services, that is, model repository.

13. Click on **Done**.

With this, our server installation is complete. We will now proceed with the client installation, which is simple and straightforward and not as complicated as the server installation.

# Getting the graphical interface ready- client installation

In this section, we will discuss the installation of the client tools.

As with the installation of the server, you will need to locate the installable by navigating to `D:\1010_Client_Installer_winem-64t | Client | Install`. In some cases, the filename can be `install.exe`, as shown in the following screenshot:

Double-click on **install** to initiate the client installation process for the client tools.

Perform the following steps:

1. Select the **Install Informatica 10.1.0 Clients** or **Upgrade to Informatica 10.1.0 Clients** option as shown in the following screenshot. Select the **Install Informatica 10.1.0 Clients** installation type if you are doing a fresh installation, or select **Upgrade to Informatica 10.1.0 Clients** to upgrade to the latest version:

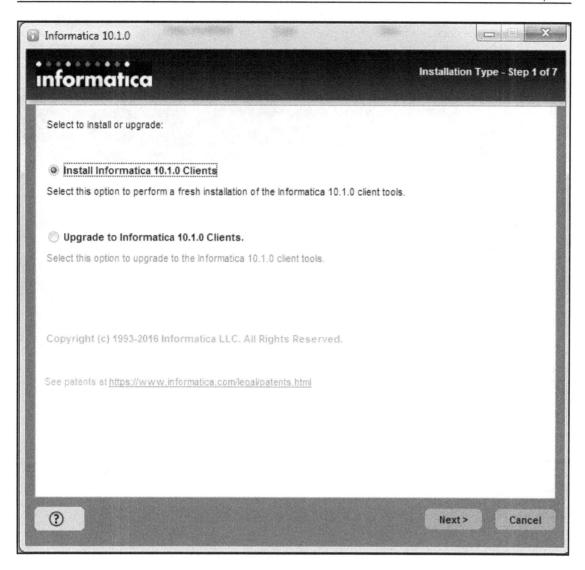

2. Click on **Next**.

3. Please check the installation prerequisites for the PowerCenter client tool as shown in the following screenshot:

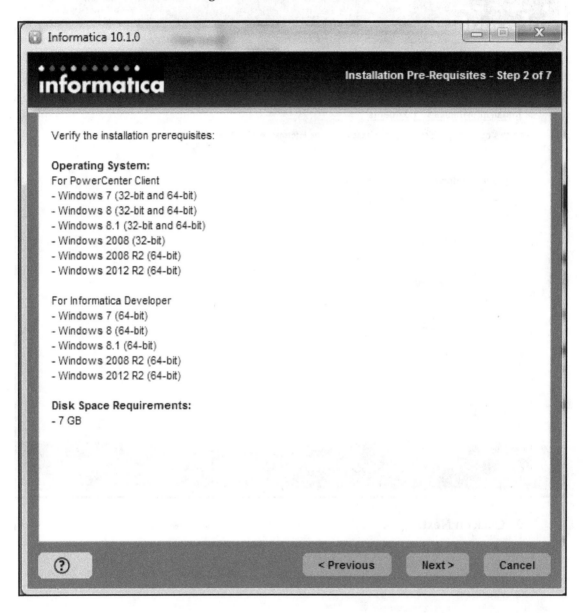

4. Verify the details, and click on **Next**.

5. On the Application Client Selection screen, select **Informatica Developer** and **PowerCenter Client** as shown in the following screenshot. Click on **Next**:

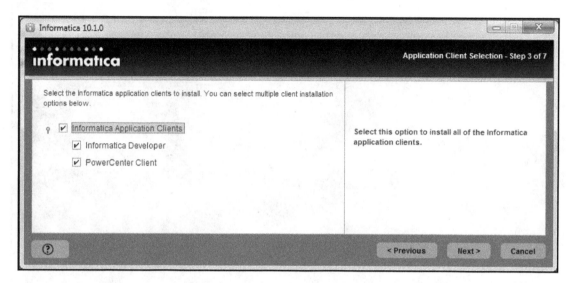

6. Enter the installation directory. You can select the same installation directory where you installed the server. Please make sure you have sufficient space in the directory. Click on **Next**:

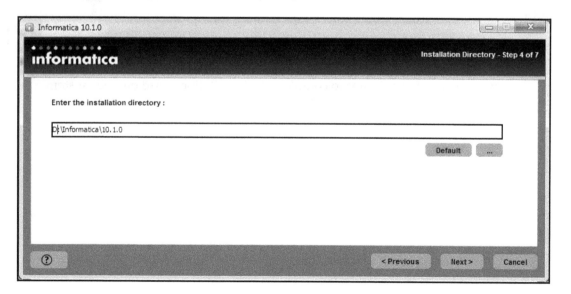

7. Cross-check the pre-installation summary, and click on **Install** to start the client installation process, as shown in the following screenshot:

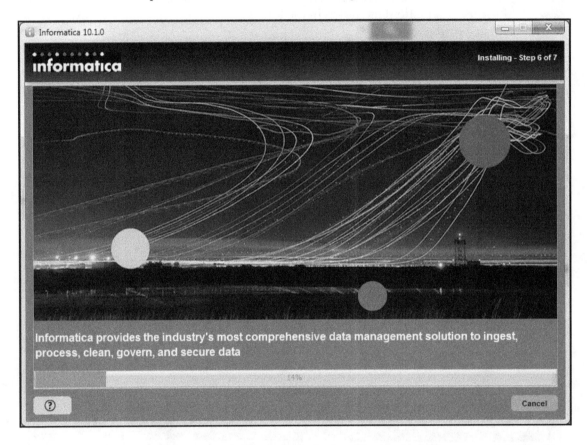

8. It will take a few minutes to complete the installation based on your system configuration.

9. Once the installation process is complete, you will get the **Post-Installation Summary** screen. Check the summary, in the following screenshot:

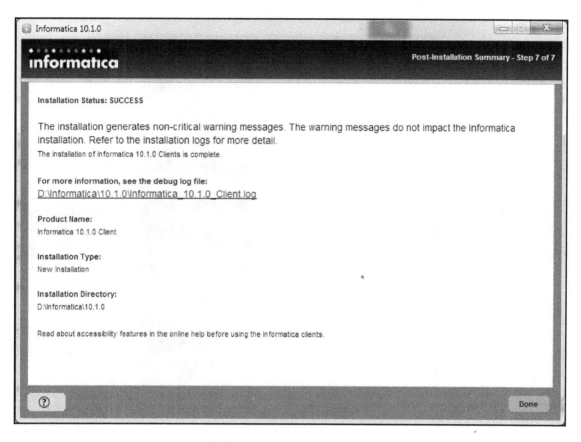

10. Click on **Done** to finish the client installation process.

With this, the installation of the server and client is complete. You will be able to see the newly installed programs in your Start menu on Windows, as shown in the following screenshot:

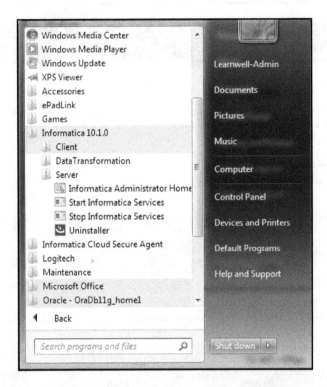

# Summary

In this chapter, we started by acquiring the files that can be installed from the Oracle e-delivery website. Later in the chapter, we learned how to extract the files properly. The later part of the chapter helped us install the server and client on our machine.

In the next chapter, we will learn about configuring various services in **Informatica Administration Console**. We will learn about the various services available in the administrator console in Informatica.

# Understanding Admin Console

**2**

In the previous chapter, we completed the installation of the Informatica PowerCenter server and client. You learned how to properly download and extract files for the purpose of installation.

In this chapter, you will be learning about the various aspects of Informatica Administration Console and other services, and also how to configure the complete administration section.

Before we move into configuring the Administration Console, let's take a look at the various services necessary to work on Informatica PowerCenter. Once we understand the services and architecture, we will start configuring the services.

## The Informatica architecture

PowerCenter has a service-oriented architecture, which gives it the ability to scale services and share resources across multiple machines. High availability functionality helps minimize service downtime due to unexpected failures or scheduled maintenance in the PowerCenter environment. To understand the architecture of Informatica PowerCenter, we will discuss the various components that form the Informatica architecture.

The Informatica architecture is divided into two sections: server and client.

The server setup can be done on Windows or UNIX operating systems, while the client installation can only be done on the Windows operating system. As a best practice, we should always install the server first and then the client.

Server is the basic administrative unit of Informatica, where we configure all the services, create users, and assign authentication. Client is the graphical interface provided to the users. Client includes Designer, Workflow Manager, Workflow Monitor, and Repository Manager.

The Informatica domain is the primary and centralized unit for the management and administration of the various services available.

The components of the Informatica PowerCenter Administrator Console are explored in the following sections.

# Domain

The domain is the first thing to be created when you start the installation process. The following points describe a domain:

- Domain is a fundamental and primary administrative unit in PowerCenter. It is a collection of nodes and services.
- There will only be a single domain for each license that you purchase.
- Usually, the domain is installed over a common server, which is accessed by software-sharing applications, such as Citrix.
- Domain configuration requires database connectivity. We will be using the Oracle Database and a SYSTEM user for domain configuration.
- When you purchase the software, you install the server over a common server, which becomes your domain and can be accessed via the client from multiple machines. The server is not installed on the personal system, which gives it the flexibility to share resources across multiple machines. The domain takes the name of the common server computer.
- A relational database is mandatory to configure the domain. The domain uses the relational database to store configuration information and user account privileges and permissions.

# Node

After the domain configuration, the node gets configured. The following points describe a node:

- It is a representation of a server running the PowerCenter Server software.
- It is a logical representation of a machine in a domain.
- The node takes the name of your machine.
- Only one node is possible per license.
- One node in the domain acts as a gateway to receive service requests from clients and route them to the appropriate service and node.
- Services and processes run on nodes in a domain.
- There are two types of nodes that are configured--worker node and gateway node.
- Gateway node is created when you install Informatica. When we installed Informatica Server in the previous chapter, a default node was created; that node will act as the gateway node.
- The machine on which the domain is configured will be used as the gateway node.
- When you install the Informatica services on other machines, you create additional gateway nodes or worker nodes which you join to the domain.
- One gateway node serves as the master gateway node for the domain. The master gateway node receives service requests from clients and routes them to the appropriate service and node.
- A worker node is any node not configured to serve as a gateway. A worker node can run application services, but it cannot serve as a gateway. The service manager performs limited domain operations on a worker node.

The following figure represents the domain and node configuration:

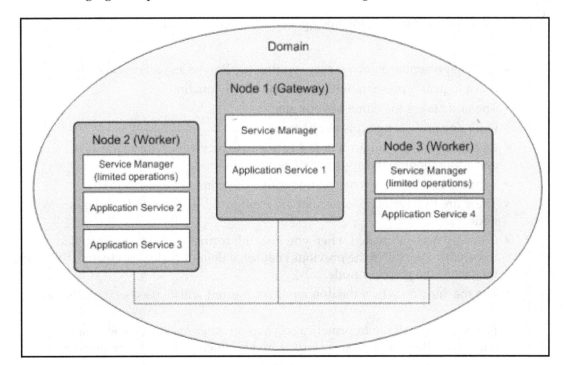

# Informatica services

Informatica services include various services that start the service manager on individual nodes.

# The service manager

The service manager is the component that starts and runs the application services on the node in a domain.

# Repository

The repository is the component that stores the metadata that is created when you work on client tools. The following points describe a repository:

- It is a centralized database of Informatica PowerCenter, which is used to store the metadata that is created when the code is designed in client tools.
- When you wish to access the existing components created in the PowerCenter client, the metadata is fetched from the repository and is displayed on the client screen.
- The repository is created in the database, which is used for installation purposes.
- Multiple repositories can be created under a domain, with each repository representing a single environment. For example, the REPO_DEV repository represents the development environment, REPO_TEST represents the test environment, and REPO_PROD represents the production environment.

# Repository services

In repository services, each service manages only one repository. All the communication with the repository (for example, from the designer or when running workflows) is managed by the repository service.

# Integration services

An integration service provides the connection required for the data flow. Integration services have the following uses:

- They manage the running of workflows and sessions in the client screen.
- They provide the services required for the flow of data from the source to the target through Informatica.
- Integration services enable the extraction of data from the source, transformations in Informatica, and loading into the target. It makes the path for data flow from the source to the target.
- One integration service is sufficient to handle different types of sources and targets.

# Model repository service

The model repository service is similar to the repository service. The difference is that it stores the metadata created in the the Informatica Developer Tool and Analyst Tool. The Developer Tool and Analyst Tool are different from the PowerCenter tool, and hence, out of the scope of this book.

Apart from these services, there are numerous other services and configuration stuff that an Informatica Administrator needs to create and set up. For our purposes, wherein our major focus is on development activities, the previously mentioned services and configuration details are sufficient.

Let's move on to create the various services in the administrator console.

# The Administration Console - configuration

The Informatica administration home page is the single place where all Informatica components can be created and configured. The Administration Console home page opens in the web browser. It does not require an internet connection. You can use any browser to open the admin console. You might need to check the browser settings if the administrator home page will not open. Based on your system configuration and settings, you might need to try using a different browser.

Perform the following steps to configure the Informatica components:

1. Informatica Administrator Home Page can be located under **All Programs** in your **Start** menu.
2. Navigate to **Start** I **All Programs** I **Informatica 10.1.0** I **Server** I **Informatica Administrator Home Page**:

    This will open Informatica Administrator in your default web browser.

3. Log in to the Informatica Administrator using the username and password that you defined when creating the domain.

In this book, we are using the default username `Administrator`, and the password is **Administrator**:

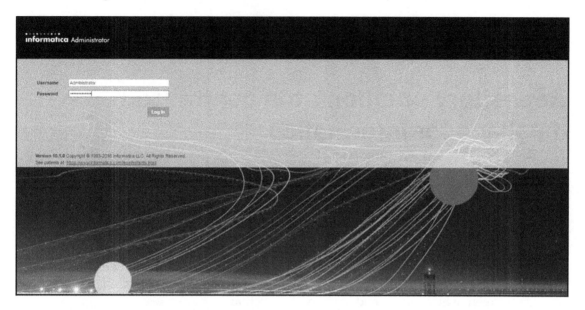

4. Click on **Log In**.
5. Once you log in, you will see the following screen:

Spare a few minutes to view all the options present on the screen. Try browsing through the various options available.

Our next process is to create and configure the various PowerCenter components, which we discussed in the preceding section.

# Repository creation - the centralized database for Informatica

Our first step is to create a repository. As mentioned earlier in the book, the repository is the centralized database of Informatica, which is used to store metadata generated in the client tools.

To create the first repository, follow the process mentioned in the preceding section. Refer to the following screenshot.

1. Click on the **Services and Nodes** option. You will be presented with various services. You will see the domain name and the node name on the left side of the screen, which we created in the earlier section:

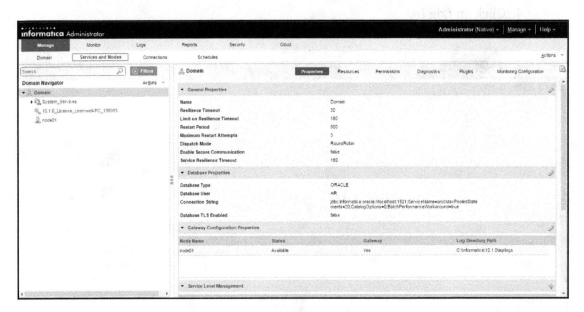

2. Navigate to **Domain** under **Domain Navigator** I **Actions** I **New** I **PowerCenter Repository Service...**:

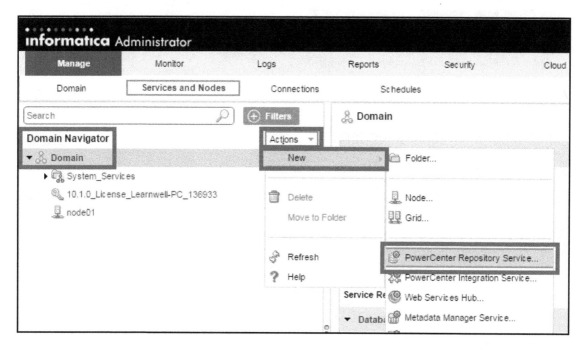

3. This will open a pop-up window, which will allow you to provide details for creating the repository, as shown in the following points. Insert the details:

- **Repository name**: Add the name of the repository. You can specify any name as per your wish. We are using REPO for our reference in this book.

- **Description**: Write a description of the repository. This is an optional field.

- **Location**: Specify the domain name we created earlier. The domain name we created earlier will appear by default, as we currently have only one domain.

- **License**: Select the license key from the drop-down list. This is the default key, as we have only one key.

- **Node**: Specify the node name from the drop-down list. This is the default key, as we have only one key.

The details are shown in the following screenshot:

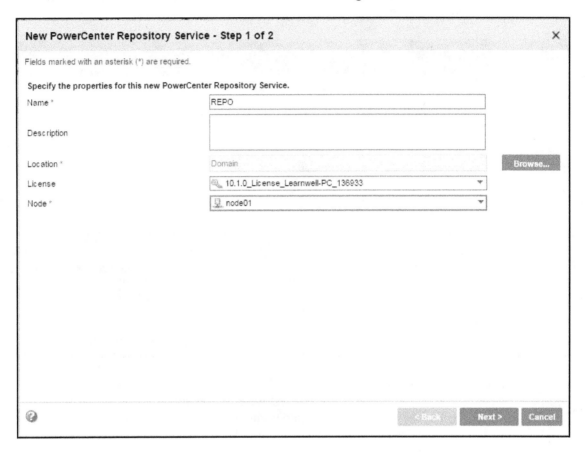

4. Click on **Next**.

5. A new screen will appear. Provide the repository database details as follows:

   - Select your repository database from the drop-down list. We are using Oracle as our user (Oracle/SQL Server).

   - Specify the repository database username that we created earlier to connect to the database. We are using **SYSTEM** as our database user.

   - Specify the repository database user password. We are using oracle as our password.

   - Specify the database connection string. We are using **orcl** as our connection string.

- The code page is required to read the data in different formats. We will be using *MS Windows Latin 1* (ANSI) as the default code page to read the data in English font. You can later specify multiple code pages to read the data in different fonts.
- **Tablespace Name** is an optional field and can be left blank.
- Choose **No content exists under the specified connection string. Create new content**.
- Check **Create as Global Repository (May not be reverted to local)**.
- Check **Enable Version control (A versioned repository cannot be unversioned)**.

The details are shown in the following screenshot:

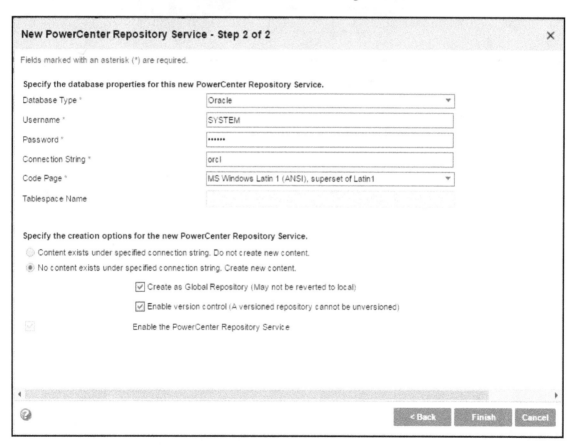

New PowerCenter Repository Service - Step 2 of 2 ✕

Fields marked with an asterisk (*) are required.

Specify the database properties for this new PowerCenter Repository Service.

| | |
|---|---|
| Database Type * | Oracle |
| Username * | SYSTEM |
| Password * | •••••• |
| Connection String * | orcl |
| Code Page * | MS Windows Latin 1 (ANSI), superset of Latin1 |
| Tablespace Name | |

Specify the creation options for the new PowerCenter Repository Service.

○ Content exists under specified connection string. Do not create new content.
◉ No content exists under specified connection string. Create new content.

☑ Create as Global Repository (May not be reverted to local)

☑ Enable version control (A versioned repository cannot be unversioned)

☑ Enable the PowerCenter Repository Service

< Back    Finish    Cancel

6. Click on **Finish**.

The process will take a few minutes to finish. Once done, you will see the REPO (repository) created under **Domain Navigator**, as shown in the following screenshot:

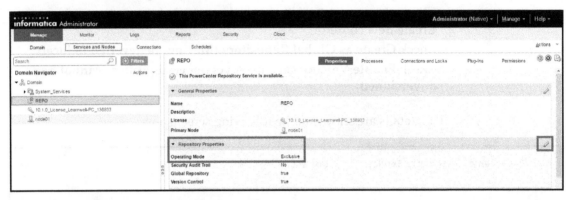

7. As you can see, the repository service is running in Exclusive mode. We need to change that to Normal before we proceed further. This can be done in the following way:

1. Click on the **Edit** option in Repository Properties. A pop-up window will appear, which will allow you to select the following properties:

   • **Operating Mode**: Select Normal from the drop-down list
   • **Security Audit Trail**: This should be set to No as default, as shown in the following screenshot:

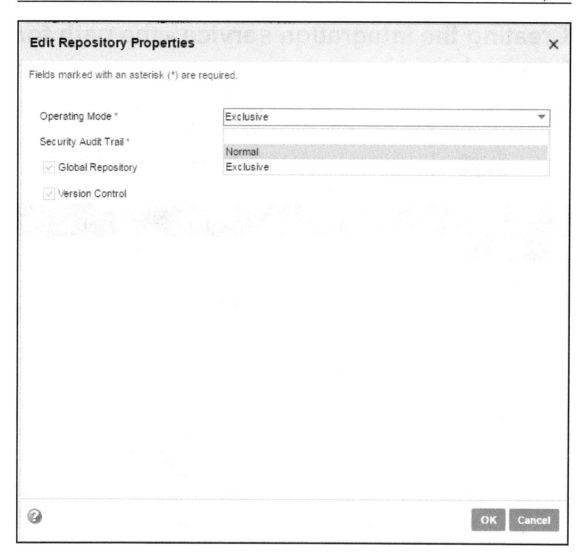

2. Click on **OK**.

8. This will change the repository mode to **Normal**.

With this, we have successfully configured the repository under the domain. Next, we will configure the integration service.

# Creating the integration service - the path for flow of data

Integration Service is required for the flow of data from the source to the target through Informatica. We discussed integration service in detail in the earlier section in this book. Perform the following process to configure the integration service:

1. Navigate to Domain under **Domain Navigator** | **Actions** | **New** | **PowerCenter Integration Service...**:

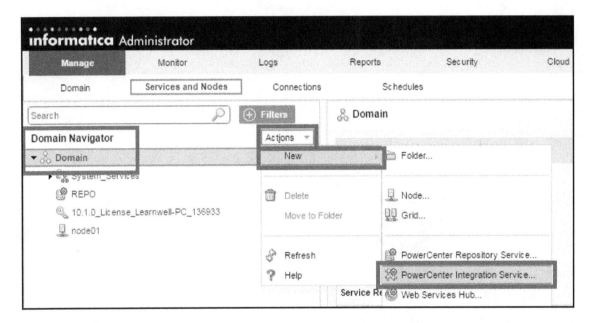

2. This will open a new screen, which will allow you to provide details for creating integration services, as shown in the following screenshot.
   - Mention the following details:
   - **Name:** Add the name of the integration service. You can specify any name as per your liking. We are using INTE for our reference in this book.
   - **Description:** You can write some description of the integration service. This is an optional field.
   - **Location:** Specify the domain name we created earlier. The domain name we created earlier will appear by default, as we have only one domain currently.

- **License:** Select the license key from the drop-down list. This is the default key, as we have only one key.
- **Node:** Specify the node name from the drop-down list. This is the default node, as we have only one node:

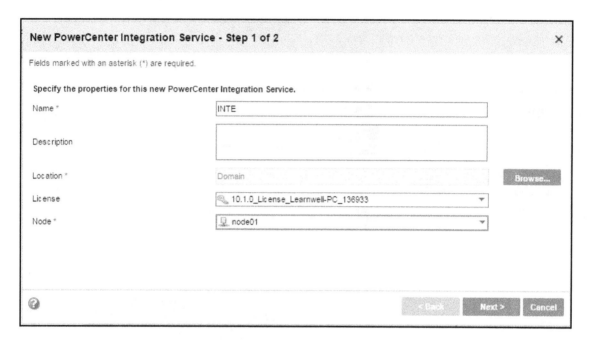

3. Click on **Next**.
4. On the next screen, we need to configure the integration service with the repository we created in the previous step, as follows:
    - **PowerCenter Repository Service**: Choose your repository service name from the drop-down list. Currently, we have only one repository present, that is REPO, which will come by default in the drop-down list.
    - **Username**: Specify the Administrator username you assigned while creating the domain. We are using Administrator as an admin username for our reference in this book.

- **Password:** Specify the Administrator password you assigned while creating the domain. We are using Administrator as the admin password for our reference in this book.
- **Data Movement Mode**: Select ASCII.

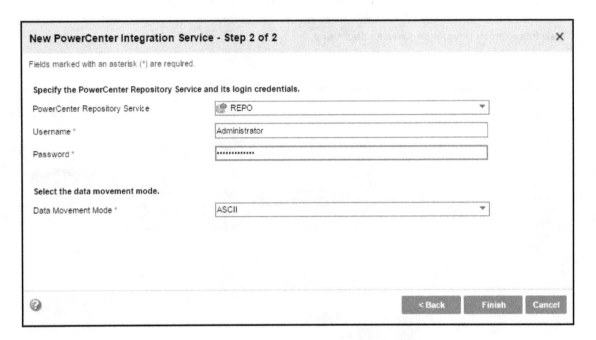

5. Click on **Finish.**
6. On the next screen, select the code page for configuration with the integration service. We will be using the default code page MS Windows Latin 1 (ANSI):

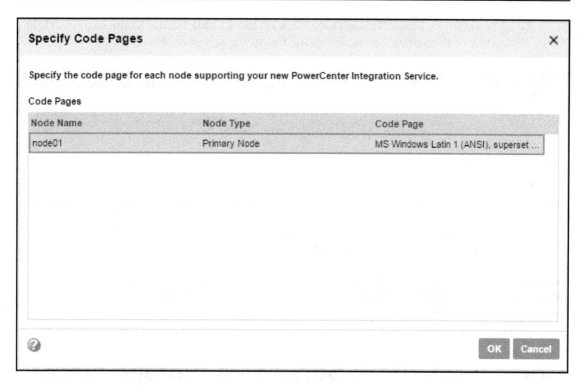

7. Click on **OK.**

8. The next screen will indicate the creation of the integration service INTE under the domain in **Domain Navigator**.

9. In some cases, the integration service might be in disabled mode, as shown in the following screenshot. We will need to enable the service.

10. To enable the integration service, click on the **Enable** button in the extreme right corner of the screen, as shown in the following screenshot:

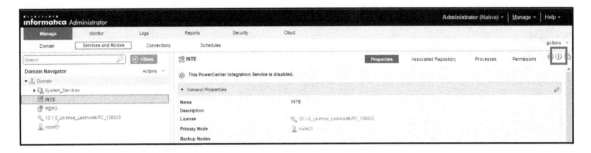

Once you are done with the process, the screen will indicate that the integration service is available.

With this, we have completed the installation and configuration of Informatica PowerCenter integration service. We are now all set to configure users and work on Informatica client tools.

# Model Repository Service - a storage place for other developer tools

As mentioned earlier, Model Repository Service stores the metadata for other developer tools of Informatica.

 Note that this service is optional and will not hamper the usage of Informatica client tools. Feel free to skip the creation of this service.

To create **Model Repository Service**, follow the mentioned steps:

1. Navigate to Domain under **Domain Navigator** | **Actions** | **New** | **Model Repository Service...**:

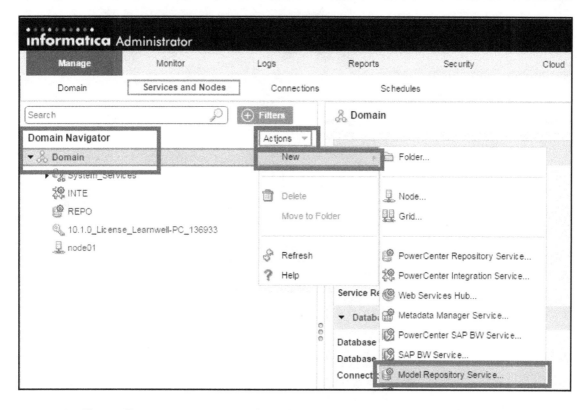

2. This will open a pop-up window that will allow you to provide details for creating the Model Repository, as shown in the following points. Insert the details.

   - **Name**: Add the name of the repository. You can specify any name as per your wish. We are using REPO_MODEL for our reference in this book.
   - **Description**: Write a description of the repository. This is an optional field.
   - **Location**: Specify the domain name we created earlier. The domain name we created earlier will appear by default, as we have only one domain currently.
   - **License**: Select the license key from the drop-down list. This is the default key, as we have only one key.
   - **Node**: Specify the node name from the drop-down list. This is the default key, as we have only one key.

The details are shown in the following screenshot:

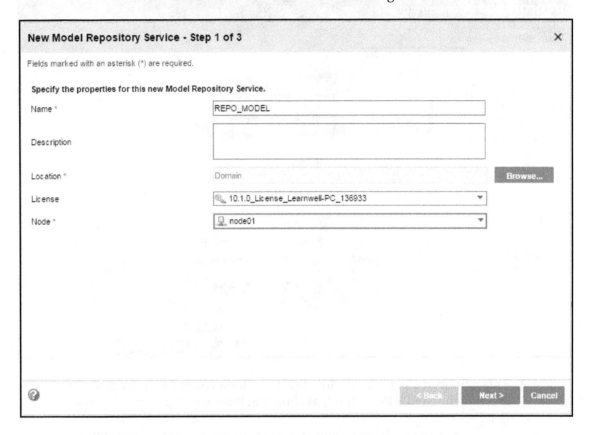

3. Click on **Next**.
4. A new screen will appear. Provide the Model Repository database details as follows:
    - Select your repository database from the drop-down list. We are using ORACLE as our user (Oracle/SQL Server).
    - Specify the repository database username that we created earlier to connect to the database. We are using BI as our database user.
    - Specify the repository database user password. We are using oracle as our password.

- Specify the connection string. The connection string looks like this:
  `jdbc:Informatica:oracle://<machinename>:<port_name>;Ser viceName=<string>;`. It will be a very long string value. We are replacing `<machinename>` with localhost, `<port_name>` with 1521, and `<string>` with orcl. Replace the value as per your database credentials. Keep the rest of the link as it is.
- **Secure JDBC Parameters** can be left blank, it's an optional field.
- Click on **Test Connection...**. If the values you specified for database details are correct, the connection will succeed.
- Choose **No content exists under specified connection string. Create new content.**
- Check **EnableService**.

The details are shown in the following screenshot:

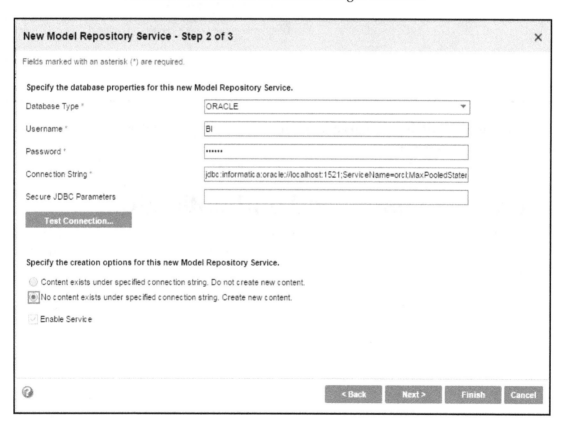

5. Click on **Finish**.

6. This will create a **Model Repository Service** under **Domain**, as shown in the following screenshot:

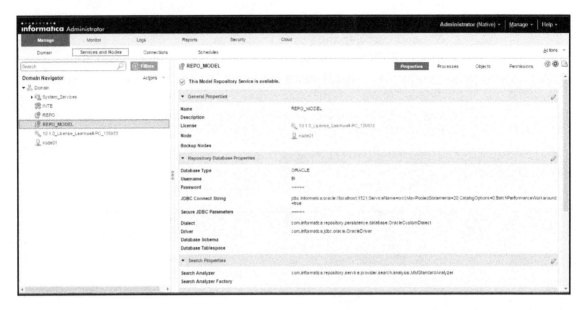

This completes the installation and configuration of the Informatica PowerCenter administration components.

# Informatica users and authentications

The next step is to create a new Informatica user and assign roles and privileges to the Informatica user. This user will be used for logging in to the Informatica client screens in the future. We need to perform the following steps:

1. Click on the **Security** tab on the **Administrator** home page, as shown in the following screenshot

- This screen allows you to create Informatica users and assign roles and responsibilities to them.

2. To add a new user, click on **Actions** in the extreme right corner of the administrator home page, and click on **Create User**:

3. In the next pop-up window, specify the username and password for the new user. The fields marked with are mandatory. The rest of the fields can be left vacant.

 It is very important to remember the username and password you define here, as this will be used for logging in to the client screens.

A user, learnwell, is created under Users, as you can see in the following screenshot:

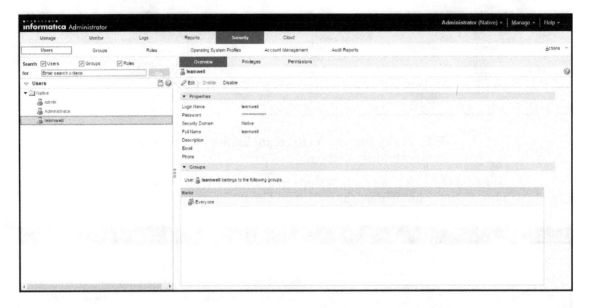

4. The next step is to assign roles and privileges to the newly created user.

5. Click on the **Privileges** tab, as shown in the following screenshot:

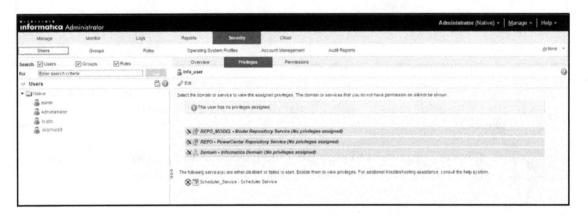

6. Click on any of the cross marks against **REPO_MODEL** or **REPO** or **Domain**, as shown in the following screenshot. A pop-up window will allow you to define the roles and privileges for the user, as shown in the following screenshot:

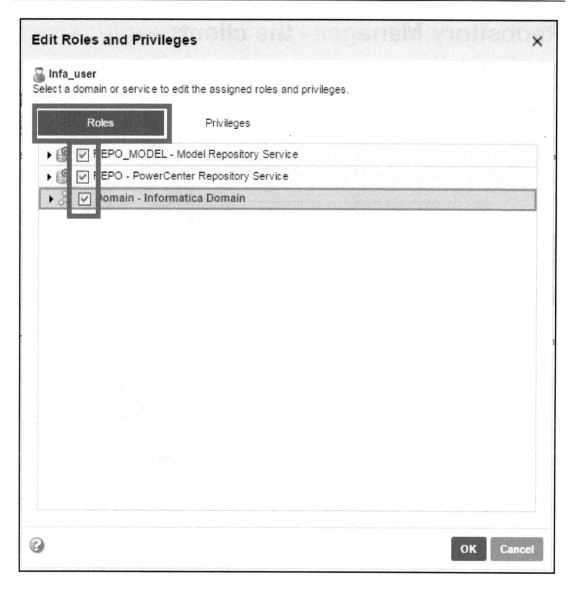

Similarly, click on the **Privileges** tab besides **Roles** and click on three
checkboxes, as done for the **Roles** tab.

With this, we have assigned all the roles and privileges to the new user, and we are all set to
configure the client tools now.

# Repository Manager - the client configuration

This is our first look at the client tools, and before we can start working on them, we need to configure the client tools with the server components:

1. To complete the configuration, open the Repository Manager. To open the Repository Manager screen, go to **Start** | **All Programs** | **Informatica 10.1.0** | **Client** | **PowerCenter Client** | **PowerCenter Repository Manager**:

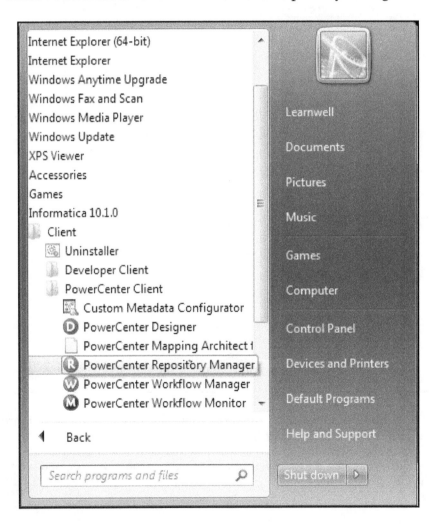

2. The Repository Manager screen will open, as shown in the following screenshot:

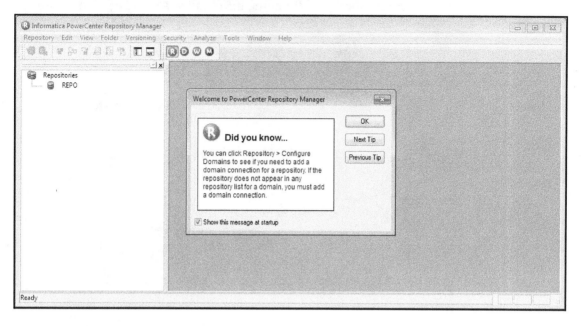

Click on **OK**.

3. To configure the domain and repository with Repository Manager, navigate to **Repository | Configure Domains**:

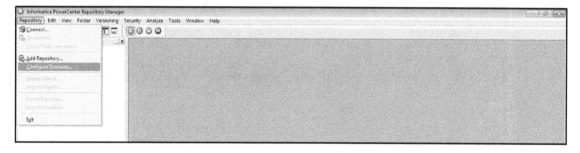

4. In the next pop-up window, provide the details for configuring the domain.
   - Click on **Add a new domain**, and specify the following details:
   - **Domain name:** Domain
   - **Gateway Hostname:** node1
   - **Gateway Port number:** 6005

Note that you need to define these values based on the domain and node configuration you did in the Informatica Administration Console.

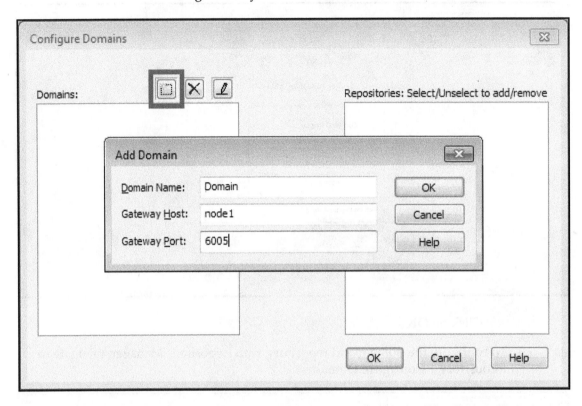

Click on **OK**.

5. Once you specify the details, a new domain and the REPO repository will appear in the box, as shown in the following screenshot:

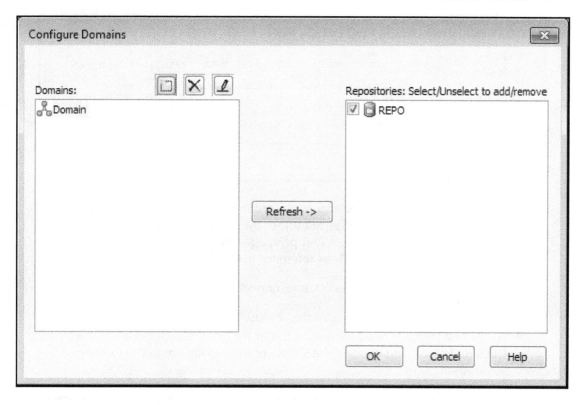

Click on **OK**.

6. This will configure your domain and repository REPO, which we created in the administrator console with the client tools. With this, you will see a repository named REPO added under Repositories in Informatica Repository Manager.

7. As a final step, right-click on REPO, and click on Connect, as shown in the following screenshot:

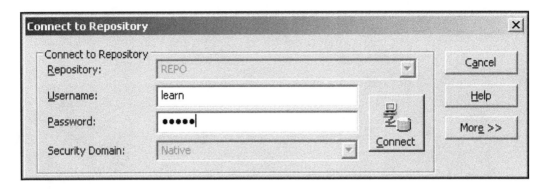

Enter a valid username and password in the pop-up window. This is the same user that we configured under the Security tab in Administrator console and granted roles and privileges. We have created two users-- Infa_user and learnwell--as reference in this book.

Enter valid details, and click on Connect.

8. As you will notice, we are connected to REPO using the username we created.

9. As the last step, we need to create a folder for doing the development activities. Click on Folder, and click on the Create option, as shown in the following screenshot:

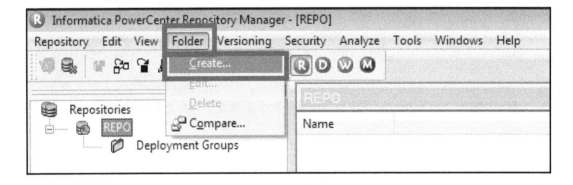

10. The next pop-up window will allow you to specify the username you wish to create. Specify the name as per your choice, as shown in the following screenshot:

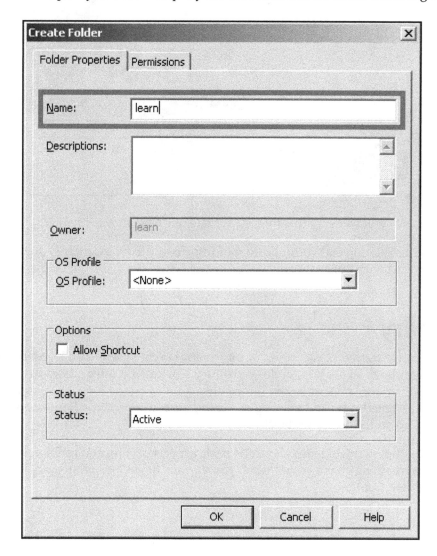

Note that we are using two users for reference in this book, Infa_user and learnwell.

Click on **OK**.

11. A message will pop up to confirm the creation of the new folder. The user can be seen added under Repositories, as shown in the following screenshot:

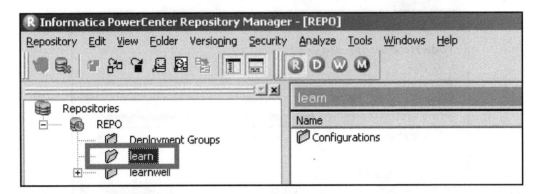

We will be using this folder to create our code in Informatica.

With this, the installation and configuration of Informatica PowerCenter is done, and we are now ready to start with our first code.

# Summary

In this chapter, we started our learning of Informatica architecture. You learned about various services, such as domain, node, repository service, and integration service. Then, we configured various services on the Informatica administrator console. We also created the user, and assigned roles and privileges. Lastly, we configured the Repository Manager client screen and added a user to the client.

In the next chapter, you will learn about the basic aspects of Informatica PowerCenter client tools. All the remaining chapters will teach you various developer-related aspects of Informatica PowerCenter.

# 3

# Understanding Designer Screen and its Components

With the installation phase over, we are all set to give the PowerCenter Client tools our first try. Client tools allow us to design code, execute the code, and check the results, and they also help in configuration activities. We have four client tools available:

- PowerCenter Designer
- PowerCenter Workflow Manager
- PowerCenter Workflow Monitor
- PowerCenter Repository Manager

Each client tool allows us to do different activities that help in the complete designing and execution of code.

In this chapter, we are going to discuss the basics of the Informatica PowerCenter Designer screen. We will also have a look at the following:

- Understanding Designer Interface
- Working with Sources
- Working with Targets
- Creating source definition from the Target structure
- Feel of the data inside Repository--a preview
- Creating a database table
- Creating a mapping and using Transformation features

# Understanding Designer Interface

The Designer screen lets you build the structural representation of sources, targets, and transformations, also known as mapping.

To open the PowerCenter Designer screen, follow these steps:

1. Go to **Start** | **All Programs** | **Informatica 10.1.0** | **Client** | **PowerCenter Client** | **Designer**
2. This will open the Designer screen as shown in the following screenshot:

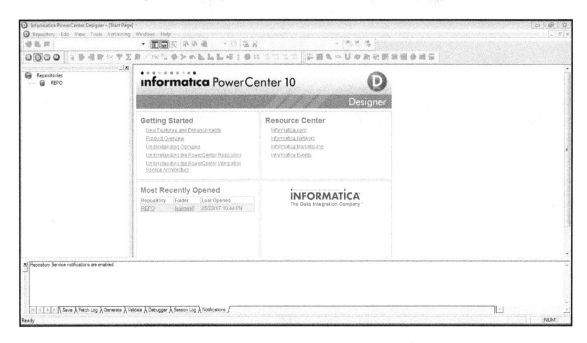

3. We will now have a look at the Designer Screen components.

# Designer screen components

The Designer screen, as can be seen in the following screenshot, is divided into five sections as described next. Each section has its own purpose. Understand each component properly as we will be referring to these components regularly in the next chapters.

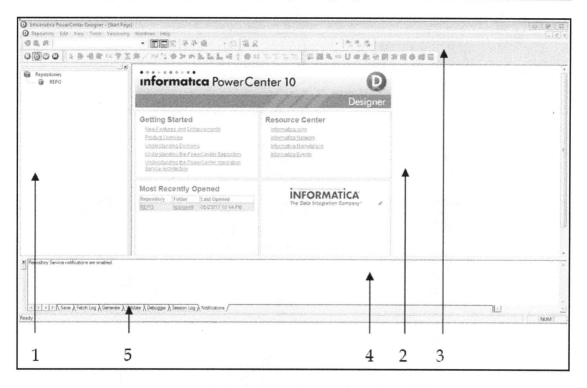

The components indicated in the preceding screenshot are explained here:

- **Navigator:** It is used to connect to repositories and open folders. You can copy objects and create shortcuts within the Navigator. The Navigator allows you to reuse the existing components.
- **Workspace**: This is the space where you actually do the coding. Open different tools in this window to create and edit repository objects such as sources, targets, mapplets, transformations, and mappings. The Designer workspace shows you different tabs -- Source Analyzer, Target Designer, Transformation Developer, Mapplet Designer, and Mapping Designer.
- **Toolbar**: This comprises the various components to be used in the Designer Screen and other shortcuts.
- **Output/control panel**: This is where you can view details about tasks you perform, such as saving your work or validating a mapping. You can view whether your code is valid or invalid. If invalid, the output panel shows you the reason for the error.

- **Status bar**: This displays the status of the current operation.It shows the error message if you are trying to perform any activity which is not supported in PowerCenter, like if you try to drag the columns from Source directly to transformation by skipping Source Qualifier.

To connect to Repository, right-click on **REPO** (as shown in the previous screenshot), and enter your username and password.

The Designer has five tools, as shown in the following screenshot, to analyze sources, design targets, and build mappings using different types of transformations:

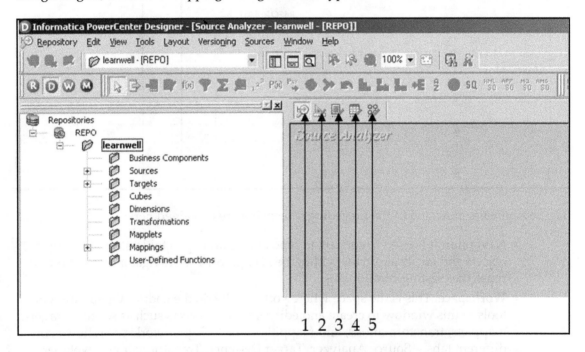

The components indicated in the preceding screenshot are explained as follows:

- **Source Analyzer**: This section allows you to import or create source definitions. You can work on various types of files (flat files, .xml files, .xls files, and so on.) and tables. Source Analyzer lets you modify existing source definitions.
- **Target Designer**: This section allows you to import or create Target definitions. You can work on various types of files (flat files, xml, .xls, and so on) and tables. Target Designer lets you modify existing Target definitions.

- **Transformation Developer**: This section allows you to create reusable transformations to use in mappings. Reusable components are important as they allow you to use the existing transformation.
- **Mapplet Designer**: This section allows you to create groups of transformations to use in mappings. Mapplets are a group of reusable transformation that can be used in multiple mappings as reusable components.
- **Mapping Designer**: This section allows you to create mappings that the integration service uses to extract, transform, and load data. mappings contain Sources, Targets, and transformations linked to each other through links. You can add multiple Sources, Targets, and Transformations in a mapping.

As a general rule, we should work first on sources, then targets, and at last transformations, which complete the mappings.

# Working with Sources

Any file or table from where we can extract the data in PowerCenter is referred to as the Source. You can import or create the source definition.

When you import the source definition in Designer, we import only the metadata, that is column names, data type, size, indexes, constraints, dependencies, and so on. Actual data never comes with the Source structure in Designer. The data flows through the mapping in a row-wise manner when we execute the workflow in Workflow Manager.

PowerCenter allows you to work on various types of sources as listed here:

- **Relational Database**: PowerCenter supports all the Relations Databases, such as Oracle, Sybase, DB2, Microsoft SQL Server, SAP HANA, and Teradata.
- **File**: This includes flat files (fixed width and delimited files), COBOL Copybook files, XML files, and Excel files.
- **High-end applications**: Hyperion, PeopleSoft, TIBCO, Web Sphere MQ, and so on can also be used.
- **Mainframe**: Additional features of Mainframe such as IBM DB2 OS/390, IBM DB2 OS/400, IDMS, IDMS-X, IMS, and VSAM can be purchased.
- **Other**: PowerCenter also supports Microsoft Access and external web services.

We will now explore different tasks we can accomplish with sources in the subsequent sections.

# Adding new Open Database Connectivity (ODBC) data source

To add a new Database data source connection to import tables, follow the following procedure:

1. In the Designer, go to **Tools | Source Analyzer** to open the Source Analyzer as indicated in the previous screenshot.
2. Go to **Sources | Import from Database** as indicated.
3. To add a new Database connection, click on the tab as shown in the following screenshot:

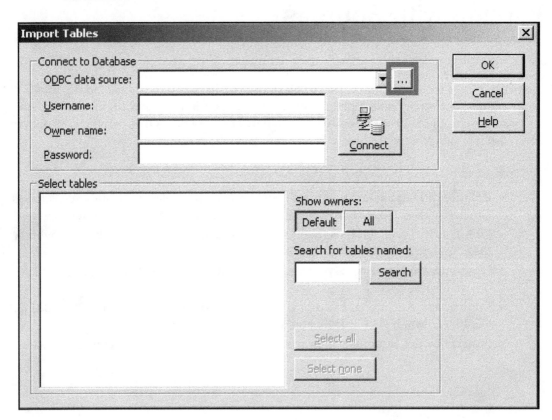

4. A popup to add a new connection will appear on the screen.

5. We need to add a new **User DSN** as shown in the following screenshot:

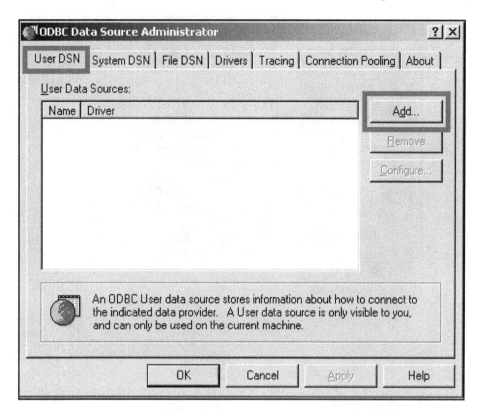

6. The next screen will allow you to select the desired database from the list of databases. For our reference, we are using Oracle Database in this book.

7. Select the type of Database you wish to add, and click on **Finish** as shown in the following screenshot:

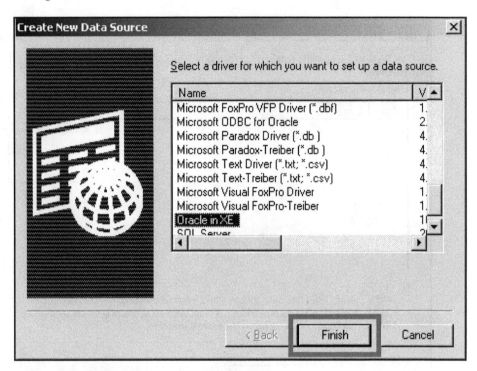

8. A new window will pop up on your screen. Mention the following details to add a new connection, as shown in the following screenshot.

- **Data Source Name**: Enter the name of the Data Source. This can be any name for your reference.
- **Description**: Specify some description for the connection.
- **TNS Service Name**: Mention the service name for your connection. We are using XE as the service name (this is the default service name for Oracle 10g Database).
- **User ID**: Mention the user ID. We are using HR as our user ID for making the connection.

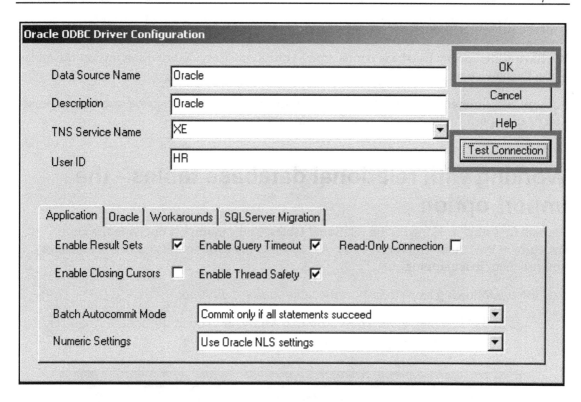

9.  After providing all the details, click on **Test Connection**.
10. A new window will pop up as shown in the following screenshot.
11. Specify the password for Oracle database, and click on **OK**.

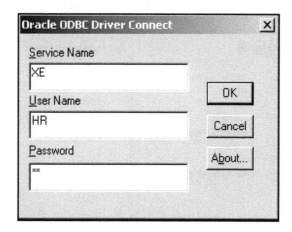

If all the values mentioned by you are correct, the Test Connection will be successful.

We have added a new Database connection to our Repository, and we can import the tables using the new connection.

You can add different types of Databases to your repository. This is just a one-time process you need to perform before you can start using the tables.

# Working with relational database tables - the Import option

We will first start working on the relational tables. You can import or create the table structure in the Source Analyzer. After you add these source definitions to the repository, you use them in a mapping.

Perform the following steps to import the table source definition:

1. In the Designer, go to **Tools | Source Analyzer** to open the Source Analyzer.
2. Go to **Sources | Import from Database**.

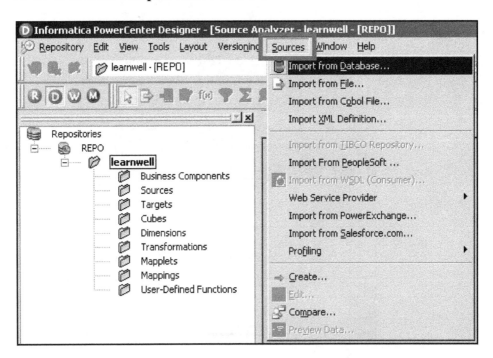

3. From the ODBC data source button, select the ODBC data source that you created to access source tables.

4. Enter the username and password to connect to the database. Also, enter the name of the source table owner, if necessary.

5. Click on **Connect**.

6. In the **Select tables** list, expand the database owner and the **TABLES** heading.

7. Select the tables you wish to import, and click on **OK**.

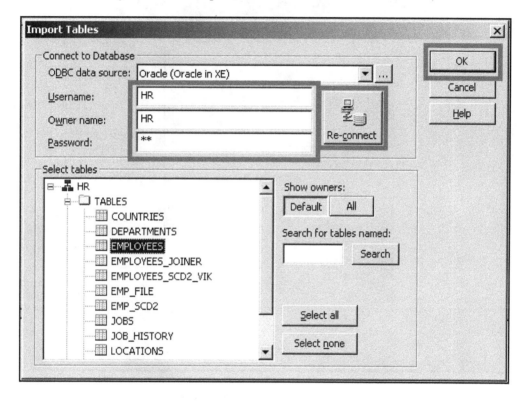

The structure of the selected tables will appear in the workspace as shown in the following screenshot:

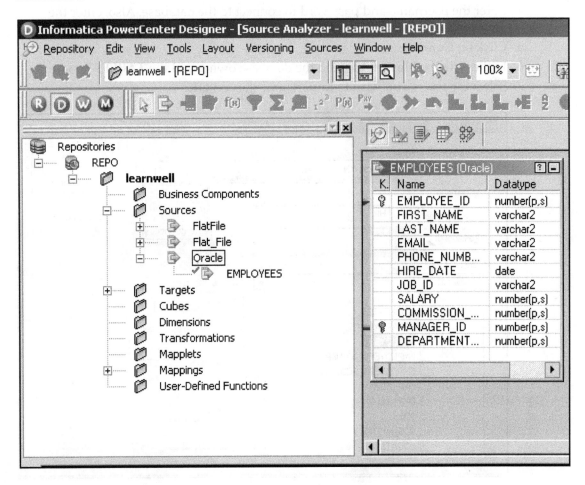

We will now have a look at working with the Import option.

# Working with flat files - Import option

In the previous section, we discussed the importing of relational tables. Before we start working on importing flat files, we will discuss some important aspects about Flat Files.

Flat files form a very important aspect of any ETL tool.

Flat files are of two types -- delimited and fixed width.

- In delimited files, the values are separated from each other by a delimiter. Any character or number can be used as the delimiter, but usually, for better interpretation, we use special characters as delimiters. In delimited files, the width of each field is not a mandatory option as each value gets separated by another using a delimiter. Refer to the following screenshot to understand a delimited file. The delimiter used in the file is the comma (,).

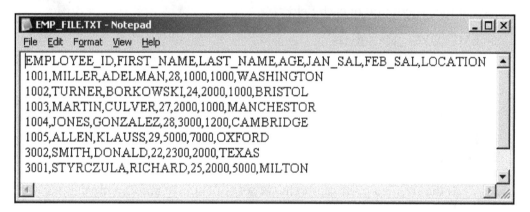

```
EMP_FILE.TXT - Notepad
File  Edit  Format  View  Help
EMPLOYEE_ID,FIRST_NAME,LAST_NAME,AGE,JAN_SAL,FEB_SAL,LOCATION
1001,MILLER,ADELMAN,28,1000,1000,WASHINGTON
1002,TURNER,BORKOWSKI,24,2000,1000,BRISTOL
1003,MARTIN,CULVER,27,2000,1000,MANCHESTOR
1004,JONES,GONZALEZ,28,3000,1200,CAMBRIDGE
1005,ALLEN,KLAUSS,29,5000,7000,OXFORD
3002,SMITH,DONALD,22,2300,2000,TEXAS
3001,STYRCZULA,RICHARD,25,2000,5000,MILTON
```

- In fixed width files, the width of each field is fixed. The values are separated from each other by the fixed size of the column defined. There can be issues in reading the data if the size of each column is not maintained properly. As shown in the following screenshot, in the fixed width file, the width of each field is fixed:

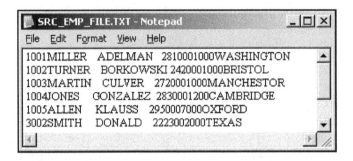

Take a look at the description of each field:

- **EMPLOYEE_ID**: 4 Bytes
- **FIRST_NAME**: 10 Bytes
- **LAST_NAME**: 10 Bytes
- **AGE**: 2 Bytes
- **JAN_SAL**: 4 Bytes
- **FEB_SAL**: 4 Bytes
- **LOCATION**: 10 Bytes

 If the size of a particular value is not equal to the size mentioned, we need to *pad* the value with *spaces*.

We move on to working with both the types of Flat Files in the subsequent two subsections.

# Working with delimited files

Following are the steps that you will have to perform to work with delimited files:

1. In the Designer, go to **Tools** | **Source Analyzer** to open the Source Analyzer.
2. Go to **Sources** | **Import from File...**.

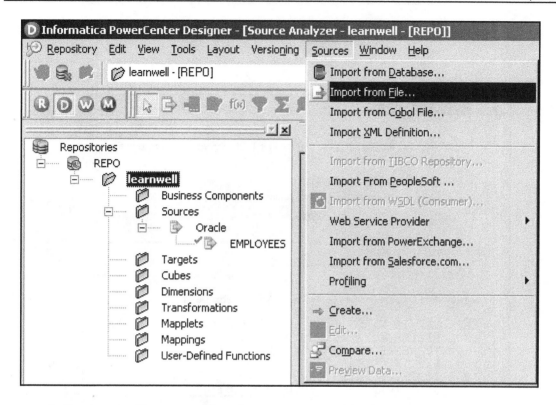

3. Browse the files you wish to import as source files.

   The Flat file import wizard will come up on the screen. The File import wizard screen will help you specify the properties for importing the file in a proper format.

4. Complete the following steps:

    i. Select the file type as **Delimited**:

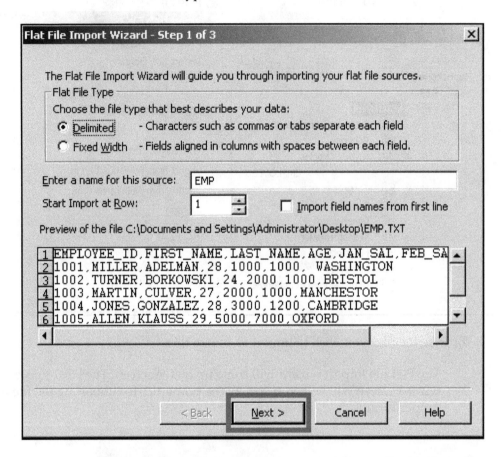

    ii. If the file contains column names as headers in the first line, then we will need to start importing at row 2 as this option indicates from which row the actual data has to be imported. If the file doesn't contain the headers in the first line, we will import the data from the first line only.

iii. Files may contain the column names in the first line as headers. You need to verify the file properly before you start working on it. Import field names from the first line enable us to import the header names into the Source Definition. If you do not select this option, the header names will not be imported.

iv. Click on **Next**, as shown in the following screenshot:

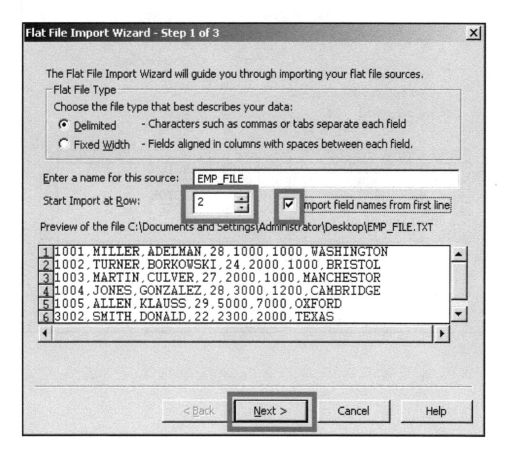

5. Select the type of delimiter used in the file. In our case, we are using the comma as the delimiter. You can select the delimiter as per the file you are using.

6. Also check the quotes option--No Quotes, Single Quotes, and Double Quotes--to work with the quotes in the text values. This option enables us to import the data with single or double quotes in text values. We are using No quotes as our option since the sample file we are using does not have any data with quotes.

7. Click on **Next**:

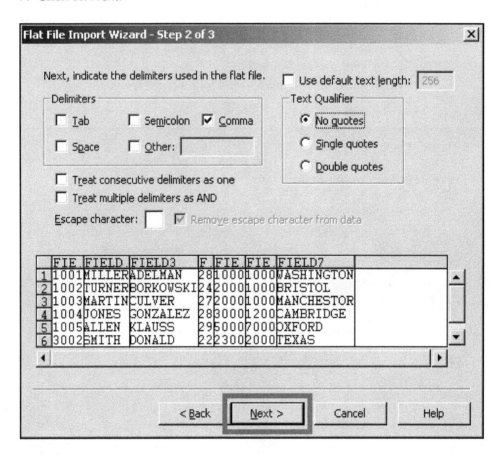

8. Verify the columns name, data type, and precision in the data view option. You can edit the column names and other details in this view as shown in the following screenshot. Generally, you do not need to do so.

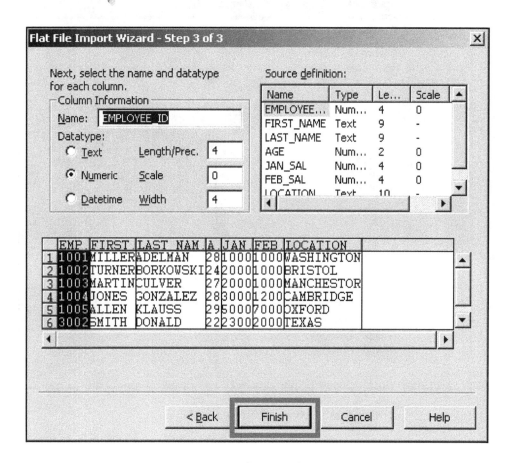

9. Click on **Finish** to get the source imported in the Source Analyzer as shown in the following screenshot:

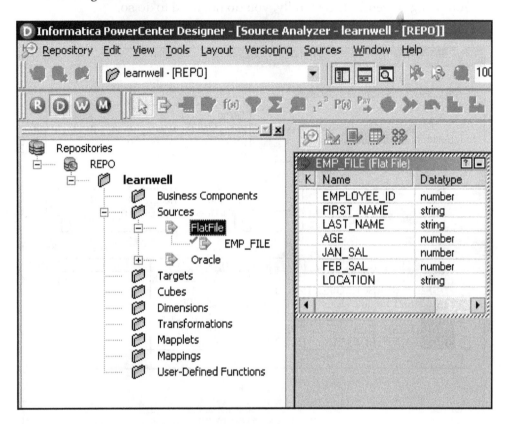

We now move on to the other Flat file type--the fixed width files.

# Working with fixed width files

Following are the steps that you will have to perform to work with fixed width files:

1. In the Designer, go to **Tools | Source Analyzer** to open the Source Analyzer.
2. Go to **Sources | Import from File...**:

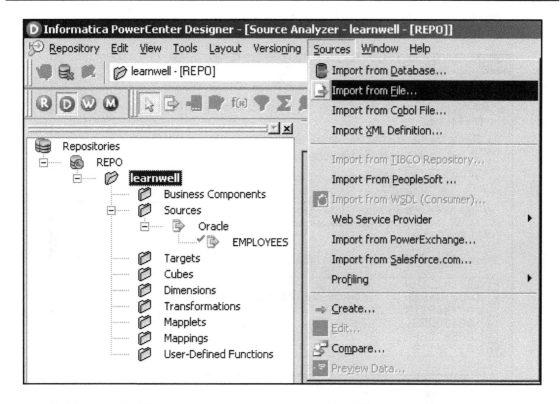

3. Browse the files you wish to use as source files. We are using `EMP_SRC_FILE` as reference to import the fixed width file.

4. The flat file import wizard will come up.

5. Select the file type--fixed width.

6. Click on **Next**:

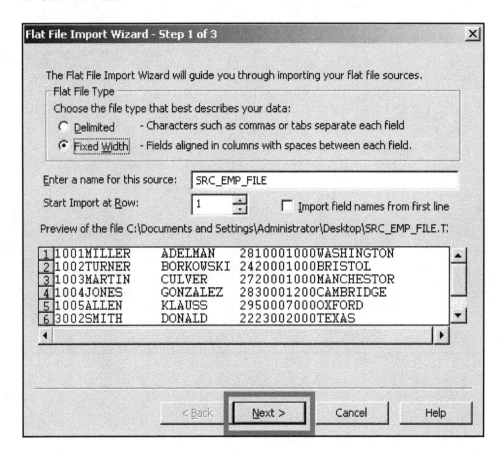

7. As against the delimited files, we will now need to set the width of each column as per the requirement. This will help us in dividing the file in a proper column-wise manner.

8. Click on **Next**:

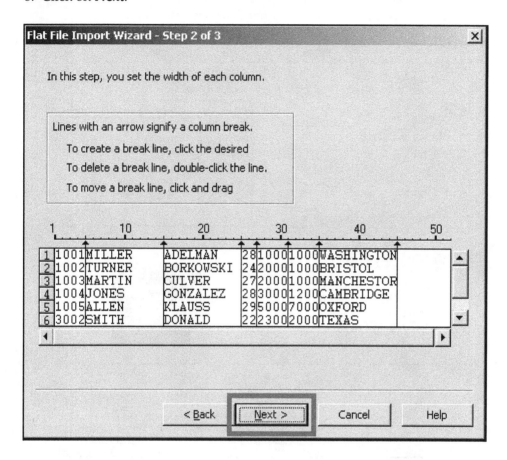

9. Specify the columns name, data type, and precision in the data view option. You can edit the column names and other details in this view:

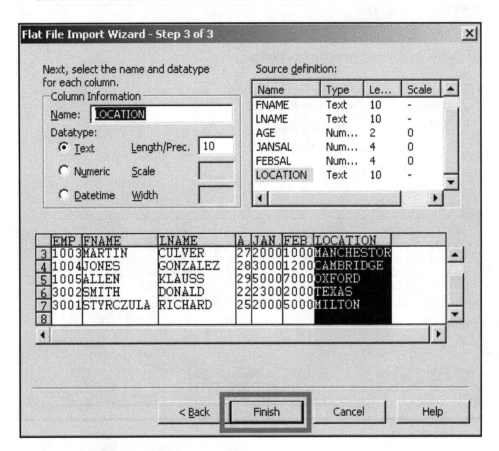

10. Click on **Next**.
11. Click on **Finish** to get the source imported in the Source Analyzer as shown in the following screenshot:

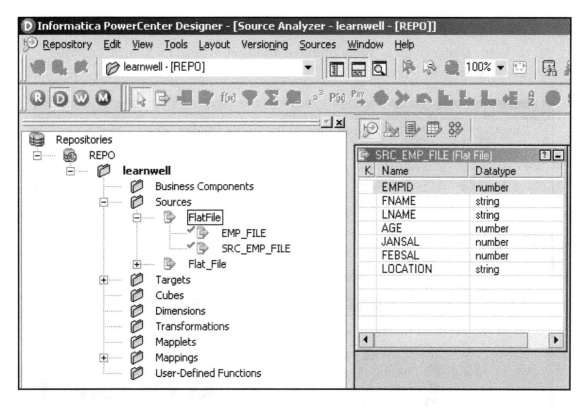

We now move on to the last section of working with sources, that is creating Source options.

# Working with Sources - the Create option

Apart from importing the file or table structure, we can manually create the Source Definition. When the sample source file or the table structure is not available, we need to manually create the source structure. When we select the create option, we need to define every details related to the file or table manually, such as the name of the source, type of source, column names, column data type, column data size, indexes, constraints, and so on. When you import the structure, the import wizard automatically imports all these details.

Following are the steps that you will have to perform to create option.

1. In the Designer, go to **Tools** | **Source Analyzer** to open the Source Analyzer.
2. Go to **Sources** | **Create**:

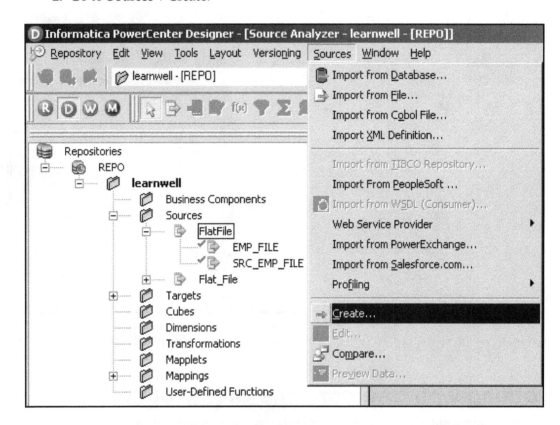

3. Mention the name of the Source as per your requirement, and select the type of Source you wish to create from the drop-down list. For our reference, we are using Flat File as our source type and SRC_STUDENT as the source file name.
4. Also, select the Database type for the new source to be created. Since we wish to create a Flat File, we have selected Flat File as shown in the following screenshot:

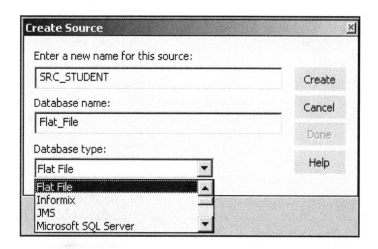

5. Click on **Create** and then on **Done**.

6. An empty source structure with the name SRC_STUDENT will appear in the Source Analyzer as shown in the following screenshot:

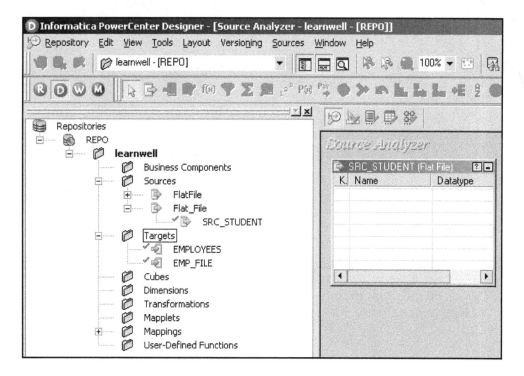

7. Since we are using the create option, we need to manually specify all the details such as the column names, data type, precision, and so on.

8. Double-click on the title bar of SRC_STUDENT to open the source definition.

9. The Edit Tables dialog box appears and displays all the properties of this source definition. The Table tab shows the name of the table, the name of the owner, and the database type. You can add a comment in the description section. The Business name field is empty since we don't use it.

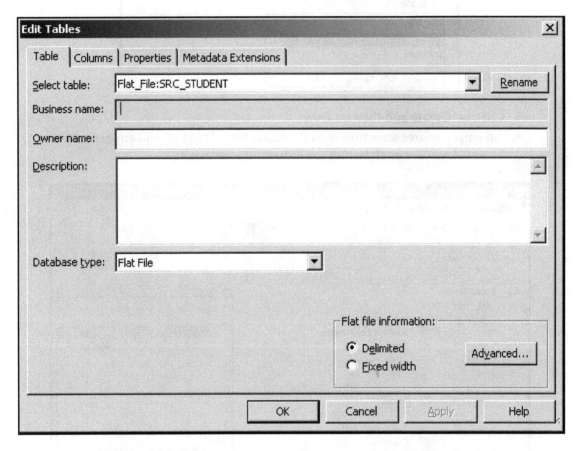

10. Click on the **Columns** tab, which displays the column descriptions for the source. Here, we have options to add a new column, delete an existing column, and so on.

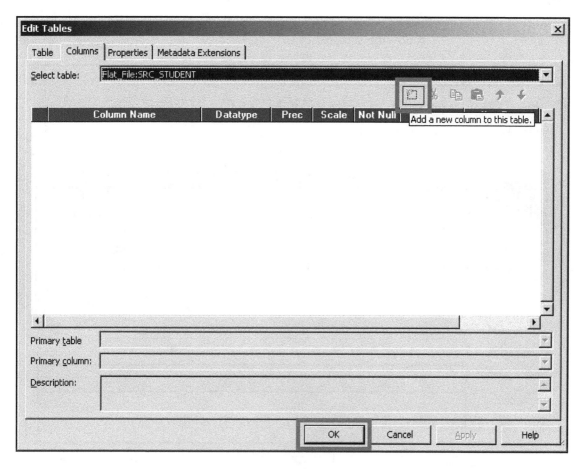

- **Add a new column**: Click on this option to add a new column as shown in the previous screenshot. You can add multiple columns as per your requirement. Once you add a new column, specify the other details such as data type, precision, and so on for the column you added.

- **Delete a column**: To delete a column, click on the column you wish to delete, and click on the delete button.

- **Copy an existing column**: You can copy an existing column if you wish to make a column similar to an existing column.

- **Paste the copied column**: You can paste the copied column as per requirement.

- Move up or down the column to rearrange the columns inside the source definition.

We have added few columns to the Source as can be seen in the following screenshot:

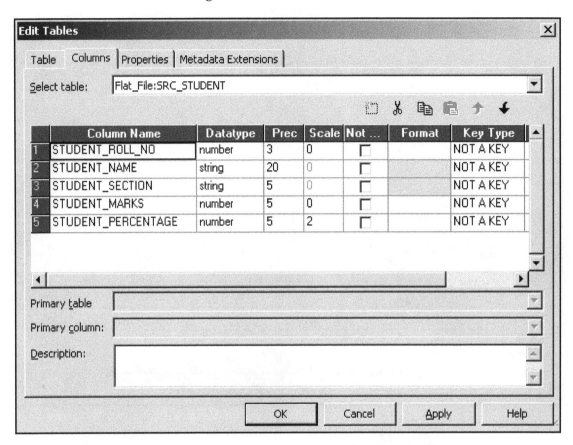

11. Click on the Metadata Extensions tab. Metadata extensions allow you to extend the metadata stored in the repository by associating information with individual repository objects. For example, you can store contact information, such as name or e-mail address, with the sources you create. This is an option and usually left empty.

12. Click on **Apply** and then on **OK** to close the dialog box to get the source definition in the Source Analyzer:

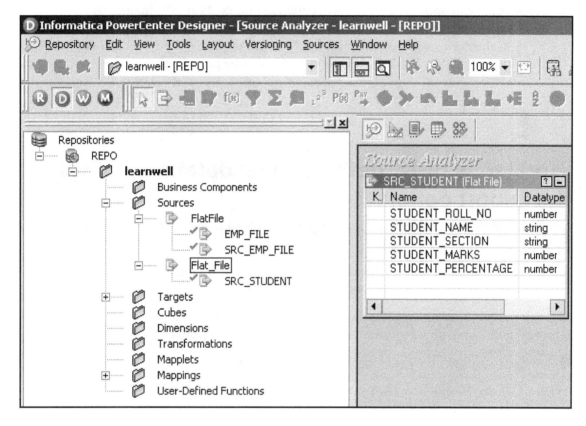

13. Go to **Repository** | **Save** or press *Ctrl + S* to save the changes to the repository.

We're done working with sources. Let's now move on to Targets!

# Working with Targets

As we saw in the previous section, PowerCenter can use different types of Sources. Similarly, PowerCenter is capable of working with different types of targets to load data:

- **Relational Database**: PowerCenter supports all the relations databases such as Oracle, Sybase, DB2, Microsoft SQL Server, SAP HANA, and Teradata.

- **File**: This includes flat files (fixed width and delimited files), COBOL Copybook files, XML files, and Excel files.
- **High-end applications**: PowerCenter also supports applications such as Hyperion, PeopleSoft, TIBCO, WebSphere MQ, and so on.
- **Mainframe**: Additional features of Mainframe such as IBM DB2 OS/390, IBM DB2 OS/400, IDMS, IDMS-X, IMS, and VSAM can be purchased
- **Other**: PowerCenter also supports Microsoft Access and external web services.

Let's start!

# Working with Target relational database tables - the Import option

Just as we discussed importing and creating source files and source tables, we need to work on target definitions.

The process of importing the target table is exactly same as importing the Source table, the only difference is that you need to work in the Target Designer.

You can import or create the table structure in the Target Designer. After you add these target definitions to the repository, you can use them in a mapping.

Follow these steps to import the table target definition:

1. In the Designer, go to **Tools | Target Designer** to open the Target Designer.
2. Go to **Targets | Importfrom Database**.
3. From the ODBC data source button, select the ODBC data source that you created to access source tables. We have already added the data source while working on the sources.
4. Enter the username and password to connect to the database.
5. Click on **Connect**.
6. In the Select tables list, expand the database owner and the TABLE heading.
7. Select the tables you wish to import, and click on **OK**.

The structure of the selected tables will appear in the Target Designer in workspace.

As mentioned, the process is the same as importing the source in the Source Analyzer. Follow the preceding steps in case of some issues.

# Working with Target Flat Files - the Import option

The process of importing the target file is exactly same as importing the Source file, the only difference is that you need to work on the Target Designer.

## Working with delimited files

Following are the steps that you will have to perform to work with delimited files.

1. In the Designer, go to **Tools | Target Designer** to open the Target Designer.
2. Go to **Target | Import from File...**.
3. Browse the files you wish to import as source files.
4. The flat file import wizard will come up.
5. Select the file type -- **Delimited**. Also, select the appropriate option to import the data from second row and import filed names from the first line as we did in case of importing the source. Click on **Next**.
6. Select the type of delimiter used in the file. Also, check the quotes option -- No Quotes, Single Quotes, and Double Quotes -- to work with the quotes in the text values. Click on **Next**.
7. Verify the column names, data type, and precision in the data view option. Click on **Next**.
8. Click on **Finish** to get the target file imported in the Target Designer.

We now move on to fixed width files.

## Working with fixed width Files

Following are the steps that you will have to perform to work with fixed width Files:

1. In the Designer, go to **Tools | Target Designer** to open the Target Designer.
2. Go to **Target | Import from File...**.
3. Browse the files you wish to use as source files.
4. The Flat file import wizard will come up.
5. Select the file type -- fixed width. Click on **Next**.

6. Set the width of each column as required by adding a line break. Click on Next.
7. Specify the column names, data type, and precision in the data view option. Click on Next.
8. Click on **Finish** to get the target imported in the Target Designer.

Just as in the case of working with sources, we move on to the create option in target.

# Working with Target - the Create option

Apart from importing the file or table structure, we can manually create the Target Definition. When the sample Target file or the table structure is not available, we need to manually create the Target structure. When we select the create option, we need to define every detail related to the file or table manually, such as the name of the Target, the type of the Target, column names, column data type, column data size, indexes, constraints, and so on. When you import the structure, the import wizard automatically imports all these details.

1. In the Designer, go to **Tools | Target Designer** to open the Target Designer.
2. Go to **Target | Create**.
3. Select the type of **Target** you wish to create from the drop-down list.
4. An empty target structure will appear in the Target Designer.
5. Double-click on the title bar of the target definition for the T_EMPLOYEES table. This will open the T_EMPLOYEES target definition.
6. A popup window will display all the properties of this target definition. The Table tab will show the name of the table, the name of the owner, and the database type. You can add a comment in the **Description** section. Usually, we keep the Business name empty.
7. Click on the **Columns** tab. This will display the column descriptions for the target. You can add, delete, or edit the columns.
8. Click on the Metadata Extensions tab (usually, you keep this tab blank). You can store some Metadata related to the target you created. Some personal details and reference details can be saved. Click on **Apply** and then on **OK**.
9. Go to **Repository | Save** to save the changes to the repository.

Let's move on to something interesting now!

# Working with Target - the Copy or Drag-Drop option

PowerCenter provides a very convenient way of reusing the existing components in the Repository. It provides the Drag-Drop feature, which helps in reusing the existing components.

Using the Drag-Drop feature, you can copy the existing source definition created earlier to the Target Designer in order to create the target definition with the same structure.

Follow these steps:

1. In the Designer, go to **Tools** | **Target Designer** to open the Target Designer.
2. Drag the SRC_STUDENT source definition from the Navigator to the Target Designer workspace as shown in the following screenshot:

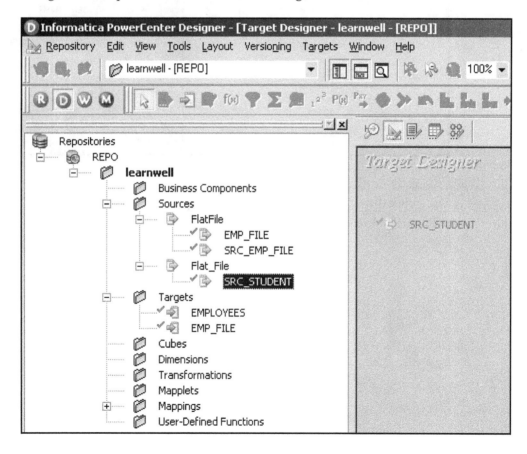

3. The Designer creates a target definition, SRC_STUDENT, with the same column definitions as the SRC_STUDENT source definition and the same database type:

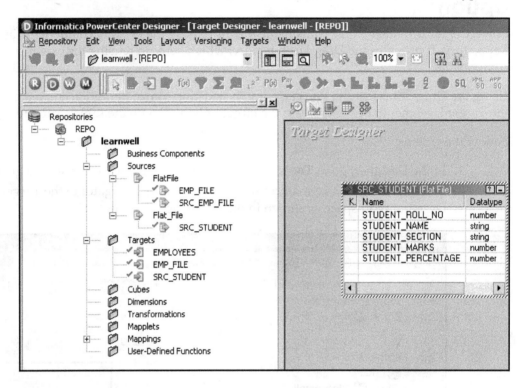

4. Double-click on the title bar of the SRC_STUDENT target definition to open it and edit properties if you wish to change some properties.
5. Click on **Rename**:

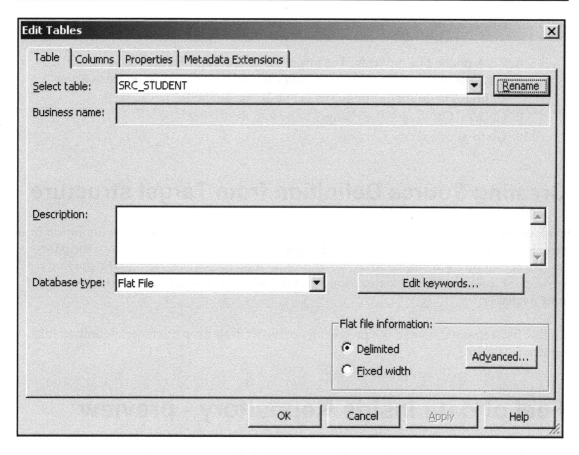

6. A new pop-up window will allow you to mention the new name. Change the target definition name to TGT_STUDENT:

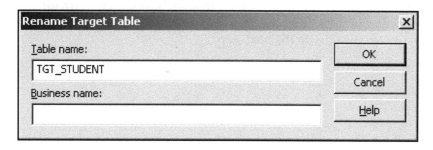

7. Click on **OK**.

8. Click on the Columns tab. The target column definitions are the same as the `SRC_STUDENT` source definition. You can add new columns, delete existing columns, or edit the columns as per your requirement.
9. Click on OK to save the changes and close the dialog box.
10. Go to `Repository` | `Save`.

# Creating Source Definition from Target structure

With Informatica PowerCenter 10.1.0, now you can drag and drop the target definition from target designer into Source Analyzer. In the previous topic, we learned to drag-drop the Source definition from Source Analyzer and reuse it in Target Designer. In the previous versions of Informatica, this feature was not available. In the latest version, this feature is now available.

Follow the steps as shown in the preceding section to drag-drop the target definition into Source Analyzer.

# Feel of data inside Repository - preview

Now that we have learned how to use Sources and Targets in PowerCenter. We will now start using these sources and targets in mappings. As mentioned earlier in the PowerCenter Designer, we only deal with the metadata of sources and targets, we do have an option to preview the data of the source and target that we imported by providing the path/connection for files or tables. This gives us an option to understand the data clearly before we move ahead with the next step.

# Previewing the source data - flat files

Follow these steps to preview the data in source:

1. Drag and drop the ource from Navigator to Source Analyzer. We are using
   `EMP_FILE` as our reference to preview data.

2. Right-click on Source Definition, and click on **Preview Data...** as shown in the
   following screenshot:

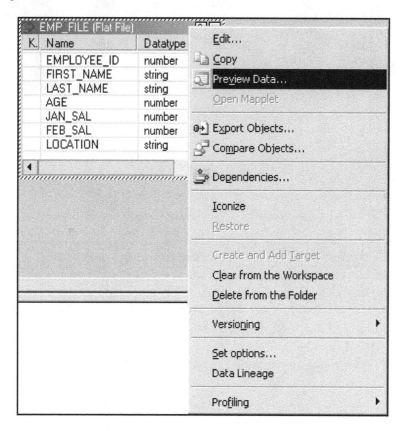

3. A new window will pop up asking you to provide the path where your file is stored. Look at the following screenshot below for your reference:

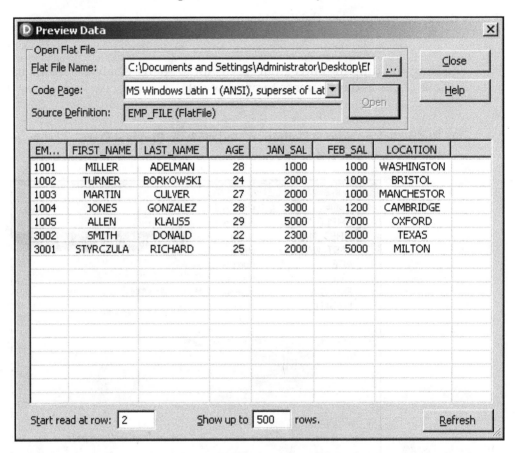

4. Click on **Open** to view the preview the data.
5. Once you are done, click on **Close**.

We now move on to relational tables.

# Previewing the Source Data - relational tables

Follow these steps to preview the data in relational data source:

1. Drag and drop the Source table from Navigator to Source Analyzer. We are using **EMPLOYEES (Oracle)** table as our reference to preview the data.

2. Right-click on **EMPLOYEES** Source Definition, and click on **Preview Data...** as shown in the following screenshot:

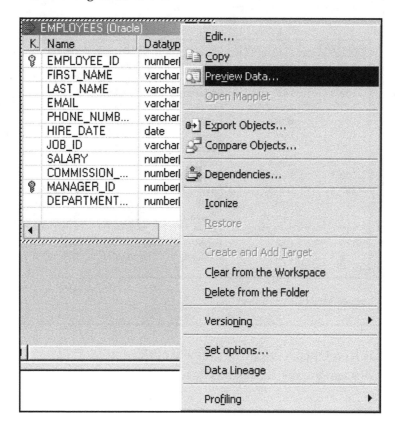

3. A new window will pop up asking you to provide the database connection details. Refer to the following screenshot for your reference:

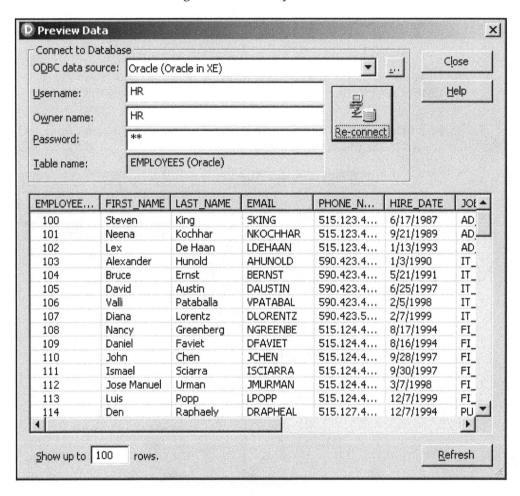

4. Click on **Open** to view the preview of the data.
5. Once you are done, click on **Close**.

# Creating a Database Table

In the earlier section, we saw the steps to import the Database table into Informatica.

Informatica PowerCenter tools allow you to create a database table from Informatica itself. If you have a table structure available in PowerCenter but the corresponding table is not available in database, you will not be able to use the table for your mapping purpose as you will not be able to provide the required connections for loading the data. PowerCenter provides a very efficient and faster way to generate a database table directly. So you need not write a CREATE SQL statement to generate a table in your Database.

For our reference, we will create a table named TGT_EMPLOYEES in oracle database.

1. In the Designer, got o **Tools** | **Target Designer** to open the Target Designer.

2. In the workspace, select the TGT_EMPLOYEES target definition.
3. Go to **Targets** | **Generate/Execute SQL**.

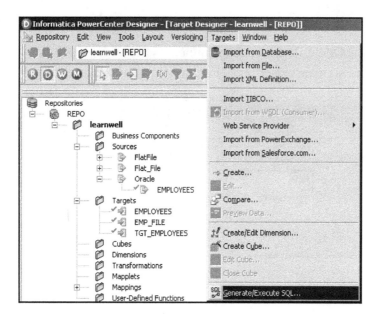

4. The Database Object Generation dialog box appears.

5. In the File Name field, enter the following text to generate an SQL script called MKTABLES.SQL - C:\MKTABLES.SQL. You can provide any path. Informatica PowerCenter will generate the SQL file at the specified location.

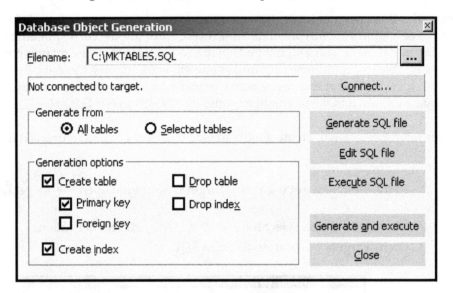

6. Select the ODBC data source to connect to the target database.

7. Enter the necessary username and password, and then click on **Connect**:

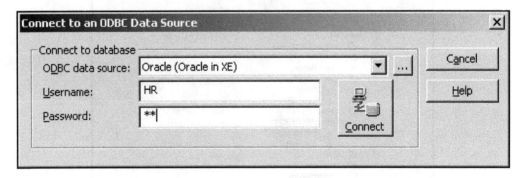

8. Select the appropriate option for generating a table:

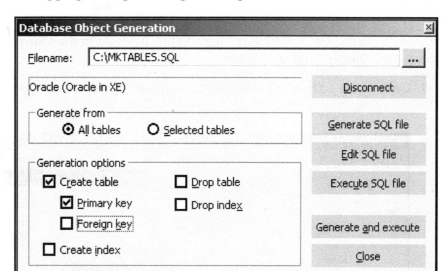

9. Click on **Generate and execute**.
10. Click on **Close** to exit the Database Object Generation dialog box.

With this, the table TGT_EMPLOYEES will be generated in the Oracle database, which can be cross-checked by writing a query in the database.

# Creating a mapping and using transformation features

In the earlier section, we learned about all the prerequisites for creating mapping. Mapping is a structural flow of data from the source to the target through transformations.

To understand the basic steps of creating mapping, let's start by creating a pass-through mapping. A pass-through mapping inserts all the source rows into the target without any modification. A pass-through mapping is a simple flow from source to target without any changes in data.

We will use the EMPLOYEE Oracle table as the source and the TGT_EMPLOYEE as the target for creating a pass-through mapping.

In the following steps, you create a mapping and link columns in the source EMPLOYEES table to a Source Qualifier transformation.

1. Go to **Tools** | **Mapping Designer** | **Mappings** | **Create...** to create a new mapping:

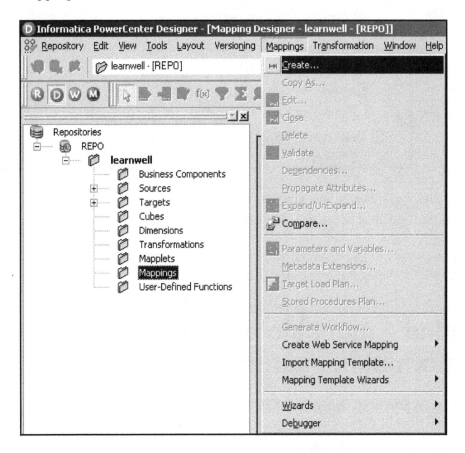

2. In the **Mapping Name** dialog box, enter m_PASS_THROUGH_EMPLOYEES, and click on **OK**.

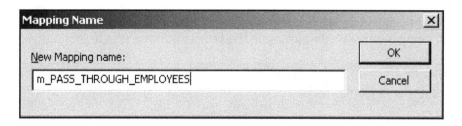

3. Drag the EMPLOYEES source definition into the Mapping Designer workspace.

4. The source definition appears in the workspace. The Designer creates a Source Qualifier transformation and connects it to the source definition. Source Qualifier is a default transformation that comes automatically with a source. We will see the usage of the Source Qualifier transformation in the next section.

5. Expand the Target node in the Navigator to open the list of all the target definitions. Drag the TGT_EMPLOYEES target definition into the workspace. The target definition appears in the Mapping Designer as shown in the following screenshot:

6. The final step is to connect the Source Qualifier transformation to the target definition.

7. Drag the columns from Source Qualifier Transformation to Target as shown in the following screenshot. Make sure you are linking the ports properly as any mismatch in linking the ports will make the data movement incorrect.

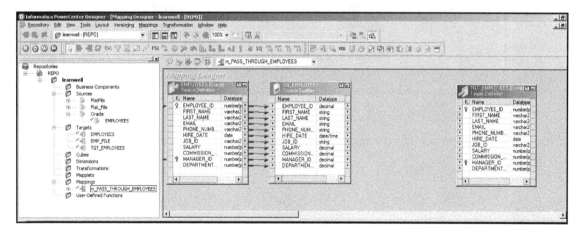

8. If you connect the links incorrectly by mistake, you can delete the links by clicking on the link and pressing the **Delete** button on your keyboard.

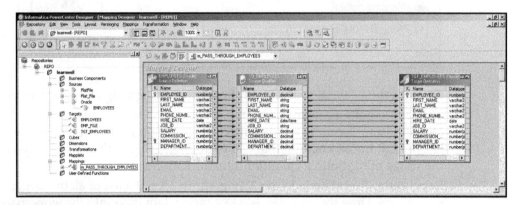

9. Go to **Repository** | **Save to** save the contents in repository:

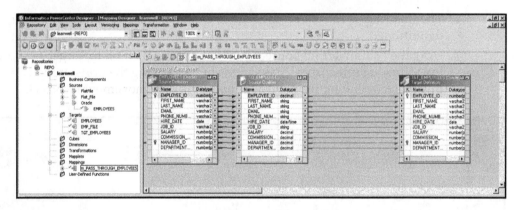

With this, the mapping is complete and saved in Repository. You can check the details in the Output panel.

# Summary

We started the chapter with the basic components of PowerCenter Designer screen, that is Source Analyzer, Target Designer, Transformation Developer, Mapplet Designer, Mapping Designer. You then learned to work on different types of sources, including flat files (delimited files and fixed width files) and relational databases. Similarly, we worked on different types of targets. We also worked upon the import and create functionality of sources and targets. Later in the chapter, we saw how to preview the data. The last and most important aspect you learned in this chapter is creating the mappings using Sources and Targets.

Informatica PowerCenter Designer screen, of course, cannot be that simple. Moving ahead, in the next chapter, we will see the advanced concepts of the Designer Screen. There are lot of high-level functionalities that are added in the Designer window to help in better and faster processing.

In the next chapter, we will see how to process the data by managing the constraints in the database. We will also see the utility to debug the mapping, which will help in finding the error. We will also see the concept of reusable functionality of transformations and mapping.

# 4
# The Lifeline of Informatica - Transformations

Transformations form the most important aspect of the **Informatica PowerCenter** tool. The functionality of any ETL tool lies in the transformations. Needless to say at this point, transformations are used to transform data. Informatica PowerCenter provides multiple transformations, each serving a particular functionality. Transformations can be created as reusable or non-reusable based on the requirement. The transformations created in workflow manager are non-reusable, and those created in task developer are reusable. You can create mapping with a single transformation or with multiple transformations.

When you run the workflow, integration service extracts the data in a row-wise manner from the source path/connection you defined in the session task and makes it flow from the mapping. The data reaches the target through the transformations you defined.

The data always flows in a row-wise manner in Informatica, no matter what your calculation or manipulation is. So, if you have 10 records in the source, there will be 10 source-to-target flows while the process is executed.

We will be talking about the following topics in this chapter:

- Adding transformation in mapping
- Ports of transformation
- Various transformations such as Expression, Aggregator, Sorter, Filter, Router, Lookup, Sequence Generator, Update Strategy, and so on
- Classification of transformation
- Tracing levels

# Creating the transformation

There are various ways in which you can create the transformation in the designer tool. They are discussed in the following sections.

## Mapping Designer

To create transformations using **Mapping Designer**, perform the following steps:

1. Open the Mapping in Mapping Designer. Then open the mapping in which you wish to add transformation, and click on **Transformation | Create** as shown:

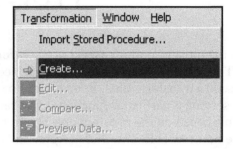

2. From the drop-down list of transformations, select the transformation you wish to create, specify the name, and click on **Create** and then **Done**:

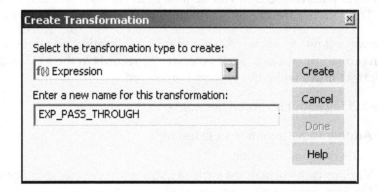

The transformation appears in the Mapping Designer workspace.

For our reference, we have created an **Expression** transformation in the preceding screenshot. You can create all other transformations in the same way.

The transformations you create in Mapping Designer are non-reusable, that is, you cannot use those transformations in other mappings. You will learn about reusable transformations in Chapter 5, *Using the Designer Screen - Advanced Features*.

# Mapplet Designer

To create transformations in Mapplet Designer, perform the following steps:

1. Open the Mapplet in Mapplet Designer, and click on **Transformation | Create** as shown previously.
2. From the drop-down list of transformations, select the transformation you wish to create, and specify the name.

# Transformation Developer

To create transformations in designer, perform the following steps:

1. Open the Transformation Developer, and go to **Transformation | Create** as shown previously under *Mapping Designer*.
2. From the drop-down list of transformations, select the transformation you wish to create, and specify the name as shown in the preceding section under *Mapping Designer*.

The transformations created in the Transformation Developer are reusable, that is, you can use them across multiple Mappings or Mapplets.

With this basic understanding, we are all set to jump into the most important aspect of Informatica PowerCenter tool--the transformations.

# Expression transformation

Expression transformation is used for row-wise manipulation. For any type of manipulation you wish to do on an individual record, use expression transformation. Expression transformation accepts row-wise data, manipulates it, and passes to the target. The transformation receives the data from the input port and sends the data out from the output ports.

Use the expression transformation for any row-wise calculation, for instance, if you want to concatenate the names, calculate the total salary and convert in upper case, and so on. To understand functionality of expression transformation, let's consider the following scenario:

**Scenario for expression transformation:** Using the flat file we created in Chapter 3, *Understanding Designer Screen and its Components* as the source, concatenate FIRST_NAME and LAST_NAME to get FULL_NAME, and get TOTAL_SALARY from JAN_SALARY and FEB_SALARY of individual employee.

We are using expression transformation in this scenario because the value of FULL_NAME can be achieved by concatenating FIRST_NAME and LAST_NAME of an individual record. Similarly, we can get TOTAL_SALARY using JAN_SALARY and FEB_SALARY . In other words, the manipulation required is row wise.

We are going to learn some basic aspects about transformations such as ports of transformations, writing a function, and so on while we implement our first transformation using Expression.

Perform the following steps to achieve the functionality:

1.  Create the source using the flat file in Source Analyzer and target in Target Designer. We will be using EMP_FILE as the source and TGT_EMP_FILE as the target.
2.  Create a new mapping m_EXP_CONCAT_TOTAL in mapping designer, drag the source and target from Navigator to Workspace, and create the Expression Transformation with the name EXP_CONCAT_TOTAL.
3.  Drag all the columns from source qualifier to expression transformation. At this point, the mapping will look like this:

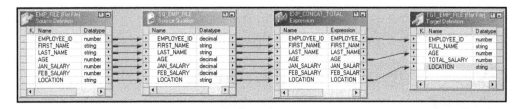

We have connected EMPLOYEE_ID, AGE and LOCATION directly to target as there is no manipulation needed for those columns.

At this step, we need to understand how to use the different types of ports in the transformation.

# Ports in transformations

The transformations receive the data from the input ports and send the data out using the output ports. Variable ports temporarily store the value while processing the data.

Every transformation with a few exceptions has input and output ports as shown in the following screenshot:

Double-click on the transformation, and click on **Ports** to open the edit view to see the input, output, and variable ports:

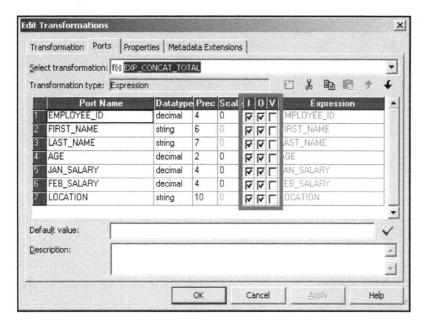

You can disable or enable input or output ports based on the requirement. In our scenario, we need to use the values coming from input port and send it by the output port using concatenate by writing the function in the expression editor.

Create two new output ports for FULL_NAME after LAST_NAME and TOTAL_SALARY after FEB_SALARY. To add new ports, double-click on the expression transformation, click on **Ports**, and add two new output ports as shown in the following screenshot:

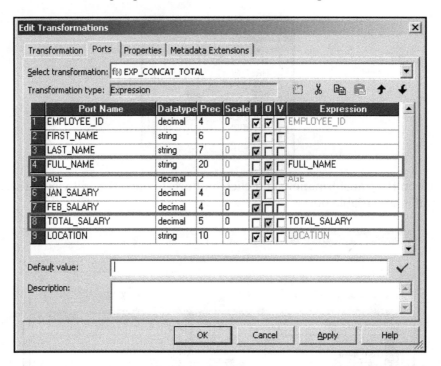

Make sure you define proper data type and size of the new ports added. As you can notice, we have disabled input ports of FULL_NAME and TOTAL_SALARY. Also, as you must have noticed, we have disabled the output ports of FIRST_NAME, LAST_NAME, JAN_SALARY, and FEB_SALARY as we do not wish to pass the data to output from those ports. This is as per the coding standards we follow in Informatica.

Once you disable the input port of FULL_NAME and TOTAL_SALARY, you will be able to write the function for the port.

# Using the expression editor

To manipulate the date, we need to write the functions in the ports. You can use the functions provided from the list of functions inside the expression editor.

1. Click on the icon as shown in the following screenshot to open the expression editor:

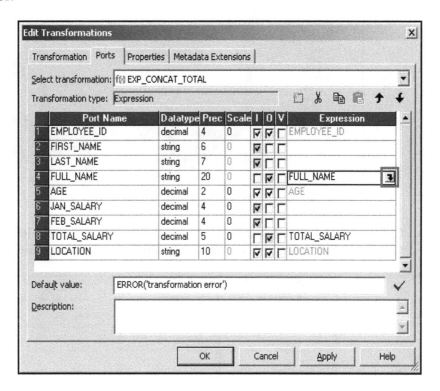

2. New windows will pop up where you can write the function. From the **Functions** tab, you can use functions. Informatica PowerCenter provides all the functions that cater to the need of SQL/Oracle functions, mathematical functions, trigonometric functions, date functions, and so on.

3. In our scenario ,we need to use the CONCAT function. Double-click on the **Concat** function under the list of functions to get the function in the editor as shown in the following screenshot:

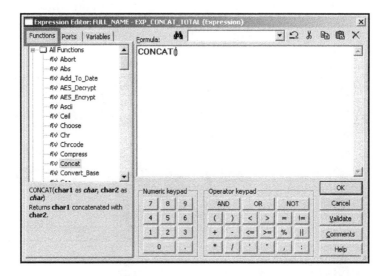

4. Click on **Ports** in the expression editor, and double-click on **FIRST_NAME** and **LAST_NAME** to get the function as shown in the following screenshot:

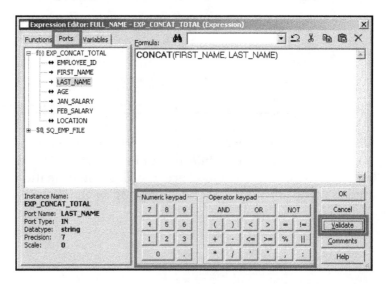

- As you can notice in the preceding screenshot, the expression editor provides a numeric keypad and an operator keypad that can be used to write the functions.
- Once you complete writing the function, click on **Validate** to make sure the function is correct syntactically. Click on **OK**.
- Similarly, write the function for calculating `TOTAL_SALARY`, which is `JAN_SAL+FEB_SAL`.

5. Link the corresponding ports to the target as shown in the following screenshot:

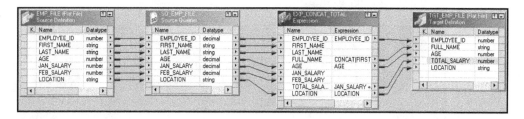

- Save the mapping to save the metadata in the repository. With this, we are done with creating the mapping using expression transformation. We have also discussed the ports and learned how to use the expression editor. You also learned how to write the function in transformation. These details will be used across all other transformations in Informatica.

# Aggregator transformation

Aggregator transformation is used for calculations using aggregate functions on a column as against in expression transformation, which is used for row-wise manipulation.

You can use aggregate functions such as **SUM, AVG, MAX, MIN** in aggregator transformation.

**Scenario for aggregator transformation:** Use the **EMPLOYEE** oracle table as the source, and get the sum of salaries of all the employees in the target.

Perform the following steps to achieve the functionality:

1.  Import the source using the **Employee Oracle** table in the Source Analyzer, and create `Target TGT_TOTAL_SALARY` in Target Designer.

2.  Create mapping `m_AGG_TOTAL_SALARY`, and drag the source and target from the Navigator to Workspace. Create the aggregator transformation with the name `AGG_TOTAL_SAL`.

3.  As we need to calculate `TOTAL_SALARY`, drag only the `SALARY` column from the Source Qualifier to aggregator transformation, as shown here:

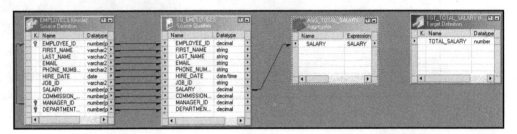

4.  Add a new column `TOTAL_SALARY` in the aggregator transformation to calculate the total salary as shown in the following screenshot:

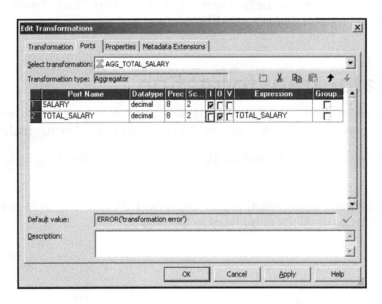

5. Add the function in the `TOTAL_SALARY` port by opening the expression editor as described in the preceding section. The function we need to add to get the total salary is `SUM(JAN_SAL)`:

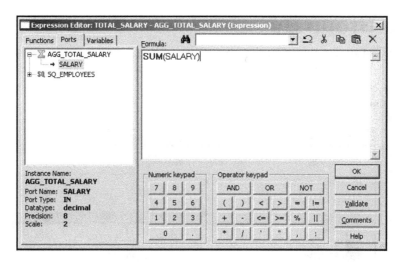

6. Connect the `TOTAL_SALARY` port to the target as shown in the following screenshot:

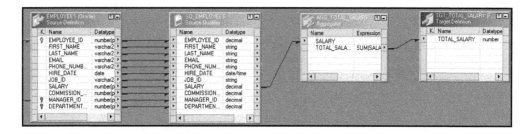

With this, we are done using the aggregator transformation. When you use aggregator transformation, integration services store the data temporarily in cache memory. Cache memory is created because the data flows in a row-wise manner in Informatica, and the calculations required in aggregator transformation are column wise. Unless we store the data temporarily in cache, we cannot calculate the result. In the preceding scenario, the cache starts storing the data as soon as the first record flows into the aggregator transformation. Cache will be discussed in detail later in the chapter under the *Lookup transformation* section.

In the next section, we will talk about added features of aggregator transformation. Aggregator transformation comes with features such as group by and sorted input.

# Using Group By

Using the **Group By** option in aggregator transformation, you can get the result of the aggregate function based on the group. Suppose you wish to get the sum of salaries of all employees based on Department_ID. We use the group by option to implement the scenario as shown in the following screenshot:

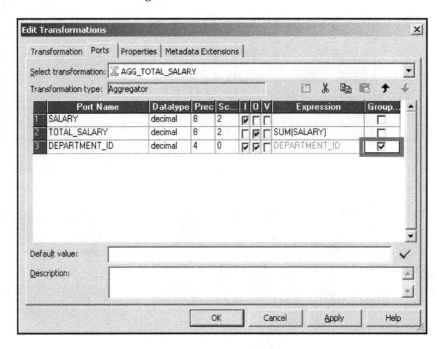

# Using Sorted Input

It is always recommended that we pass sorted input to aggregator transformation as this will enhance the performance. When you pass the sorted input to aggregator transformation, integration services enhance the performance by storing less data in cache. When you pass unsorted data, aggregator transformation stores all the data into cache, which takes more time. When you pass the sorted data to aggregator transformation, aggregator transformation stores comparatively less data. The aggregator passes the result of each group as soon as the data for the particular group is received.

Note that aggregator transformation does not sort the data. If you have unsorted data, use sorter transformation to sort the data, and then pass the sorted data to the aggregator transformation to enhance the performance.

When you pass the sorted data to the aggregator transformation, check the **Sorted Input** option in the properties as shown in the following screenshot:

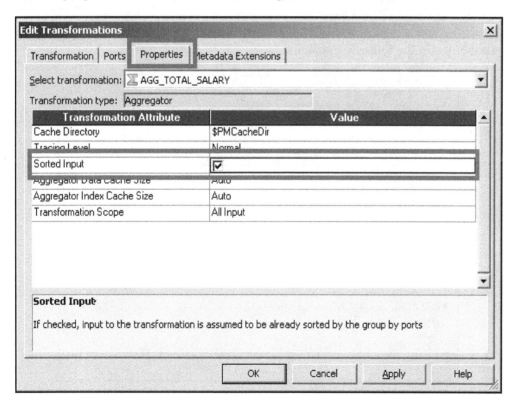

# Sorter transformation

Sorter transformation is used to sort the data in ascending or descending order based on single key or multiple keys. A sample mapping showing sorter transformation is indicated in the following screenshot:

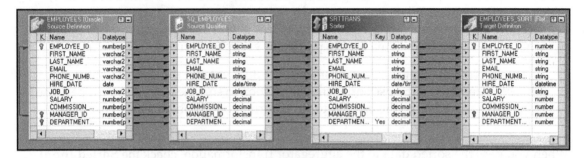

In the preceding mapping, we wish to sort the data based on the DEPARTMENT_ID field. To achieve this, mark the key port for the DEPARTMENT_ID columns in the sorter transformation, and select from the drop-down you wish to have **Ascending** or **Descending** sorting as shown in the following screenshot:

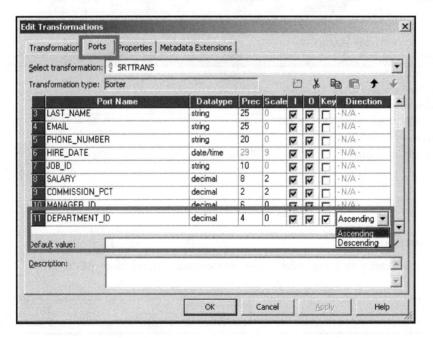

If you wish to sort the data on multiple columns, check the **Key** ports corresponding to the required port.

Apart from ordering the data in ascending or descending order, you can also use sorter transformation to remove duplicates from the data using the distinct option in the properties. Sorter can remove duplicates only if the complete record is duplicate, and not only a particular column. To remove the duplicate, check the **Distinct** option in sorter transformation as shown in the following screenshot:

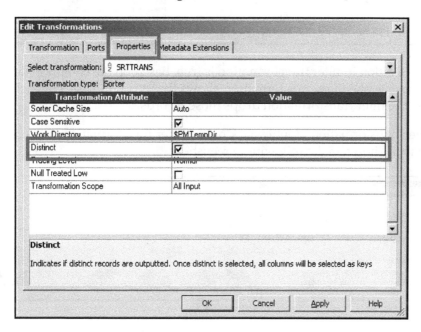

Sorter transformation accepts the data in a row-wise manner and stores the data in cache internally. Once the data in received completely, it sorts the data in ascending or descending order based on the condition and sends the data to the output port.

# Filter transformation

Filter transformation is used to remove unwanted records from the mapping. You define the filter condition in the filter transformation, based on which the records will be rejected or passed further in mapping.

A sample mapping showing the filter transformation is shown in the following screenshot:

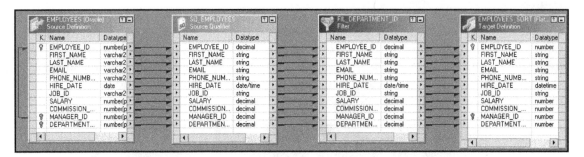

The default condition in filter transformation is true. Based on the condition defined, if the record returns true, the filter transformation allows the record to pass. For each record that returns false, the filter transformation drops those records.

To add a filter transformation, double-click on the filter transformation, and click on the **Properties** tab as shown in the following screenshot:

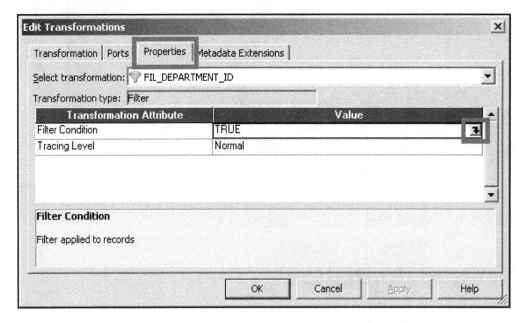

Click on the button as shown in the preceding screenshot to open the expression editor to add the function for the filter condition. Add the required condition. We have used DEPARTMENT_ID=100 as the condition. This will allow records with DEPARTMENT_ID =100 to reach the target, rest all records will get filtered.

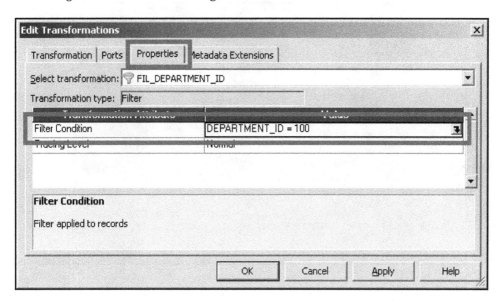

# Router transformation

Router transformation is a single input and multiple output group transformation. Router can be used in place of multiple filter transformations. Router transformation accepts the data once through the input group, and based on the output groups you define, it sends the data to multiple output ports. You need to define the filter condition in each output group.

A mapping using router transformation where we wish to load all the records from LOCATION as INDIA in one target records from UK in another target, and all other non-matching records in the third target is indicated in the following screenshot:

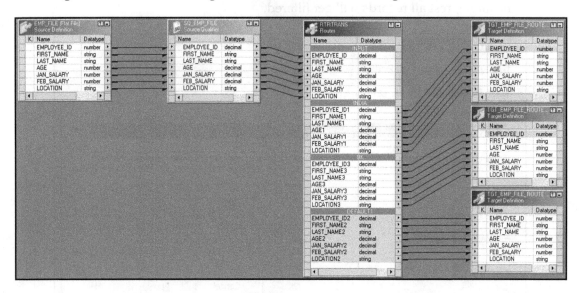

When you drag the columns to the router, the router transformation creates an input group with only input ports and no output port. To add the output groups, click on the **Groups** tab, and add two new groups. Mention the name of each group under the group name, and define the filter condition for each group. Click on **OK** to get the output groups created in router transformation:

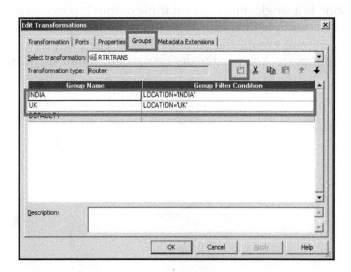

When you add the group, a default group gets created automatically. All non-matching records from the other groups will pass through the default group if you connect the default group output ports to the target.

When you pass the records to router transformation through the input group, the router transformation checks the records based on the Filter condition you define in each output group. For each record matching, the condition passes further. For each record that fails, the condition is passed to the default group.

As you can understand now, router transformation is used in place of multiple Filter transformations.

# Rank transformation

Rank transformation is used to get the top or bottom specific number of records. Consider that you need to take the top five salaried employees from the EMPLOYEE table; you can use rank transformation and define the property. A sample mapping indicating the Rank transformation is shown in the following screenshot:

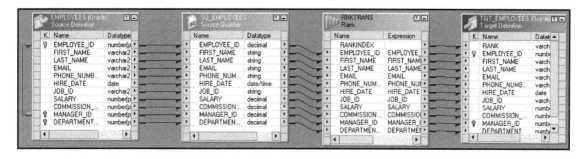

When you create a Rank transformation, a default output port RANKINDEX comes with the transformation. It is not mandatory to use the RANKINDEX port. We have connected the RANKINDEX port to the target as we wish to denote the rank of the employees based on their **SALARY**.

When you use Rank transformation, you need to define the port on which you wish to rank the data. As shown in the following screenshot, we have ranked the data based on **SALARY**:

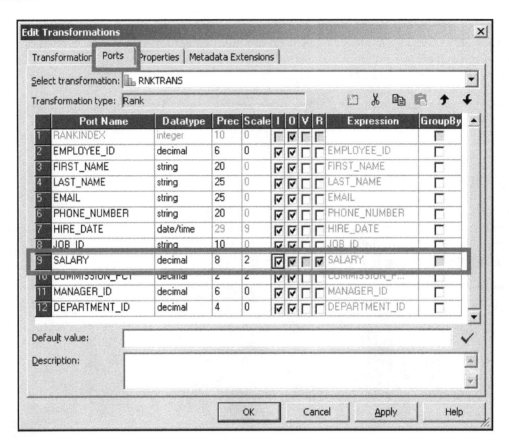

You cannot rank the data on multiple ports.

Also, you need to define either the **Top** or **Bottom** option and the number of records you wish to rank in the **Properties** tab. In our case, we have selected **Top** and **5** numbers to implement the scenario as shown in the following screenshot:

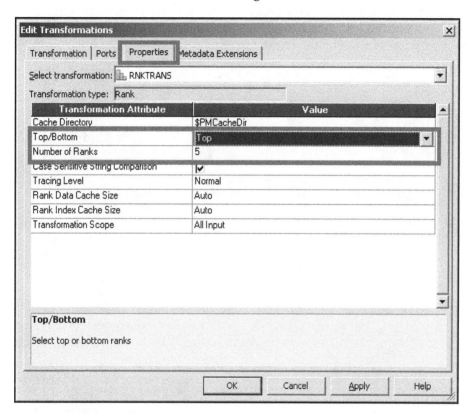

Rank transformation accepts the data in a row-wise manner and stores the data in cache. Once the data in received completely, it checks the data based on the condition and sends the data to the output port.

Rank transformation allows you to get the data based on a particular group. In the next section, we will talk about the group by key present in Rank transformation.

# Group by Ranking

Rank transformation also provides a feature to get the data based on a particular group. Consider the scenario discussed in the preceding section. We need to get the top five salaried employees from each department. To achieve the functionality, we need to select the **Group by** option as shown in the following screenshot:

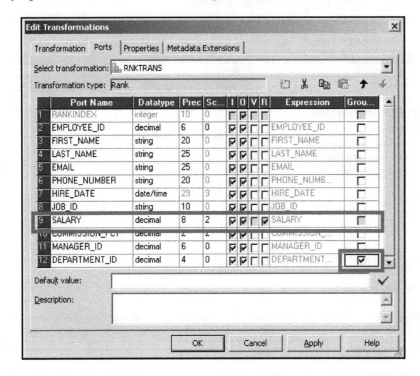

As we proceed in the chapter, we will talk about the default port of the Rank transformation, that is, Rank Index.

# Rank Index

When you create a Rank transformation, a default column gets created called Rank Index. This port, if required, can generate numbers indicating the Rank. This is an optional field that you may use if required. If you do not wish to use Rank Index, you can leave the port unconnected.

Suppose you have following data belonging to the SALARY column in the source:

| SALARY |
|--------|
| 100 |
| 1000 |
| 500 |
| 600 |
| 1000 |
| 800 |
| 900 |

When you pass the data through Rank transformation and define the condition to get the top five salaried records, the Rank transformation generates the Rank index as indicated here:

| Rank_Index | Salary |
|------------|--------|
| 1 | 1000 |
| 1 | 1000 |
| 3 | 900 |
| 4 | 800 |
| 5 | 600 |

As you can see, Rank index assigns rank 1 to the same salary value and assigns 3 to the next salary since it is actually $3^{rd}$ in the sequence. So, if you have five records with 1,000 as salary in the source along with other values and you defined the condition to get the top five salaries, Rank transformation will give all five records with 1,000 salary and reject all others.

With this, you have learned all the details about Rank transformation.

# Sequence Generator transformation

Sequence Generator transformation is used to generate a sequence of unique numbers. Based on the property defined in the Sequence Generator transformation, the unique values are generated. A sample mapping showing the Sequence Generator transformation in shown in the following screnshot:

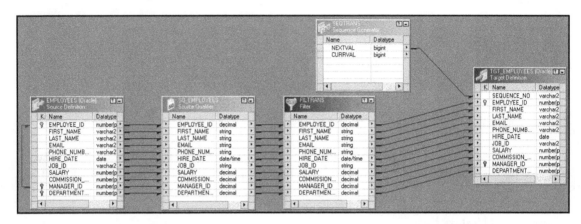

As you can notice in the mapping, the Sequence Generator transformation does not have any input port. You need to define the `Start` value, `Increment by` value, and `End` value in the properties. Based on properties, the sequence generator generates the value. In the preceding mapping, as soon as the first record enters the target from the Source Qualifier transformation, `NEXTVAL` generates its first value and so on for other records. The sequence Generator is built for generating numbers.

# Ports of Sequence Generator transformation

Sequence Generator transformation has only two ports, namely `NEXTVAL` and `CURRVAL`. Both the ports are output ports. You cannot add or delete any port in the Sequence Generator. It is recommended that you always use the `NEXTVAL` port first. If the `NEXTVAL` port is utilized, then use the `CURRVAL` port. You can define the value of `CURRVAL` in the properties of the Sequence Generator transformation.

Consider a scenario where we are passing two records to transformation; the following events occur inside the Sequence Generator transformation. Also, note that in our case, we have defined the `Start` value as *0*, the `Increment by` value as *1*, and the `End` value is *default* in the property. Also, the current value defined in properties is 1. The following is the sequence of events:

1. When the first record enters the target from the Filter transformation, the current value, which is set to 1 in the properties of the Sequence Generator, is assigned to the NEXTVAL port. This gets loaded into the target by the connected link. So, for the first record, SEQUENCE_NO in the target gets the value as 1.

2. The Sequence Generator increments CURRVAL internally and assigns that value to the current value, which is 2 in this case.

3. When the second record enters the target, the current value, which is set as 2, now gets assigned to NEXTVAL. The Sequence Generator increments CURRVAL internally to make it 3.

So at the end of the processing of record 2, the NEXTVAL port will have value 2 and the CURRVAL port will have value set as 3. This is how the cycle keeps on running till you reach the end of the records from the source.

It is a little confusing to understand how the NEXTVAL and CURRVAL ports are behaving, but after reading the preceding example, you will have a proper understanding of the process.

# Properties of Sequence Generator transformation

There are multiple values that you need to define inside the Sequence Generator transformation. Double-click on the Sequence Generator, and click on the **Properties** tab as shown in the following screenshot:

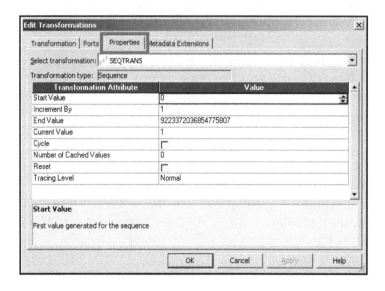

Let's discuss the properties in detail:

- **Start Value:**This comes into the picture only if you select the **Cycle** option in the properties. It indicates the integration service to start over from this value as soon as the end value is reached when you have checked the cycle option.
- The default value is 0, and the maximum value is 9223372036854775806.
- **Increment By:** This is the value by which you wish to increment the consecutive numbers from the NEXTVAL port.
- The default value is 1, and the maximum value is 2147483647.
- **End Value:** This is the maximum value Integration service can generate. If the Sequence Generator reaches the end value and if it is not configured for the cycle, the session will fail, giving the error as data overflow. The maximum value is 9223372036854775807.
- **Current Value:** This indicates the value assigned to the CURRVAL port. Specify the current value that you wish to have for the first record. As mentioned in the preceding section, the CURRVAL port gets assigned to NEXTVAL, and the CURRVAL port is incremented.
- The CURRVAL port stores the value after the session is over, and when you run the session the next time, it starts incrementing the value from the stored value if you have not checked the reset option. If you check the reset option, Integration service resets the value to 1. Suppose you have not checked the **Reset** option and you have passed 17 records at the end of the session, the current value will be set to 18, which will be stored internally. When you run the session the next time, it starts generating the value from 18.
- The maximum value is 9223372036854775807.
- **Cycle:**If you check this option, Integration services cycles through the sequence defined. If you do not check this option, the process stops at the defined End Value.
- If your source records are more than the End value defined, the session will fail with the overflow error.
- **Number of Cached Values:** This option indicates how many sequential values Integration service can cache at a time. This option is useful only when you are using reusable sequence generator transformation.
- The default value for non-reusable transformation is 0. The default value for reusable transformation is 1,000. The maximum value is 9223372036854775807.

- **Reset:**If you do not check this option, the Integration services store the value of the previous run and generate the value from the stored value. Else, the Integration will reset to the defined current value and generate values from the initial value defined. This property is disabled for reusable Sequence Generator transformation.
- **Tracing Level:**This indicates the level of detail you wish to write into the session log. We will discuss this option in detail later in the chapter.

With this, we have seen all the properties of the Sequence Generator transformation.

Let's talk about the usage of Sequence Generator transformation:

- **Generating Primary/Foreign Key:**Sequence Generator can be used to generate primary key and foreign key. Primary key and foreign key should be unique and not null; the Sequence Generator transformation can easily do this as seen in the preceding section. Connect the NEXTVAL port to both the targets for which you wish to generate the primary and foreign keys as shown in the following screenshot:

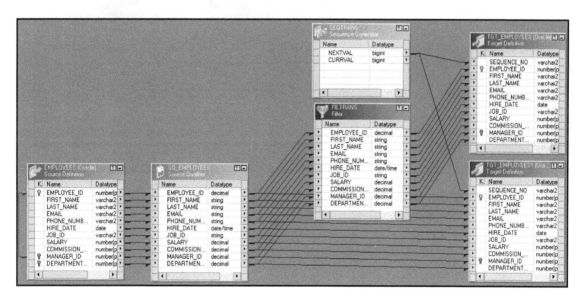

- **Replace missing values:** You can use the Sequence Generator transformation to replace missing values by using the IIF and ISNULL functions. Consider you have some data with JOB_ID of Employee. Some records do not have JOB_ID in the table. Use the following function to replace those missing values:

```
IIF( ISNULL (JOB_ID), NEXTVAL, JOB_ID)
```

- The preceding function interprets if the JOB_ID is null, then assign NEXTVAL, else keep JOB_ID as it is. The following screenshot indicates the preceding requirement:

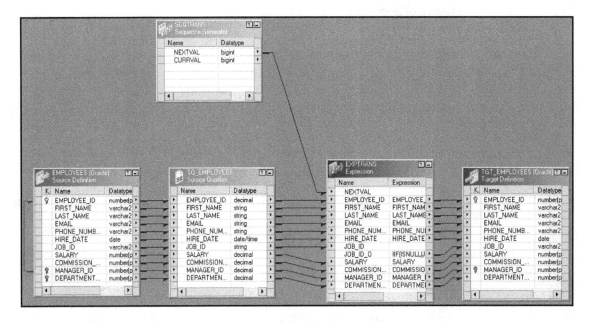

With this, you have learned all the options present in the Sequence Generator transformation. Next, we will talk about Joiner transformation.

# Joiner transformation

Joiner transformation is used to join two heterogeneous sources. You can join data from same the source type also. The minimum criteria for joining the data are a matching column in both the sources. A mapping indicating the Joiner transformation is shown in the following screenshot:

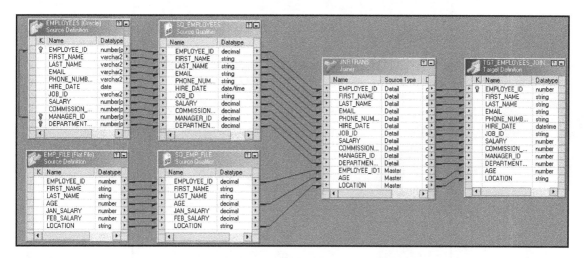

Joiner transformation has two pipelines, one is called **Master** and the other is called **Detail**. We do not have any left or right Join as we have in SQL database.

To use Joiner transformation, drag all the required columns from the two sources into Joiner transformation, and define the Join condition and Join type in the properties.

# Master and Detail Pipeline

By default, when you add the first source, it becomes Detail and the other becomes Master. You can decide to change the master or detail source. To make a source the Master source, check the **Master** port for the corresponding source as shown in the following screenshot:

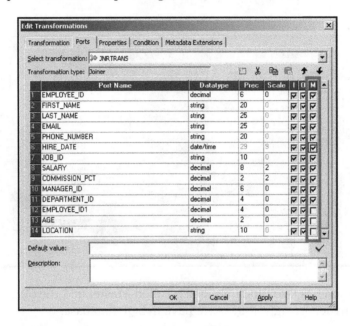

Always verify that the Master and Detail sources are defined to enhance the performance. It is always recommended to make the table with less number of records the Master and the other one Details. This is because Integration service picks the data from the Master source and scans the corresponding record in the Details table. So, if we have less number of records in the Master table, there will be less iteration scanning. This enhances the performance.

# Join condition

As aforementioned, Join condition is the most important element to join the data. To define the Join condition, you need to have a common port in both the sources. Also, make sure the data type and precision of the data you are joining are the same. You can join the data based on multiple columns as well. Joining the data on multiple columns increases the processing time. Usually, you join the data based on key columns such as the primary key of both the table and the primary/foreign key relation of the tables.

Joiner transformation does not consider NULL as matching data. If it receives NULL in the data, it does not consider them matching.

To define the Join Condition, double-click on the Joiner transformation, click on the **Condition** tab, and define the new condition:

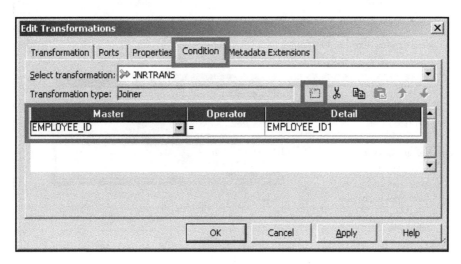

You can define multiple conditions to join two tables.

# Join type

Based on the join type defined, the Joiner transformation matches the data. Similar to SQL, joiner transformation uses the join type to join the data. Let's discuss the join type in detail by taking the following example. We have two sources, EMPLOYEE_TABLE as the master source and EMPLOYEE_FILE the other detail source:

```
EMPLOYEE_TABLE (Master Source - Oracle`)
EMPLOYEE_ID,AGE
101,20
102,30
103,20
EMPLOYEE_FILE (Detail Source - Flat File)
EMPLOYEE_ID,SAL
101,1000
103,4000
105,2000
106,4000
110,5000
```

As you can notice, we have made a table with fewer records as the master source to enhance the performance. To assign the Join type, double-click on Joiner transformation, and click on the **Properties** tab. Select the join type out of four types from the drop-down as shown here:

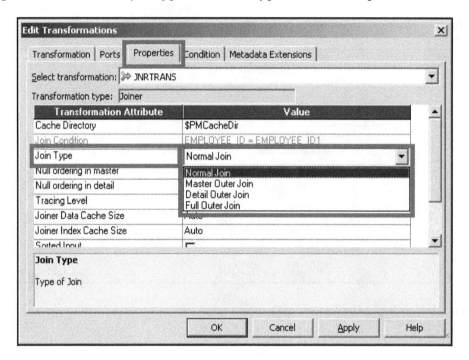

## Normal join

When you define a normal join, Integration service allows only matching records from both master and detail sources and discards all other records.

For the preceding scenario, we will put `EMPLOYEE_ID = EMPLOYEE_ID` as the join condition.

The result of the Normal join for the aforementioned data is shown here:

```
EMPLOYEE_ID,AGE,SAL
101,20,1000
103,20,4000
```

As mentioned, with Normal join, all non-matching records will get rejected.

# Full join

When you define a full join, Integration service allows all the matching and non-matching records from both the Master and Detail sources.

The result of the Full join for the aforementioned data is shown next:

```
EMPLOYEE_ID,AGE,SAL
101,20,1000
102,30,NULL
103,20,4000
105,NULL,2000
106,NULL,4000
110,NULL,5000
```

# Master Outer join

When you define a Master Outer join, Integration service allows all matching records from both the Master and Detail sources and also allows all other records from the Details table.

The result of the Master Outer join for the aforementioned data is shown here:

```
EMPLOYEE_ID,AGE,SAL
101,20,1000
103,20,4000
105,NULL,2000
106,NULL,4000
110,NULL,5000
```

# Detail Outer join

When you define a Detail Outer join, Integration service allows all matching records from both the Master and Detail sources and also allow all other records from the Master table.

The result of the Detail Outer join for the aforementioned data is shown here:

```
EMPLOYEE_ID,AGE,SAL
101,20,1000
102,30,NULL
103,20,4000
```

With this, you have learned about the various options available in Joiner transformation.

# Union transformation

Union transformation is used to the merge data from multiple sources. A union is a multiple-input-single-output transformation. This is the opposite of the router transformation that we discussed earlier. The basic criterion for using union transformation is that you should have data with matching data type. If you do not have data with matching data type coming from multiple sources, union transformation will not work. Union transformation merges the data coming from multiple sources and does not remove duplicates, that is. it acts as **UNION ALL** of SQL statements.

As mentioned previously, Union requires data coming from multiple sources. It reads the data concurrently from multiple sources and processes the data. You can use heterogeneous sources to merge the data using Union transformation.

A mapping indicating the Union transformation is shown in the following screenshot:

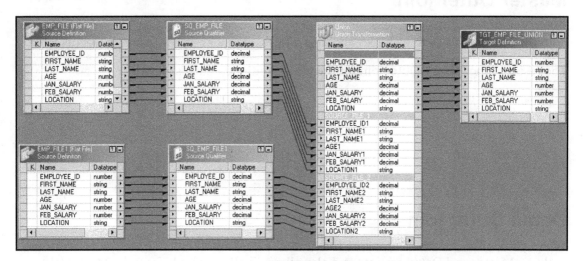

Working on Union transformation is a little different from working on other transformations, which we will discuss in this section. To create union transformations, follow these steps:

1. Once you create a Union transformation, drag all the required ports from one source to Union transformation. As soon you drag the port, Union creates an Input group and another Output group with the same ports as Input.

2. Add the Output groups from the **Group** tab in Union transformation. Add as many groups as many input sources you have, as shown in the following screenshot:

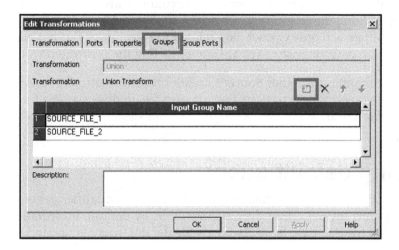

3. Once you add the groups, Union transformation creates the groups with the same ports as shown in the preceding mapping.
4. Link the ports from other sources to the input ports of other groups in Union transformation.

With this, we have created mapping using Union transformation.

# Source Qualifier transformation

Source Qualifier transformation acts as a virtual source in Informatica. When you drag a relational table or flat file in Mapping Designer, Source Qualifier transformation comes along. Source Qualifier is the point where Informatica processing actually starts. The extraction process starts from the Source Qualifier.

Note that it is always recommended that the columns of Source and Source Qualifier match. Do not change the columns or their data type in the Source Qualifier. You can notice the difference in the data type in the Source Definition and Source Qualifier, which is because Informatica interprets the data in that way only.

To discuss Source Qualifier, let's take an example of the Joiner transformation mapping we created earlier.

As you can notice, there are two Source Qualifier transformations present in mapping: one for flat file and the other for relational database. You can notice that we have connected only three columns from the Source Qualifier transformation of flat files to Joiner transformation. To reiterate the point, all the columns are dragged from Source to Source Qualifier, and only three columns are linked to Joiner transformation. This indicates that Source Qualifier will only extract data related to three ports, but not all. This helps in improving the performance as we are not extracting the unwanted columns data.

In the same mapping, another Source Qualifier transformation is connected to relational source. There are multiple options that are possible in this case. We have discussed each option in detail next.

# Viewing default query

When you use the relational database as source, source qualifier generates a default SQL query to extract the data from the database table. By default, Informatica extracts all the records from the database table. To check the default query generated by Informatica, follow these steps:

1. Double-click on the Source Qualifier transformation, click on the **Properties** tab, and select SQL query:

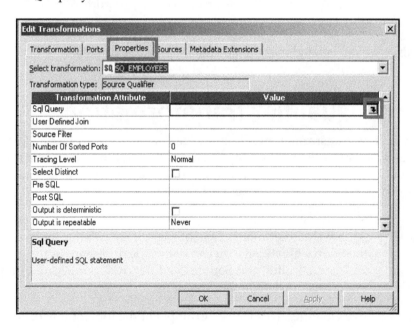

2. The SQL editor opens. Click on the **Generate SQL** option. If required, specify the database username and password:

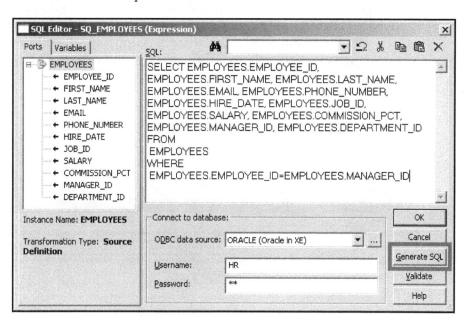

Informatica shows the default query based on the links connected from the Source Qualifier transformation.

# Overriding default query

We can override the default query generated by Source Qualifier transformation. If you override the default query generated by Source Qualifier, it is called **SQL override**. You should not change the list of ports or the order of the ports in the default query. You can write a new query or edit the default query generated by Informatica. You can perform various operations while overriding the default query.

# Using the WHERE clause

You can add the WHERE clause in the SQL query while you override the default query. When you add the WHERE clause, you reduce the number of records extracted from the source. This way, we say that our Source Qualifier transformation is acting as Filter transformation. You can also define the WHERE condition in the Source filter. If you define the source filter, you need not add the WHERE clause in the SQL query. You can add the source filter as shown in the following screenshot:

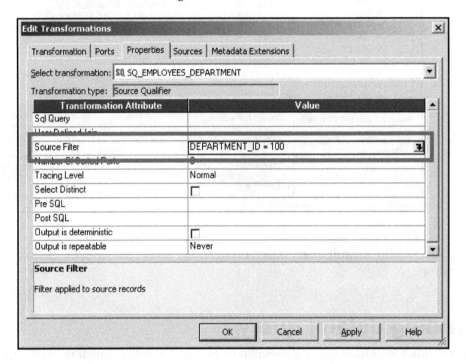

# Joining Source Data

You can use the Source Qualifier transformation to define the user-defined join types. When you use this option you can avoid using Joiner transformation in the mapping. When you use Source Qualifier transformation for joining the data from two database tables, you will not use Master or Detail join. You will use the Database level join types, like left and right join. We will use the EMPLOYEE and DEPARTMENT oracle tables to join the data using Source Qualifier transformation. Perform the following steps to use the Source Qualifier to perform join functionality:

1. Open the Mapping Designer, and drag the **EMPLOYEE** and **DEPARTMENT** oracle tables into mapping. Once you drag both the sources into Mapping Designer, delete the **Source Qualifier** from the **DEPARTMENT** table, and drag all the columns from the **DEPARTMENT Source Definition** into the **EMPLOYEE Source Qualifier** as shown in the following screenshot:

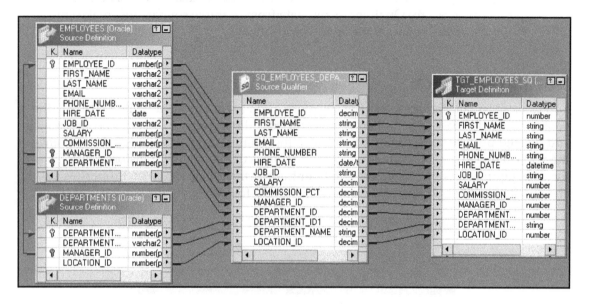

Link the required columns from Source Qualifier to target as per your requirement.

2. Open the **Properties** tab of the Source Qualifier transformation and generate the default SQL as discussed in the preceding section. Now you can modify the default generated query as per your requirement to perform the join on the two tables.

Using this feature helps in making our mapping simple by avoiding Joiner transformation and, in turn, helps in faster processing.

Note that you cannot always replace Joiner with Source Qualifier. This option can be utilized only if you wish to join data at the source level and both your sources are relational tables in the same database. You can use a single Source Qualifier to join data from multiple sources, just make sure the tables belong to same database scheme.

## Sorting the data

You can also use the **Source Qualifier** transformation to sort the data while extracting the data from the database table. When you use the sorted port option, Integration Service will add defined ports to the **ORDER BY** clause in the default query. It will keep the sequence of the ports in the query similar to the sequence of ports defined in the transformation. To sort the data, double-click on the Source Qualifier transformation, click on the **Properties** tab, and specify **Number Of SortedPorts** as shown in the following screenshot:

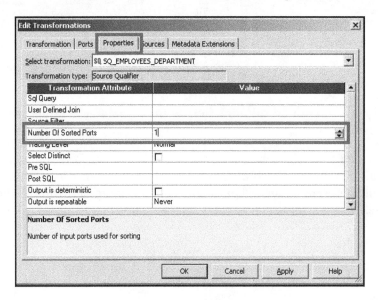

It will be possible only if your source is a database table and only if you wish to sort the data at the source level. If you wish to sort the data in between the mapping, you need to put Sorter transformation.

# Selecting distinct records

You can use Source Qualifier to remove the duplicates from the database tables using the Select Distinct option. By default, Integration Service writes the SELECT * statement, that is, it writes the query with all the columns in the default query. When you select the distinct option, Integration Service adds the **Select Distinct** statement into the query that it generates. Usually, we use the distinct option on the primary key of the database table. To add the Distinct command in your query, double-click on the Source Qualifier transformation, click on the **Properties** tab, and check the **Select Distinct** option as shown in the following screenshot:

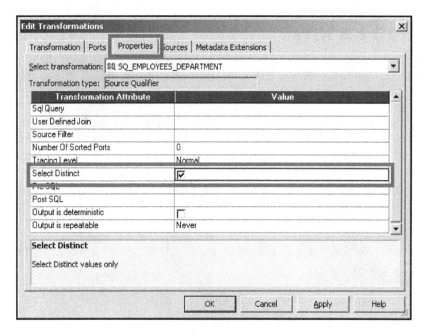

It will be possible only in case your source is a Database table and only if you wish to select unique records at the source level. If you wish to get unique records in between the mapping, you need to put Sorter transformation, which also provides features to remove duplicates.

# Classification of transformations

At this point, we have seen quite a few transformations and their functionality. Before we take the next transformations, let's talk about classification of transformations. The transformations based on their connectivity with other components are divided as Connected or Unconnected. The transformation based on the number of records at the input and output ports are divided as Active or Passive.

Let's first discuss Active and Passive Classification.

# Active and Passive

This classification of transformations is based on the number of records at the input and output ports of the transformation. This classification is not based on the number of ports or the number of groups.

If the transformation does not change the number of records at its input and output ports, it is said to be a Passive transformation. If the transformation changes the number of records at the input and output ports of the transformation, it is said to be an Active transformation. Also, if the transformation changes the sequence of records passing through it, it will be an Active transformation as in case of Union transformation. Let's take an example to understand the classification.

Consider the Expression transformation from the mapping we took in case of the preceding Expression transformation, where we concatenated FIRST_NAME and LAST_NAME as shown in the following screenshot:

As you can notice, the number of input ports is **7** and output ports is **5**. In that mapping, let's say our source contains **10** records. When we pass all the records to the transformation, the total records that will reach the input ports will be 10 and the total records that will reach the output ports will also be 10, so this makes Expression transformation Passive. We are not concerned about the number of ports at input and output.

Consider the example of Filter transformation, which filters out unwanted records. Since it changes the number of records, it is Active transformation.

# Connected and Unconnected

A transformation is said to be connected if it is connected to any source or any target or any other transformation by at least a link. If the transformation is not connected by any link, it is classed as Unconnected. Only Lookup and Stored Procedure transformations can be connected and unconnected, rest all transformations are connected.

# Lookup transformation

Lookup transformation is used to look up the source, Source Qualifier, or target to get the relevant data. You can look up in flat files and relational tables. Lookup transformation works on the similar lines as Joiner with a few differences, such as Lookup does not require two sources. Lookup transformations can be connected and unconnected. They extract the data from the lookup table or file based on the lookup condition. Perform the following steps to create and configure Lookup transformation:

# Creating the Lookup transformation

We will talk about the steps needed to create a lookup transformation:

1. In the Mapping Designer, click on **Transformations**, and create Lookup transformation. Specify the name of the Lookup transformation, and click on **OK**.

2. A new window will ask you to select the source, target, or Source Qualifier on which you wish to look up. You will get a list of all the sources, targets, and **Source Qualifier** available in your **Repository**. Click on the required component and then on **OK** as shown in the following screenshot:

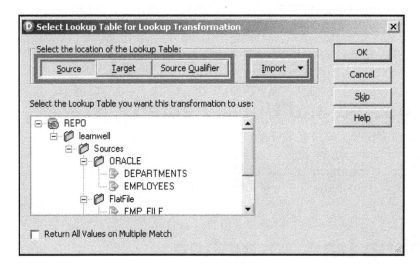

If the required source or target is not available in the Repository, you can import it before you can use it to look up. Click on the **Import** button to import the structure as shown in preceding screenshot.

The Lookup transformation with the same structure of the source or target or Source Qualifier appears in the workspace.

## Configuring the Lookup transformation

You have learned how to create the lookup transformation in the preceding section. We will implement the similar mapping shown in Joiner transformation using Lookup transformation. We will use the EMPLOYEE oracle table as source and look up on the EMP_FILE flat file. Follow these steps to implement the mapping:

1. Drag the **EMPLOYEE** table as the source in **Mapping Designer**, and drag the target.
2. We have already created the Lookup transformation in the preceding section.

3. To get the relevant data based on the matching condition of the **EMPLOYEE** table and the `EMP_FILE` file, drag the `EMPLOYEE_ID` column from the **EMPLOYEE** table to Lookup transformation. Drag the corresponding columns from the **EMPLOYEE Source Qualifier** and Lookup transformation to the target as shown in the following screenshot:

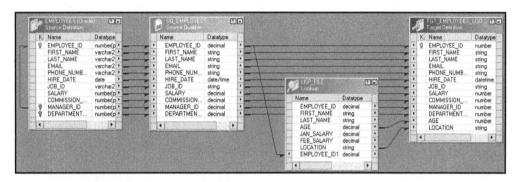

4. Click on the **Condition** tab, and create a new condition as shown in the following screenshot:

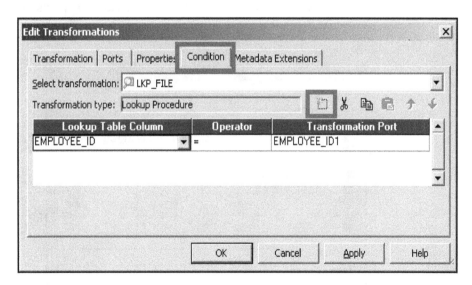

# Configuring the Lookup transformation

When you create the Lookup transformation, you can configure the lookup transformation to cache the data. Caching the data makes the processing faster since the data is stored internally after the cache is created. Once you select to cache the data, Lookup transformation caches the data from the file or table once, and then, based on the condition defined, lookup sends the output value. Since the data gets stored internally, the processing becomes faster as it does not require checking the lookup condition in the file or database. Integration services query the cache memory as against checking the file or table for fetching the required data.

When you select to create cache, Integration service creates cache files in the default directory $PMCacheDir. The cache is created automatically and also it is deleted automatically once the processing is complete. We will discuss about cache in the later part of the chapter under the *Types of Lookup cache* section.

# Lookup ports

Lookup transformation has four different types of ports. To view the ports of Lookup transformation, click on the **Ports** tab of Lookup transformation, as shown in the following screenshot:

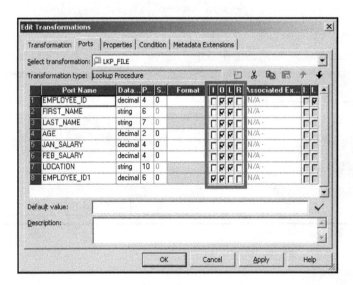

The ports are as follows:

- **Input Ports (I):**These receive the data from other transformations. This port will be used in the Lookup condition. You need to have at least one input port.
- **Output Port (O):** These pass the data out of the Lookup transformation to other transformations.
- **Lookup Port (L):** Each column is assigned a Lookup and Output port when you create the Lookup transformation. If you delete the lookup port from the flat file lookup source, the session will fail. If you delete the lookup port from the relational lookup table, Integration Services extract the data only with the Lookup port. This helps in reducing the data extracted from the lookup source.
- **Return Port (R):** This is only used in case of unconnected lookup transformation. This port indicates which data you wish to return in the Lookup transformation. You can define only one port as the return port. It is not used in case of Connected Lookup transformation.

# Lookup query

Similar to the Source Qualifier transformation, which generates a default query when you use the Source as a Relational database table, Lookup transformation also generates a default query based on the ports used in the Lookup transformation. To check the default query generated by Lookup transformation, click on the **Properties** tab, and open **Lookup Sql Override** as shown in the following screenshot:

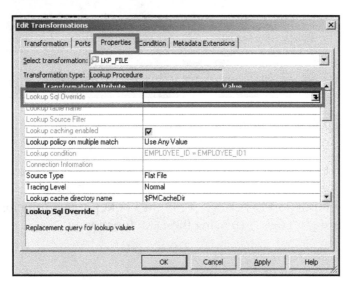

Similar to overriding the default SQL in the Source Qualifier transformation, you can override the default query generated by the Lookup transformation. If you override the default query generated by the Lookup transformation, it is referred to as Lookup SQL Override.

# Unconnected Lookup transformation

As mentioned in the preceding section, unconnected transformations are not connected to any other transformation or source or target by any links. Unconnected lookup transformation is called by another transformation using the :LKP function. Using the :LKP function, you pass the required value to the input port of the Lookup transformation, and the return port, in turn, pass the output value back to the transformation from which the lookup was called. A mapping using unconnected Lookup transformation is shown here:

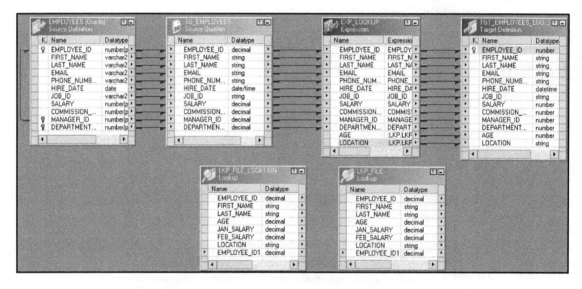

In the preceding mapping, we are implementing the same scenario we implement using Connected Lookup transformation. Follow these steps to implement the scenario:

1. Create an Expression transformation, and drag all the ports from the Source Qualifier transformation to the Expression transformation.
2. Create an input port EMPLOYEE_ID in the Lookup transformation that will accept the value of EMPLOYEE_ID using the :LKP function.

3. Create another output port AGE in the Expression transformation that is used to call the unconnected Lookup transformation using the :LKP function. Link the AGE port to the target. Write the :LKP.LKP_FILE(EMPLOYEE_ID) function in the **Expression Editor** of the AGE column as shown in the following screenshot:

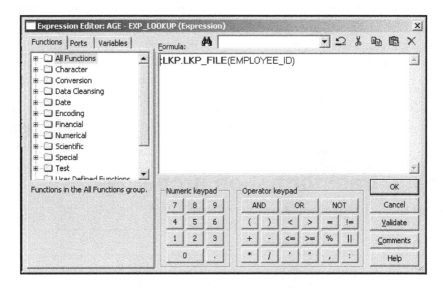

4. Double-click on the Lookup transformation, click on **Ports**, and make AGE the return port as shown in the following screenshot:

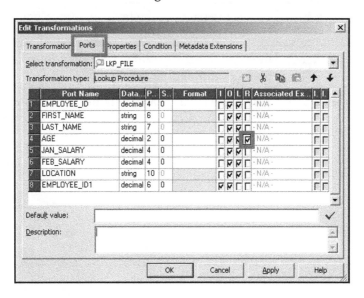

5. When you execute the mapping, row-wise data will flow from the source to the Expression transformation. The :LKP function passes the data to the Lookup transformation, which compares the data based on the condition defined in the **Condition** tab, which, in turn, returns the data from the return port to the Expression transformation from where the data is passed further in mapping.

6. Similarly, add another output port **LOCATION** in the Expression transformation. Create another Lookup transformation. We cannot use the same lookup transformation as the unconnected lookup transformation can return only one port. Follow the aforementioned process to look up for the AGE port to complete the mapping.

We have seen the implementation of Connected and Unconnected Lookup transformation.

# Lookup transformation properties

Let's discuss the properties of Lookup transformation:

| Property | Description |
|---|---|
| Lookup SQL override | This is similar to SQL override. When you override the default query generated by the Lookup transformation in order to extract the data from relational tables, it is referred to as Lookup SQL override. |
| Lookup table name | This is the name of the table on which you are looking up using Lookup transformation. |
| Lookup source filter | Integration service will extract only those records that satisfy the filter condition defined. |
| Lookup cache enabled | This property indicates whether Integration service caches data during processing. Enabling this property enhances the performance. |

| Lookup policy on multiple matches | You can decide to choose a particular value if lookup transformation returns multiple values based on the condition defined. The various options available are as follows:<br>• Use First Value: Integration service will return the first matching record.<br>• Use Last Value: Integration service will return the last matching record.<br>• Use Any Value: When you select this option, Integration services returns the first matching value.<br>• Report Error: When you select this option, Integration service gives the error in the session log. This indicates that your system has duplicate values. |
|---|---|
| Lookup condition | This is the Lookup condition you defined in the condition tab of Lookup transformation. |
| Connection information | This property indicates the database connection used for extracting data in the lookup transformation. |
| Source type | This gives information indicating lookup transformation is looking up on a flat file or relational database or Source Qualifier. |
| Tracing level | This gives the amount of details you wish to write related to Lookup transformation. |
| Lookup cache directory name | This indicates the directory where cache files will be created. Integration service also stores the persistent cache in this directory. The default is $PMCacheDir. |
| Lookup cache persistent | Check the option if you wish to make the cache permanent. If you select to make the cache persistent, Integration service stores the cache in the form of files at the $PMCacheDir location. |
| Lookup data cache size | This is the size of the data cache you wish to allocate to Integration service for storing the data. The default is Auto. |
| Lookup data index size | This is the size of the Index cache you wish to allocate to Integration service for storing the Index details like lookup condition. The default is Auto. |
| Dynamic lookup cache | Select the option if you wish to make the Lookup cache dynamic. |

| Output old value on update | If you unable the option, Integration service sends the old value from output ports, that is, if the cache is to be updated with a new value, it first sends the old value to the output ports present in the cache. You can use this option if you enable dynamic caching. |
|---|---|
| Cache file name prefix | This indicates the name of the cache file to be created when you enable persistent caching. |
| Recache from Lookup source | When you check this option, Integration service rebuilds the cache from the lookup table when the lookup is called. |
| Insert else update | If you check this option, Integration service inserts a new row into the cache and updates existing rows if the row is marked as insert. This option is used when you enable dynamic caching. |
| Update else insert | If you check this option, Integration service updates the existing row and inserts a new row if the row is marked as update. This option is used when you enable dynamic caching. |
| Datetime format | This property indicates the format of date and time. The default is MM/DD/YYYY HH24:MI:SS. |
| Thousand separator | You can choose the separator for separating the value. The default is no separator. |
| Decimal separator | You can choose the separator for separating the decimal values. The default is no period. |
| Case-sensitive string comparison | This property indicates the type of comparison to be done when comparing the strings. |
| Null ordering | This specifies how the Integration service orders the null values while processing data. The default is to sort the null value high. |
| Sorted input | Check this option if you are passing sorted data to the lookup transformation. Passing the sorted data enhances the performance. |
| Lookup source is static | This indicates that the lookup source is not changing while processing the data. |
| Pre-build Lookup cache | This indicates whether Integration service builds the cache before the data enters the Lookup transformation. The default is Auto. |
| Subsection precision | This property indicates the subsection precision you wish to set for date-time data. |

We have seen all the details of Lookup transformation.

# Update Strategy transformation

Update Strategy transformation is used to **INSERT, UPDATE, DELETE,** or **REJECT** records based on the defined condition in the mapping. Update Strategy transformation is mostly used when you design mappings for **Slowly Changing Dimensions** (**SCD**). When you implement SCDs, you actually decide how you wish to maintain historical data with the current data. We will discuss SCD in Chapter 6, *Implementing SCD Using Designer Screen Wizards*. When you wish to maintain no history, complete history, or partial history, you can achieve this functionality using either the property defined in the session task or the Update Strategy transformation.

When you use session task, you instruct the Integration service to treat all the records in the same way, that is, Insert, Update or Delete.

When you use Update Strategy transformation in the mapping, the control is no more with the session task. Update Strategy transformation allows you to Insert, Update, Delete, or Reject records based on the requirement. When you use Update Strategy transformation, the control is no more with Session task. You need to define the following functions to perform the corresponding operation:

- DD_INSERT: This is used when you wish to insert the records, also represented by numeric '0'
- DD_UPDATE: This is used when you wish to update the records, also represented by numeric '1'
- DD_DELETE: This is used when you wish to delete the records, also represented by numeric '2'
- DD_REJECT: This is used when you wish to reject the records, also represented by numeric '3'

Consider we wish to implement a mapping using Update Strategy transformation, which allows all employees with salary greater than 10,000 to target and eliminate all other records. The following screenshot depicts the mapping for the preceding scenario:

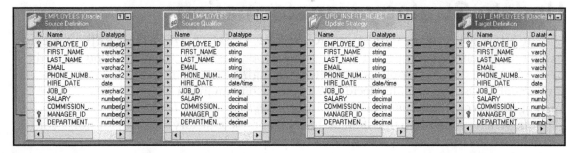

Double-click on the Update Strategy transformation, and click on **Properties** to add the condition:

```
IIF(SALARY >= 10000, DD_INSERT, DD_REJECT)
```

Update Strategy transformation accepts the records in a row-wise manner and checks each record for the condition defined, and based on that, it inserts or rejects the data into the target.

# Normalizer transformation

Normalizer transformation is used in place of Source Qualifier transformation when you wish to read the data from the **Cobol Copybook** source. Also, Normalizer transformation is used to convert column-wise data to row-wise data. This is similar to the transpose feature of MS Excel. You can use this feature if your source is a Cobol Copybook file or relational database tables. Normalizer transformation converts columns to rows and also generates an index for each converted row. A sample mapping using Normalizer transformation is shown in the following screenshot:

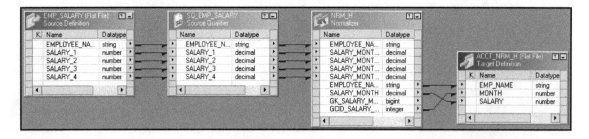

Consider the following example that contains salaries of three employees for four months:

```
STEVE 1000 2000 3000 4000
JAMES 2000 2500 3000 3500
ANDY 4000 4000 4000 4000
```

When you pass the data through Normalizer transformation, it returns the data in a row-wise form along with the index as shown here:

```
STEVE 1000 1
STEVE 2000 2
STEVE 3000 3
STEVE 4000 4
JAMES 2000 1
JAMES 2500 2
JAMES 3000 3
JAMES 3500 4
ANDY 4000 1
ANDY 4000 2
ANDY 4000 3
ANDY 4000 4
```

As you can notice, the index key is incremented for each value. It also initializes the index from 1 when processing data for a new row.

# Configuring Normalizer transformation - ports

Normalizer transformation ports are different from other transformations ports. You cannot edit the ports of Normalizer transformation. To define the ports, you need to configure the Normalizer tab of Normalizer transformation. To add multiple occurring ports in Normalizer transformation, double-click on the Normalizer transformation, and click on **Normalizer**. Add the columns in the **Normalizer** tab. You need to add the single and multiple occurring ports in the **Normalizer** tab.

When you have multiple occurring columns, you need to define those under the occurs option in the Normalizer transformation as shown in the following screenshot:

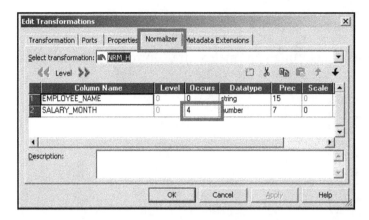

When you add the columns in the **Normalizer** tab, the columns get reflected in the **Ports** tab based on the options defined. In our case, we define SALARY_MONTH as occurs 4 times in the Normalizer transformation, it creates the port 4 times in the **Ports** tab.

Also, Normalizer transformation creates a new port called **generated column ID (GCID)** for every multi-occurring ports you define in the **Normalizer** tab. In our case, it is created for SALARY_MONTHLY. This port generates the index value to be assigned to a new multi-occurring value. The GCID is incremented automatically each time it processes a new record as shown in the following screenshot:

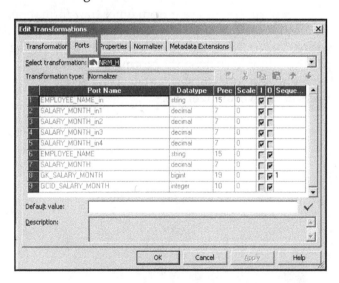

The attributes of the **Normalizer** tab are described here:

| Attribute | Description |
|---|---|
| **Column name** | This indicates the name of the column you wish to define. |
| **Level** | This defines the groups of columns in the data. It defines the hierarchy of the data. The group-level column has a lower level number. It does not contain data. |
| **Occurs** | This indicates the number of times the column occurs in the data. |
| **Datatype** | This indicates the data type of the data. |
| **Prec** | This indicates the length of the column in the source data. |
| **Scale** | This indicates the decimal position in the numeric data. |

# Stored Procedure transformation

Stored Procedure is a database component. Informatica uses the Stored Procedure similar to database tables. Stored Procedures are a set of SQL instructions that require a certain set of input values and return an output value. You can import or create the Stored Procedure in mapping the way you either import or create database tables. To use Stored Procedure in mapping, the stored procedure should exist in the database.

Similar to Lookup transformation, Stored Procedure can also be connected or unconnected transformation in Informatica. When you use connected Stored Procedure, you pass the value to Stored Procedure through links. When you use unconnected Stored Procedure, you pass the value using the :SP function.

# Importing Stored Procedure transformation

Importing the Stored Procedure is similar to importing the database tables in Informatica. We have seen earlier the process of importing database tables. Before you import the Stored Procedure, make sure the stored procedure is created and tested at the database level. Also, make sure you have the valid credentials for connecting to the database.

To import the stored procedure, open the mapping in the mapping designer. Click on **Transformation**, and select the **Import Stored Procedure...** option as shown here:

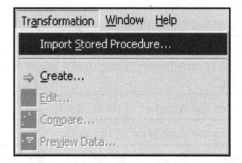

Connect with the database credentials, and click on the required procedure and then on **OK**:

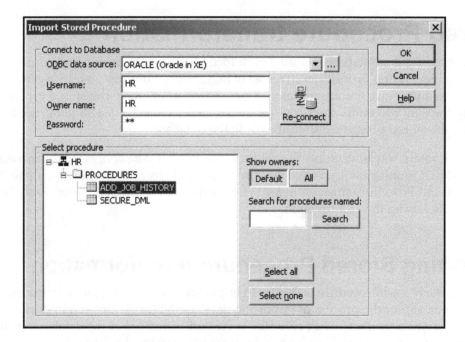

The Stored Procedure appears in the workspace. Connect the corresponding input and output ports to complete the mapping.

# Creating Stored Procedure transformation

You can create the Stored Procedure transformation instead of importing it. Usually, the best practice is to import the Stored Procedure as it takes care of all the properties automatically. When you create the transformation you need to take care of all the input, output, and return ports in the Stored Procedure transformation. Before you create the Stored Procedure, make sure the Stored Procedure is created in the database.

To create the stored procedure transformation, open the mapping in the mapping designer. Go to **Transformation | Create.** Select Stored Procedure transformation from the list of transformations, and mention the name of the transformation as shown here:

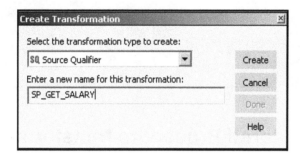

In the next window, click on **Skip.** A Stored Procedure transformation appears in the mapping Designer. Add the corresponding input, output, and variable ports. You need to be aware of the ports present in the Stored Procedure created in the database.

# Using Stored Procedure transformation in Mapping

As mentioned, Stored Procedure transformation can be connected or unconnected. Similar to Lookup transformation, you can configure connected or unconnected Stored Procedure transformation.

# Connected Stored Procedure transformation

A connected Stored Procedure transformation is connected in the mapping with the links. The connected Stored Procedure transformation receives data at the input port and sends the data out using output ports. A sample mapping showing the connected Stored Procedure transformation is shown in the following screenshot:

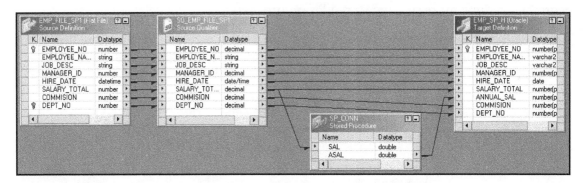

# Unconnected Stored Procedure transformation

An unconnected Stored Procedure transformation is not connected to any other source, target, or transformation by links. Unconnected Stored Procedure transformation is called by another transformation using the :SP function. It works similar to unconnected Lookup transformation, which is called using the : LKP function. A sample mapping using unconnected Stored Procedure transformation is shown here:

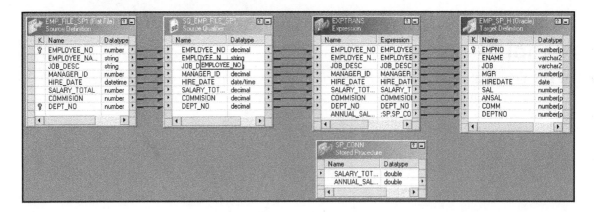

We have used Expression transformation to call the Stored Procedure. The function that is used to call Stored Procedure is this:

```
:SP.SP_CONN(SALARY_TOTAL,PROC_RESULT).
```

Follow similar steps to create unconnected Stored Procedure mapping as used in the case of unconnected Lookup transformation.

# Transaction Control transformation

Transaction Control transformation allows you to **commit** or **rollback** individual records based on a certain condition. By default, Integration service commits the data based on the properties you define at the session task level. Using the Commit Interval property, Integration service commits or rolls back the data into the target. Suppose you define the Commit interval as 10,000, Integration service will commit the data after every 10,000 records. When you use Transaction Control transformation, you get the control at each record to commit or rollback.

When you use Transaction Control transformation, you need to define the condition in the expression editor of the Transaction Control transformation. When you run the process, the data enters the Transaction Control transformation in a row-wise manner. The transaction Control transformation evaluates each row, based on which it commits or rolls back the data.

A sample mapping using Transaction Control transformation is shown in the following screenshot:

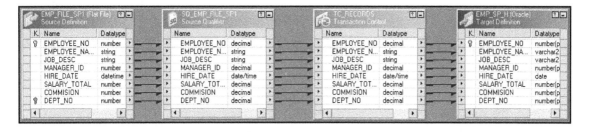

To use the Transaction Control transformation in mapping, perform the following steps:

1. Open the mapping in **Mapping Designer**, and create the **Transaction Control** transformation.
2. Drag the required columns from **Source Qualifier** transformation to Transaction Control transformation.

3. Connect the appropriate ports from **Transaction Control** transformation to the target.
4. Double-click on the **Transaction Control** transformation, and click on **Properties.** We need to define the condition in the Transaction Control transformation expression editor as shown in the following screenshot:

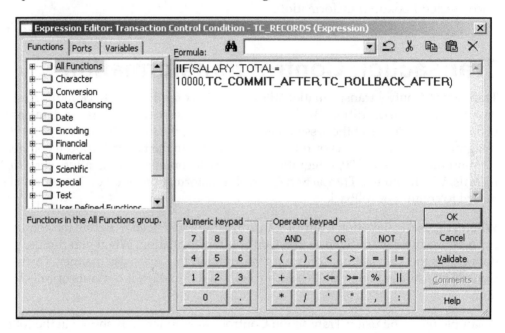

5. Click on **OK.**

The mapping using Transaction Control transformation is complete.

Transaction Control transformation supports the following built-in variables in the Expression Editor:

- TC_COMMIT_BEFORE: The Integration service commits the current record, starts the processing of new record, then writes the current row to the target.
- TC_COMMIT_AFTER: The Integration service commits and writes the current record to the target, then starts the processing of the new record.
- TC_ROLLBACK_BEFORE: The Integration service rolls back the current record, starts the processing of new record, and then writes the current row to the target.
- TC_ROLLBACK_AFTER: The Integration service writes the current record to the target, rolls back the current record, and then starts the processing of the new record.

- `TC_CONTINUE_TRANSACTION`: This is the default value for Transaction Control transformation. The Integration service does not perform any transaction operation for the record.

With this, we have seen the details related to Transaction Control transformation. It is not recommended to use Transaction Control transformation in the mapping as it hampers the performance by checking each record for commit or rollback.

# Types of Lookup cache

Cache is the temporary memory that is created when you execute the process. It is created automatically when the process starts and is deleted automatically once the process is complete. The amount of cache memory is decided based on the property you define in the transformation level or session level. You usually set the property as default, so as required, it can increase the size of the cache. If the size required for caching the data is more than the cache size defined, the process fails with the overflow error. There are different types of caches available.

# Building the Cache - Sequential or Concurrent

You can define the session property to create the cache either sequentially or concurrently.

## Sequential cache

When you select to create the cache sequentially, Integration Service caches the data in a row-wise manner as the records enter the lookup transformation. When the first record enters the lookup transformation, lookup cache gets created and stores the matching record from the lookup table or file in the cache. This way, the cache stores only the matching data. It helps in saving the cache space by not storing unnecessary data.

## Concurrent cache

When you select to create cache concurrently, Integration service does not wait for the data to flow from the source; it first caches complete data. Once the caching is complete, it allows the data to flow from the source. When you select concurrent cache, the performance enhances as compared to sequential cache since the scanning happens internally using the data stored in cache.

# Persistent cache - the permanent one

You can configure the cache to permanently save the data. By default, the cache is created as non-persistent, that is, the cache will be deleted once the session run is complete. If the lookup table or file does not change across the session runs, you can use the existing persistent cache.

Suppose you have a process that is scheduled to run every day and you are using lookup transformation to look up on the reference table that which is not supposed to change for six months. When you use non-persistent cache every day, the same data will be stored in cache; this will waste time and space every day. If you select to create persistent cache, the integration service makes the cache permanent in the form of a file in the $PMCacheDir location. So, you save the time every day, creating and deleting the cache memory.

When the data in the lookup table changes, you need to rebuild the cache. You can define the condition in the session task to rebuild the cache by overwriting the existing cache. To rebuild the cache, you need to check the rebuild option in the session property as discussed under the *Session properties* section in Chapter 7, *Using the Workflow Manager Screen*.

# Sharing the cache - named or unnamed

You can enhance the performance and save the cache memory by sharing the cache if there are multiple lookup transformations used in a mapping. If you have the same structure for both the lookup transformations, sharing the cache will help in enhancing the performance by creating the cache only once. This way, we avoid creating the cache multiple times, which in turn, enhances the performance. You can share the cache--either named or unnamed

## Sharing unnamed cache

If you have multiple lookup transformations used in a single mapping, you can share the unnamed cache. Since the lookup transformations are present in the same mapping, naming the cache is not mandatory. Integration service creates the cache while processing the first record in first lookup transformation and shares the cache with other lookup in the mapping.

# Sharing named cache

You can share the named cache with multiple lookup transformations in the same mapping or in another mapping. Since the cache is named, you can assign the same cache using the name in the other mapping.

When you process the first mapping with lookup transformation, it saves the cache in the defined cache directory and with a defined cache file name. When you process the second mapping, it searches for the same location and cache file and uses the data. If the Integration service does not find the mentioned cache file, it creates the new cache.

If you run multiple sessions simultaneously that use the same cache file, Integration service processes both the sessions successfully only if the lookup transformation is configured for read only from the cache. If there is a scenario when both lookup transformations are trying to update the cache file or a scenario where one lookup is trying to read the cache file and other is trying to update the cache, the session will fail as there is conflict in the processing.

Sharing the cache helps in enhancing the performance by utilizing the cache created. This way we save the processing time and repository space by not storing the same data multiple times for lookup transformations.

# Modifying cache - static or dynamic

When you create a cache, you can configure them to be static or dynamic.

## Static cache

A cache is said to be static if it does not change with the changes happening in the lookup table. The static cache is not synchronized with the lookup table.

By default, Integration service creates a static cache. The Lookup cache is created as soon as first record enters the lookup transformation. Integration service does not update the cache while it is processing the data.

## Dynamic cache

A cache is said to be dynamic if it changes with the changes happening in the lookup table. The static cache is synchronized with the lookup table.

You can choose from the lookup transformation properties to make the cache dynamic. Lookup cache is created as soon as first record enters the lookup transformation. Integration service keeps on updating the cache while it is processing the data. The Integration service marks the record as insert for new row inserted in dynamic cache. For the record that is updated, it marks the record as update in the cache. For every record that doesn't change, the Integration service marks it as unchanged.

You use the dynamic cache while you process the slowly changing dimension tables. For every record inserted in the target, the record will be inserted in cache. For every record updated in the target, the record will be updated in the cache. A similar process happens for the deleted and rejected records.

# Tracing level

Tracing level in Informatica defines the amount of data you wish to write in the session log when you execute the workflow. Tracing level is a very important aspect in Informatica as it helps in analyzing the error. It is very helpful in finding the bugs in the process. You can define tracing level in every transformation. The tracing level option is present in every transformation properties window. There are four types of tracing level available:

- **Normal:**When you set the tracing level as normal, Informatica stores status information, information about errors and skipped rows. You get detailed information but not at an individual row level.
- **Terse:** When you set the tracing level as terse, Informatica stores error information and information of rejected records. Terse tracing level occupies less space as compared to normal.
- **Verbose Initialization:** When you set the tracing level as verbose Initialize, it stores process details related to startup, details about index and data files created, and more details about the transformation process in addition to the details stored in normal tracing. This tracing level takes more space as compared to normal and terse.
- **Verbose Data:** This is the most detailed level of tracing level. It occupies more space and takes longer time as compared to the other three. It stores row-level data in the session log. It writes the truncation information whenever it truncates the data. It also writes the data to error log if you enable row error logging.

Default tracing level is normal. You can change the tracing level to terse to enhance the performance. Tracing level can be defined at an individual transformation level, or you can override the tracing level by defining it at the session level.

# Summary

In this chapter, we discussed the most important aspect of Informatica PowerCenter tool and most of the widely used transformations. Other transformations that have been intentionally not added in this chapter are very rarely used transformations. We talked about the functionalities of various transformations. You learned the usage of ports and expression editor in various transformations. We discussed the classification of the transformations, that is Active/Passive and Connected/Unconnected. You learned about the different types of caches and tracing levels available.

In the next chapter, we will discuss the forth client screen, **Repository Manager**. We saw the usage of other screens. We will see how the Repository Manager screen is used for deploying the code across various environments in Informatica.

# 5
# Using the Designer Screen - Advanced Features

In previous chapters, we developed our skills for using the PowerCenter Designer screen and various transformations present in Informatica.

In this chapter, we will talk about high-level aspects of the PowerCenter Designer screen. Once we are clear about the basics of the Designer screen, we are all set to work on the advanced concepts of PowerCenter Designer. Apart from the basic functionalities of creating mappings, the Designer screen offers multiple utilities to assist you in smoother execution of ETL processing. Some of these functionalities will be regularly used, and some will be rare to you. It is always good to have an understanding of these functionalities to have the upper hand when using the tool.

The topics that will be covered in this chapter are listed as follows:

- Debugger
- Reusable transformations
- Mapplets
- Target load plan
- Parameters and variables
- Comparing objects

# Debug me please - the debugger

Informatica PowerCenter provides a utility called **debugger** to debug the mapping so that you can easily find the issue in the mapping you created. Using the debugger, you can see the flow of every record across the transformations.

As you are aware, Informatica PowerCenter is not a data storage tool, it is a data manipulation tool that helps you manipulate data. This point is important in the aspect of debugger, as once you finish the process, to verify the data, you only have either the source or the target to check the result and compare. The debugger jumps in with a functionality that provides you with the option of actually seeing the data flow from each and every transformation in your mapping.

When you execute the mapping through a session task, the data automatically starts flowing from the source to the target through transformations--the same process you are carrying out manually using the debugger.

Consider an example to understand the debugger functionality.

You created a mapping with 100 transformations, and you have 1,000 records present in your source. You executed the mapping and got the results. When you started analyzing the output in your target table, you found the data in a few columns to be incorrect. Now, the problem is, you are not sure where out of the 100 transformations the issue actually started--your solution is debugger. The debugger will allow you to see the movement of each record from every transformation so that you can catch the origin of the error and rectify it accordingly.

To set up and execute the debugger, follow these steps:

1. In the Designer, go to **Tools** | **Mapping Designer** | **Mapping** | **Debugger** | **Start Debugger**, as shown in the following screenshot:

2. A new window will pop up listing prechecks for the debugger, as shown in the following screenshot:

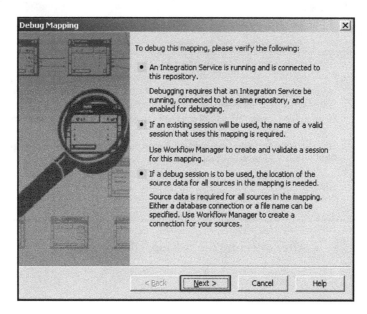

- Please read the points clearly before you proceed. Click on **Next**.
- The next screen will ask you to select the session task for the mapping you wish to debug. Please select the session task you created to execute the mapping.
- Even though running a debugger is a manual process, you still need a session task because the integration service needs to get the path for extracting and loading the data that is provided in the session task.

 Please note, you can use an existing session or create a new debug session to run the debugger. If you use an existing session, the debugger will use properties from that the session. You need to add all properties if you create a new debug session.

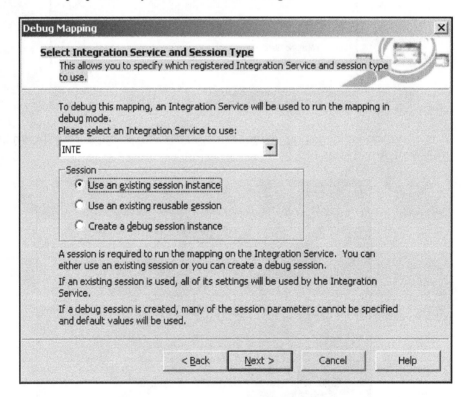

- After selecting the session, click on **Next**.

4. Select the appropriate session in the next window, and click on **Next**:

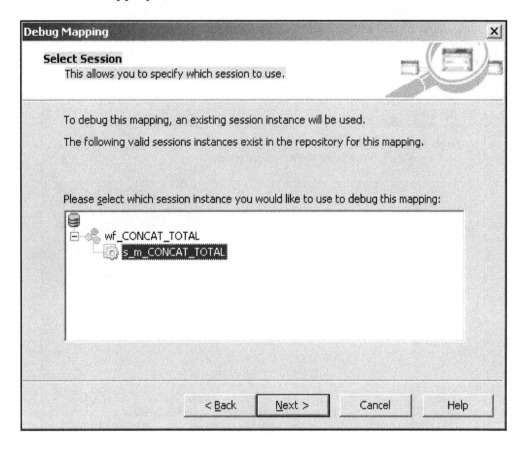

5. In the next screen, you will see an option to discard the target data. This option indicates what you wish to do with the data you loaded in the target using the debugger. Since you are running the debugger for testing purposes, you basically wish to discard the target data.

- Checking this option will discard the data in the target. Click on **Finish**:

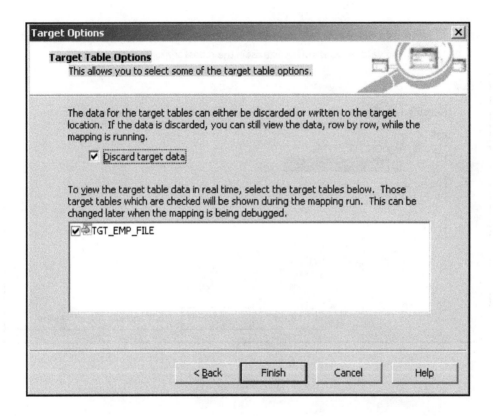

- The output panel of your screen will be divided into three sections, as seen in the following screenshot:

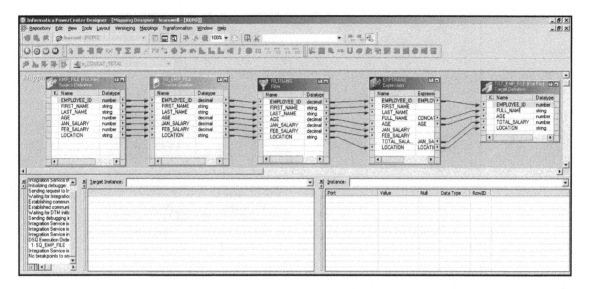

- The output panel is divided into sections as follows:
- **Notification**: This section will show general information about the debugger execution.
- **Target instance**: This section will show the data as it reaches the target of your mapping. If your mapping contains multiple targets, all the targets will be displayed in this section in the drop-down as shown in the previous screenshot. You can select the target for which you wish to see the data from the dropdown.
- **Instance**: This section will show the data when it reaches the different transformations of your mapping. If your mapping contains multiple transformations, all the transformations will be displayed in this section in the dropdown as shown in the previous screenshot. You can select the transformation for which you wish to see the data from the dropdown. The debugger shows the data in each transformation, as per the logic you coded in the mapping.

- We have completed the setup for the debugger; click on **NextInstance** to start the debugger:

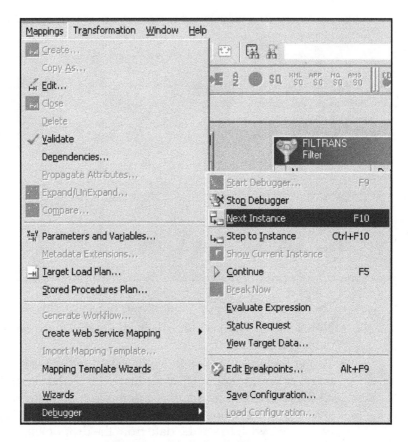

- The debugger will start showing the movement of data from each transformation under the instance and then, at the end, in the target under the target instance.
- Keep pressing **Next Instance (F10)** to step the data toward the next instance in your mapping flow.
- Once all the data reaches the target, the debugger will automatically shut down.

- If you have a very large mapping and traversing through every transformation is tough work, you can actually select particular transformations at particular intervals to understand and narrow down the issue. This can be achieved using breakpoints.
- To set a breakpoint, click on **Edit Breakpoints**:

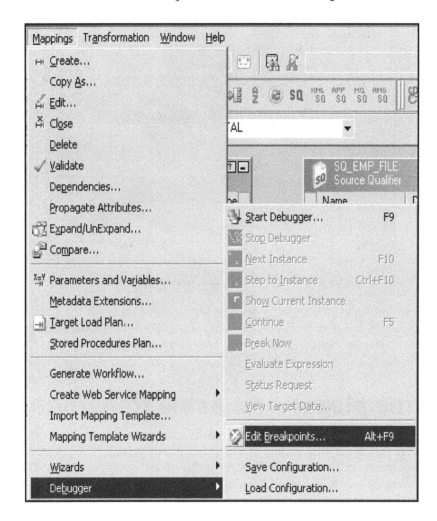

- A new window will let you add breakpoints. Click on **Add** to add a new breakpoint in the debugger. You can set a few more properties in this window:

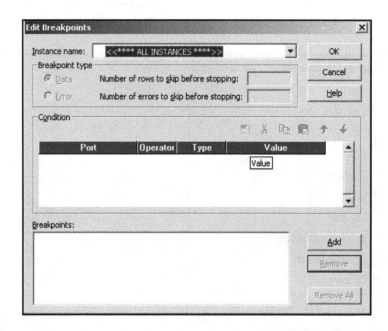

As you must have noticed, debugger is the best way to find issues in the data movement across the mapping. So, whenever you face some issues related to data loading in target or mismatches in the targets, start a debugger and solve your issues.

# Reuse me please - reusable transformation

As you are aware, sources and targets are reusable components, that is, you work on sources in Source Analyzer and targets in Target Designer respectively. Also, you must be aware that you cannot edit sources and targets in Mapping Designer; they can only be edited in Source Analyzer and Target Designer respectively.

Sources and targets are called reusable components because you can use the same source and target in multiple mappings. We can reuse the source or target across multiple mappings only if the metadata requirements of both mappings is exactly the same. Metadata, in this case, means the number of columns, their data type, their data size, indexes, constraints, and so on. Even if there are small changes, you cannot reuse the components.

On the same lines, if we have the same logic to implement across multiple mappings, we can use the reusable transformations, which allow us to reuse the same transformation across mappings. You can only reuse a transformation if the metadata requirements in the mappings are exactly the same. Even if there is a small difference, the reusable transformations will not work, as there could be a mismatch in processing.

There are two ways in which you can create reusable transformations:

- Using Transformation Developer
- Making an existing transformation reusable

# Using Transformation Developer

To use Transformation Developer, perform the following steps:

1. In the Designer, go to **Tools | Transformation**.
2. Go to **Transformation | Create...**:

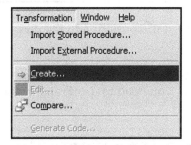

3. Select the type of transformation you wish to create from the list of transformations. We are creating an Expression Transformation as an example. Click on **Create** and then click on Done:

4. The transformation will appear on the screen. Also, you will see the transformation added in your **Navigator** under **Transformations**, as shown in the following screenshot:

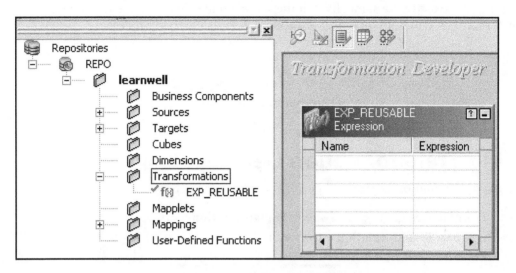

Now, you can drag and drop the transformation in the mapping in Mapping Designer to use it as a reusable component.

You will notice that you cannot edit the reusable transformation in Mapping Designer. To edit the reusable transformation, you need to use Transformation Developer.

# Making an existing transformation reusable

In the previous topic, we saw how to use a new transformation as a reusable transformation. Imagine that you already have a transformation that you wish to use in another mapping, but since it is non-reusable, you are not able to do so. To solve this issue, we have an option, using which you can make an existing non-reusable transformation reusable by following these steps:

1. A warning message will pop up advising you that the process is irreversible, as shown here:

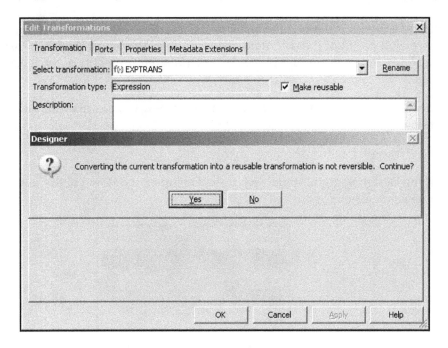

2. Open the mapping in Mapping Designer containing the transformation you wish to make reusable. We are using an existing mapping containing an Expression Transformation to make reusable.

3. Double-click on the transformation to view the properties of the transformation. You will see an option: make reusable. Click on the box, as shown in the preceding screenshot.

You can see the transformation is now added under Transformation in Navigator, which indicates that the transformation can be reused, and you can drag it into other mappings also.

# Mapplet

In the previous section, we saw how to make a transformation reusable. Going further, you may also like to reuse logic implemented using multiple transformations. A group of transformations that can be reused is called a Mapplet.

Mapplets can be created in Mapplet Designer in Informatica PowerCenter Designer. They allow you to reuse a group of transformations in multiple mappings. As in the case of reusable transformations, to use Mapplets, the metadata requirements of the mappings should be exactly the same.

You can use Mapplet Designer to create Mapplets with new transformations or use existing transformations.

To create a new Mapplet, follow the steps mentioned:

1. In the Designer, go to **Tools** | **Mapplet Designer**, as shown in the following screenshot. Click **Create**:

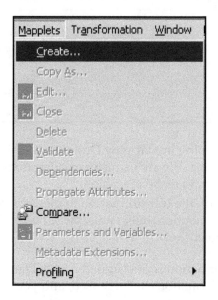

2. Specify the name of the new Mapplet MPLT_REUSABLE.
3. Add transformations in the Mapplet as per your logic. We are using the Filter and Expression Transformations to create sample logic.
4. Click on **Transformations**, create Mapplet Input and Mapplet Output, and name them MPLT_INPUT and MPLT_OUTPUT respectively.

5. Place Mapplet Input before Filter and Mapplet output after Expression. These will act as the Source and Target for Mapplet. Drag the columns from the Expression Transformation to `MPLT_OUTPUT`, and drag columns from the Filter Transformation back to `MPLT_INPUT`, as shown in the following screenshot:

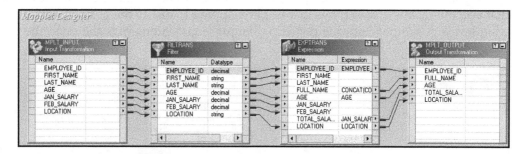

6. Press *Ctrl + S* to save the Mapplet, and you will be able to see the Mapplet added under Mapplets in **Navigator**.
7. You can now drag the Mapplet in Mapping Designer to use it as a reusable component. Drag the Mapplet into Mapping Designer, link the columns from Source Qualifier to the input ports of Mapplet, and drag the output ports from Mapplet to Target Designer, as shown in the following screenshot:

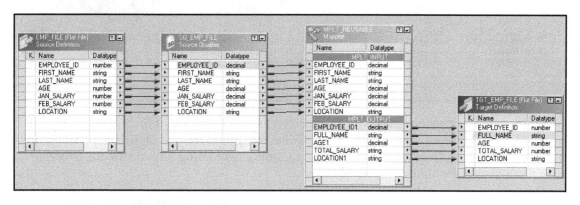

If you wish to reuse the logic implemented using multiple transformations in an existing mapping, you can simply copy the existing transformations from Mapping Designer and paste them in Mapplet Designer. This is the easiest way to use an existing group of transformations.

As you must have noticed, Mapplet serves two purposes: first, it allows you to reuse your existing transformation, and second, it makes your mapping look simpler by replacing multiple components with a single component.

# Managing the constraints - the target load plan

While you work on multiple mappings in a complex scenario, the situation may demand that you put multiple data flows in a single mapping to justify the performance and the complexity. A sample mapping depicting the previous statement is shown in the following screenshot:

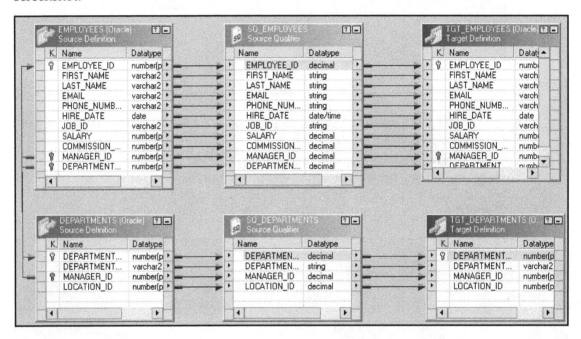

If you execute the previous mapping, the session may fail because of the primary key and foreign key violations on the database side. Since the Employee and Department tables are dependent on each other, when you run the mapping containing both flows, the process may fail if the data violates the dependency.

To avoid the issue, Informatica PowerCenter contains a utility called Target Load Plan. How do you plan to load the data into multiple targets in a mapping? We can load the data in a particular sequence in multiple targets in a mapping to avoid failure due to constraints.

Imagine that the EMPLOYEES table data depends on the DEPARTEMNTS data because of the primary key and foreign key constraints. So, to satisfy the referential integrity, the DEPARTMENTS table should be loaded first. The target load order is useful when you wish to handle referential integrity while inserting, deleting, or updating data in the tables that have the primary key and foreign key relationships.

To set the target load plan in a mapping, follow the mentioned process:

1. This will make the DEPARTMENTS table load before the EMPLOYEES table is loaded, and we can avoid the failure.

2. In the Designer, go to **Tools** | **Mapping Designer** | **Mapping** | **Target Load Plan** as shown in the following screenshot:

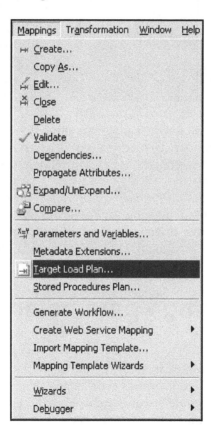

3. A new window will pop up, as shown in the following screenshot:

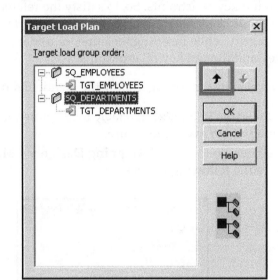

4. To set the target load plan, just move the target load group using the arrow provided in the window. To load the DEPARTMENTS table before the EMPLOYEES table, select SQ_DEPARTMENTS and click on the up arrow, as shown in the previous screenshot.

When we use the target load plan, Informatica PowerCenter actually restricts the extraction of data from the Source Qualifier. It waits for the first flow in the selected sequence to finish loading data, and then starts extracting data from the second source qualifier to load it.

# Avoid hardcoding - parameters and variables

When you work on any technology, it is always advisable that your code is dynamic. This means you should use hardcoded values as little as possible in your code. It is always recommended that you use parameters or variables in your code so that you can easily pass these values and need not frequently change the code.

We will discuss this concept in more detail in the *Parameter file - parameters and variables* section in Chapter 9, *Advanced Features of Workflow Manager Screen*.

In this section, we will discuss how to use parameters and variables in the PowerCenter Designer screen.

The value of a variable can change between session runs. The value of a parameter will remain constant across session runs. The difference is very minute, so you should define the parameter or variable properly, as per your requirements.

Consider a Filter Transformation where you have defined the filter condition as LOCATION='USA'. Since you have used a hardcoded value in the filter conditions, it is always recommended that you pass the value using a parameter or variable.

Follow these steps to use variables or parameters:

1. In the Designer, go to **Tools | Mapping Designer | Mapping | Parameters and Variables...**, as shown in the following screenshot:

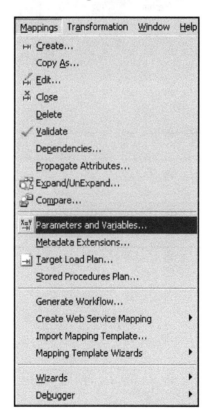

2. A new window will pop up to allow you to provide parameters and variables, as shown in the following screenshot. Add a new parameter or variable, depending on your requirement. For our reference, we are creating a parameter $$LOCATION. You can choose from the dropdown whether you wish to make it a parameter or a variable. Click on **OK**:

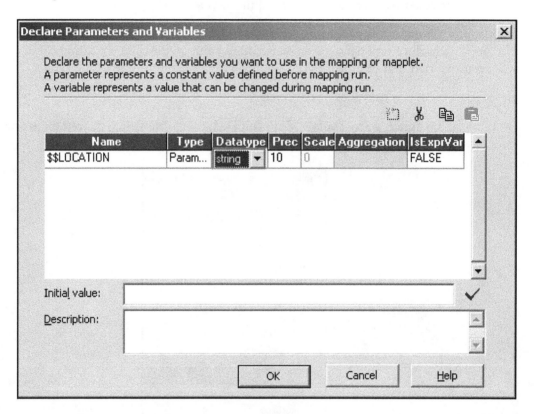

3. Once you define the parameter or variable at the mapping level, you can use those in the transformations. Refer to the following screenshot:

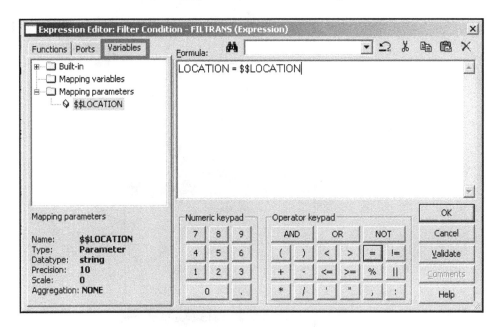

With this, we have defined a parameter/variable at the mapping level and used it in the transformations to avoid hardcoding.

# Comparing objects

Informatica PowerCenter allows you to compare objects present within a repository. You can compare sources, targets, transformations, Mapplets, and mappings in PowerCenter Designer under Source Analyzer, Target Designer, Transformation Developer, Mapplet Designer, and Mapping Designer respectively. You can compare objects in the same repository or in multiple repositories.

Follow these steps to compare two objects. We are using two sources to compare as an example.

1. In the Designer, go to **Tools** I **Source Analyzer** I **Sources** I **Compare**, as shown in the following screenshot:

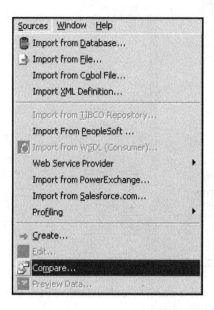

2. Select **Source 1** and **Source 2** that you wish to compare, as shown in the following screenshot:

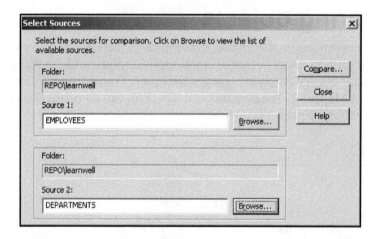

3. Click on **Compare**.

4. You can check different types of comparison options for the two sources. Informatica PowerCenter Comparison Utility gives the option to check differences in the repository and versions under the General tab. The Table tab allows you to check differences in the owner name and database type. The Column tab allows you to see differences in the column and other properties related to columns, such as data type, precision, and other constraints. Similar to this, when you compare targets and mappings, you can check out the differences using the Compare Object functionality.

This can be helpful in the analysis of components and to understand the difference between newer and existing components.

# Summary

To summarize, we started the chapter with the debugger, which helps you with debugging errors in your mapping. Using debugger, you can pinpoint an error in your mapping, using which you can easily resolve the issue. Next in the chapter, we discussed reusable transformation, which allows you to reuse a transformation across mappings. Reusable transformations are very important, as they save the time and effort of recreating the same transformations. Moving on in the chapter, we talked about Mapplets, which allow you to reuse groups of transformations, which, in turn, makes your mapping simpler by replacing multiple transformations with a single component. Also, Mapplets save you time and effort by allowing you to reuse existing components. Next in the line was the target load plan, using which you can set up the priority of loading the target tables in a single mapping. This is useful when loading the data maintaining the constraints. We also looked at some details about parameters and variables. We are finished the chapter with comparing objects, functionality, which allows you to compare two components; this is very helpful is understanding and maintaining versions on the repository.

With this, we have seen all the basic and advanced topics in Informatica PowerCenter Designer screen. The more you practice, the better you will be at building your logic. As you must have understood by now, practice is the only option to make your stand clear on the Informatica PowerCenter tool.

In the next chapter, we will take our learning to a more advanced aspect, called SCD. You will learn to implement the various types of SCDs.

# 6
# Implementing SCD Using Designer Screen Wizards

**Slowly Changing Dimensions** (**SCD**), as the name suggests, allows maintaining changes in the Dimension table in the data warehouse. Before you read the chapter, make sure you have a complete understanding of data warehousing concepts, especially SCD. Make sure you know about SCD1, SCD2, and SCD3 types. For your reference, we have described each SCD in detail in this chapter. For more details, refer to the book *The Data Warehouse Toolkit* by Ralph Kimball. Before we move ahead with the implementation of the SCD in Informatica PowerCenter, let's discuss the different types of SCDs.

Note that we are taking the general SCD in our discussion, that is, SCD1, SCD2, and SCD3. Apart from these, there will always be Hybrid SCDs that you will come across. A Hybrid SCD is nothing but a combination of multiple SCDs to serve your complex business requirements.

## Types of SCD

The various types of SCD are described as follows:

- **Type 1 dimension mapping** (**SCD1**): This keeps only current data and does not maintain historical data.

 Use SCD1 mapping when you do not want history of previous data.

- **Type 2 dimension/version number mapping (SCD2)**: This keeps current as well as historical data in the table. It allows you to insert new records and changed records using a new column (PM_VERSION_NUMBER) by maintaining the **version number** in the table to track the changes. We use a new column PM_PRIMARYKEY to maintain the history.

 Use SCD2 mapping when you want to keep a full history of dimension data, and track the progression of changes using a version number.

- Consider there is a column LOCATION in the EMPLOYEE table and you wish to track the changes in the location on employees. Consider a record for Employee ID 1001 present in your EMPLOYEE dimension table. Steve was initially working in India and then shifted to USA. We are willing to maintain history on the LOCATION field.
- **Type 2 dimension/flag mapping**: This keeps current as well as historical data in the table. It allows you to insert new records and changed records using a new column (PM_CURRENT_FLAG) by maintaining the flag in the table to track the changes. We use a new column PRIMARY_KEY to maintain the history.

 Use SCD2 mapping when you want to keep a full history of dimension data, and track the progression of changes using a flag.

- Let's take an example to understand different SCDs.
- **Type 2 dimension/effective date range mapping**: This keeps current as well as historical data in the table. SCD2 allows you to insert new records and changed records using two new columns (PM_BEGIN_DATE and PM_END_DATE) by maintaining the date range in the table to track the changes. We use a new column PRIMARY_KEY to maintain the history.

 Use SCD2 mapping when you want to keep a full history of dimension data, and track the progression of changes using start date and end date.

- **Type 3 Dimension mapping**: This keeps current as well as historical data in the table. We maintain only **partial history** by adding a new column `PM_PREV_COLUMN_NAME`, that is, we do not maintain full history.

 Use SCD3 mapping when you wish to maintain only partial history.

| EMPLOYEE_ID | NAME | LOCATION |
|---|---|---|
| 1001 | STEVE | INDIA |

Your data warehouse table should reflect the current status of `Steve`. To implement this, we have different types of SCDs.

# SCD1

As you can see in the following table, `INDIA` will be replaced with `USA`, so we end up having only current data, and we lose historical data:

| PM_PRIMARY_KEY | EMPLOYEE_ID | NAME | LOCATION |
|---|---|---|---|
| 100 | 1001 | STEVE | USA |

Now if `Steve` is again shifted to `JAPAN`, the `LOCATION` data will be replaced from `USA` to `JAPAN`:

| PM_PRIMARY_KEY | EMPLOYEE_ID | NAME | LOCATION |
|---|---|---|---|
| 100 | 1001 | STEVE | JAPAN |

The advantage of SCD1 is that we do not consume a lot of space in maintaining the data.

The disadvantage is that we don't have historical data.

# SCD2 - Version number

As you can see in the following table, we are maintaining the full history by adding a new record to maintain the history of the previous records:

| PM_PRIMARYKEY | EMPLOYEE_ID | NAME | LOCATION | PM_VERSION_NUMBER |
|---|---|---|---|---|
| 100 | 1001 | STEVE | INDIA | 0 |
| 101 | 1001 | STEVE | USA | 1 |
| 102 | 1001 | STEVE | JAPAN | 2 |
| 200 | 1002 | MIKE | UK | 0 |

We add two new columns in the table: PM_PRIMARYKEY to handle the issues of duplicate records in the primary key in the EMPLOYEE_ID (supposed to be the primary key) column, and PM_VERSION_NUMBER to understand current and history records.

# SCD2 - FLAG

As you can see in the following table, we are maintaining the full history by adding new records to maintain the history of the previous records:

| PM_PRIMARYKEY | EMPLOYEE_ID | NAME | LOCATION | PM_CURRENT_FLAG |
|---|---|---|---|---|
| 100 | 1001 | STEVE | INDIA | 0 |
| 101 | 1001 | STEVE | USA | 1 |

We add two new columns in the table: PM_PRIMARYKEY to handle the issues of duplicate records in the primary key in the EMPLOYEE_ID column, and PM_CURRENT_FLAG to understand current and history records.

Again, if Steve is shifted, the data looks like this:

| PM_PRIMARYKEY | EMPLOYEE_ID | NAME | LOCATION | PM_CURRENT_FLAG |
|---|---|---|---|---|
| 100 | 1001 | STEVE | INDIA | 0 |
| 101 | 1001 | STEVE | USA | 0 |
| 102 | 1001 | STEVE | JAPAN | 1 |

# SCD2 - Date range

As you can see in the following table, we are maintaining the full history by adding new records to maintain the history of the previous records:

| PM_PRIMARYKEY | EMPLOYEE_ID | NAME | LOCATION | PM_BEGIN_DATE | PM_END_DATE |
|---|---|---|---|---|---|
| 100 | 1001 | STEVE | INDIA | 01-01-14 | 31-05-14 |
| 101 | 1001 | STEVE | USA | 01-06-14 | 99-99-9999 |

We add three new columns in the table: PM_PRIMARYKEY to handle the issues of duplicate records in the primary key in the EMPLOYEE_ID column, and PM_BEGIN_DATE and PM_END_DATE to understand the versions in the data.

The advantage of SCD2 is that you have complete history of the data, which is a must for data warehouse.

The disadvantage of SCD2 is that it consumes a lot of space.

# SCD3

As you can see in the following table, we are maintaining the history by adding new columns:

| PM_PRIMARYKEY | EMPLOYEE_ID | NAME | LOCATION | PM_PREV_LOCATION |
|---|---|---|---|---|
| 100 | 1001 | STEVE | USA | INDIA |

An optional column PM_PRIMARYKEY can be added to maintain the primary key constraints. We add a new column PM_PREV_LOCATION in the table to store the changes in the data. As you can see, we added a new column to store data as against SCD2,where we added rows to maintain history.

If Steve is now shifted to JAPAN, the data changes to this:

| PM_PRIMARYKEY | EMPLOYEE_ID | NAME | LOCATION | PM_PREV_LOCATION |
|---|---|---|---|---|
| 100 | 1001 | STEVE | JAPAN | USA |

As you can notice, we lost INDIA from the data warehouse, that is why we say we are maintaining partial history.

 To implement SCD3, decide how many versions of a particular column you wish to maintain. Based on this, the columns will be added in the table.

SCD3 is best when you are not interested in maintaining the complete but only partial history.

The drawback of SCD3 is that it doesn't store the full history.

At this point, you should be very clear about the different types of SCDs. We need to implement these concepts practically in Informatica PowerCenter. Informatica PowerCenter provides a utility called wizard to implement SCD. Using the wizard, you can easily implement any SCD. In the next topics, you will learn how to use the wizard to implement SCD1, SCD2, and SCD3.

Before you proceed to the next section, please make sure you have a proper understanding of the transformations in Informatica PowerCenter. You should be clear about the source qualifier, expression, filter, router, lookup, update strategy, and sequence generator transformations. Wizard creates a mapping using all these transformations to implement the SCD functionality.

When we implement SCD, there will be some new records that need to be loaded into the target table, and there will be some existing records for which we need to maintain the history.

 The record that comes for the first time in the table will be referred to as the NEW record, and the record for which we need to maintain history will be referred to as the CHANGED record. Based on the comparison of the source data with the target data, we will decide which one is the NEW record and which is the CHANGED record.

To start with, we will use a sample file as our source and the Oracle table as the target to implement SCDs. Before we implement SCDs, let's talk about the logic that will serve our purpose, and then we will fine-tune the logic for each type of SCD.

1. Extract all records from the source.
2. Look up on the target table, and cache all the data.
3. Compare the source data with the target data to flag the NEW and CHANGED records.

4. Filter the data based on the NEW and CHANGED flags.

5. Generate the primary key for every new row inserted into the table.

6. Load the NEW record into the table, and update the existing record if needed.

Based on the specific SCD, the preceding logic will be modified to a certain extent.

# SCD1 - I hate history!

To implement SCD1 using wizard, follow these steps:

1. In the Designer, go to **Tools** | **Mapping Designer** | **Mapping** | **Wizard** | **Slowly Changing Dimensions** as shown in the following screenshot:

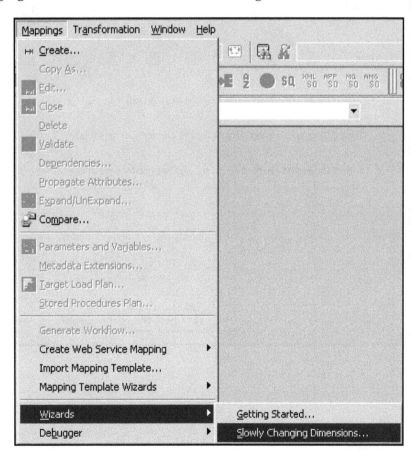

2.  A new window will pop up asking the name (m_SCD1) of the new SCD mapping. Select **Type 1 Dimension - Keep most recent values in the target** as we are implementing SCD1. Click on **Next**:

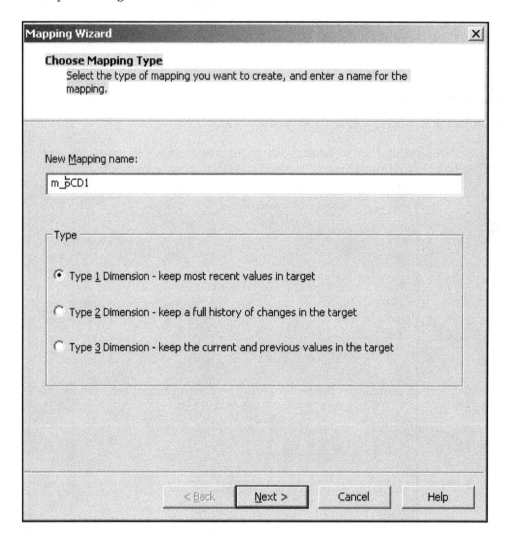

3. The next screen will ask you to select the source. Select a source from the drop-down. All the sources present in your repository will be listed in this drop-down list. We are using EMP_FILE.txt as the source file for our reference. Also, specify the name of the target you wish to create. We will name the target EMPLOYEE_SCD1 for our reference in this book. Click on **Next**:

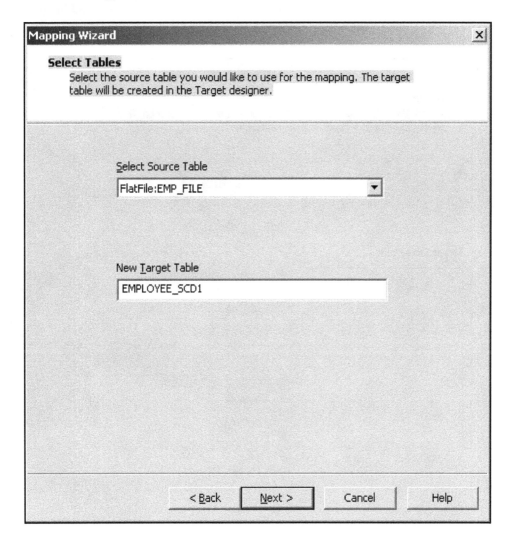

4.  In the next window, select **EMPLOYEE_ID** as **Logical Key Field**. This specifies which column will be used to check the existence of data in the target. Make sure the column you use is the key column of the source.

    - Also, add LOCATION under **Fields to compare for changes**. This specifies for which column you wish to maintain the history. Click on **Finish:**

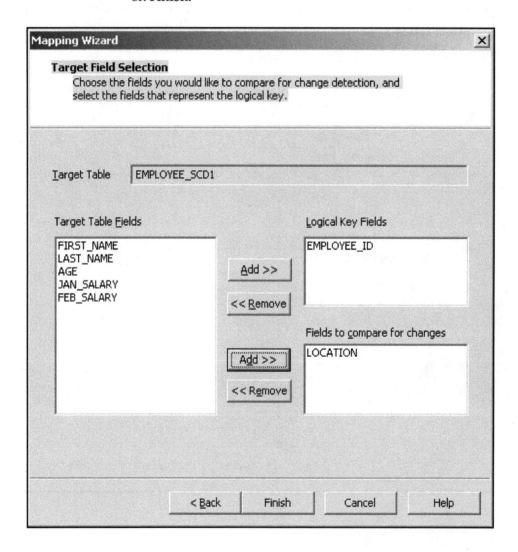

- The wizard creates a complete mapping in your mapping designer workspace. Make the necessary changes into the mapping if required:

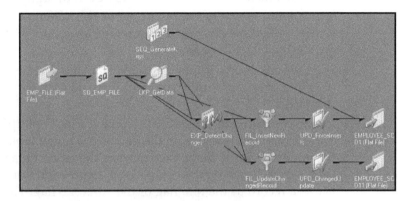

Before we proceed further, we need to make some points clear:

- Since we have used flat file as a source, Informatica PowerCenter wizard generates the target also as a file. We cannot maintain SCDs on files, so make sure you target type to database. We will be changing it to the Oracle table as reference in this book. You can do this in the target designer. Drag the target (EMPLOYEE_SCD1) created by wizard in the target designer, double-click to open the properties, and change the database type of Oracle. This will change the type of the target from file to oracle. Once you modify the target table to oracle database, the mapping will look like this:

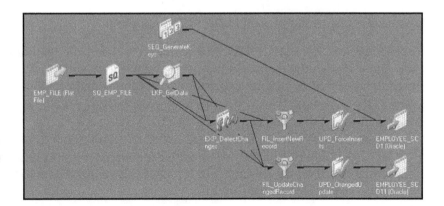

- The wizard creates two instances of the same oracle target table in the mapping load the data from NEW and CHANGED flow respectively. Understand clearly that these two structures refer to the same oracle table EMPLOYEE_SCD1 even though the name (EMPLOYEE_SCD1 and EMPLOYEE_SCD11) is different in the view. When you double-click on the target instances, in the table tab, you can see the table name as EMPLOYEE_SCD1.

- Since we are done with the mapping, it's time to analyze the mapping. It is very important to understand each component of the mapping.

- Informatica PowerCenter SCD1 mapping uses Lookup transformation to lookup on the data in the target table and uses Expression Transformation to compare the target data with the source data. Based on the comparison, Expression transformation marks a record as the NEW flag or the CHANGED flag. The mapping divides into two flows.

- Filter transformation FIL_InsertNewRecord allows only the NEW record to pass further and filter the records marked as CHANGED from the first flow. It passes new records to UPD_ForceInserts, which inserts these records into the target. The sequence generator generates the primary key for each new record.

- Filter transformation FIL_UpdateChangedRecord allows only the CHANGED record to pass further and filters the records marked as NEW from the second flow. It passes changed records to UPD_ChangedUpdate, which replaces the existing rows in the target to reflect the latest changes.

Let's understand each transformation used in the SCD1 mapping:

- **Source Qualifier (SQ_EMP_FILE)**: This extracts the data from the file/table you used as the source in the mapping. It passes data to the downstream transformations, that is, lookup, expression, and filter transformation

- **Lookup (LKP_GetData)**: This is used to lookup on the target table. It caches the existing data from the table *EMPLOYEE_SCD1*.
  - The EMPLOYEE_ID=IN_EMPLOYEE_ID condition in the condition tab will compare the data with the source table and target table. Based on the comparison, it passes the required data to the expression transformation.

- **Expression (EXP_DetectChanges)**: This receives the data from upstream transformation, and based on comparison, it create two flags: `NewFlag` and `ChangedFlag`. In our case, we are using the `LOCATION` field for comparison.
- Wizard created the condition for `NewFlag` as `IIF(ISNULL(PM_PRIMARYKEY), TRUE, FALSE)`.
- The condition for `ChangedFlag` is `IIF(NOT ISNULL(PM_PRIMARYKEY) AND (DECODE(LOCATION,PM_PREV_LOCATION,1,0)=0), TRUE, FALSE)`.
- For every record coming from source, if there is no matching record in the target, we can flag that record as `NewFlag`, that is, the condition `EMPLOYEE_ID !=` `EMPLOYEE_ID` signifies `NewFlag`. If no matching record is present for `EMPLOYEE_ID` in target, it signifies that `PM_PRIMARYKEY` will not be available. So, Lookup transformation will return `NULL` for the `PM_PRIMARYKEY` column.
- For every record coming from the source, if there is a matching record in the target and if the location from the source does not match the location for a particular `EMPLOYEE_ID` from the target, we can flag that record as `ChangedFlag`, that is, `EMPLOYEE_ID = EMPLOYEE_ID AND LOCATION !=` `PM_PREV_LOCATION`.

Based on the condition, it passes the data to downstream filter transformations:

- **Filter (FIL_InsertNewRecord)**: This filters the records coming from the upstream Expression transformation that are marked `ChangedFlag` and allows only records with `NewFlag` to pass to the `UPD_ForceInserts` update strategy.
- **Filter (FIL_UpdateChangedRecord)**: This filters the records coming from the upstream expression transformation that are marked as `NewFlag` and allows only records with `ChangedFlag` to pass to the `UPD_ChangedUpdate` update strategy.
- **Update Strategy (UPD_ForceInserts)**: This uses the `DD_INSERT` condition to insert data into the `EMPLOYEE_SCD1` target.
- **Update Strategy (UPD_ChangedUpdate)**: This uses the `DD_UPDATE` condition to overwrite existing `LOCATION` into the `EMPLOYEE_SCD11` target instance.
- **Sequence Generator (SEQ_GenerateKeys)**: This generates a sequence of values for each row marked as `NewFlag` to be loaded into the target incrementing by 1. It populates the value into `PM_PRIMARYKEY` in the `EMPLOYEE_SCD1` target instance.
- **Target (EMPLOYEE_SCD1)**: This is the target table instance to accept `NewFlag` records into the target table.

- **Target (EMPLOYEE_SCD11)**: This is the target table instance to accept the `ChangedFlag` records into the target table.

# SCD2 (version number) - I need my ancestors!

To implement SCD2 using wizard, follow these steps:

1. In the **Designer**, go to **Tools** | **Mapping Designer** | **Mapping** | **Wizard** | **Slowly Changing Dimensions** as shown in the following screenshot:

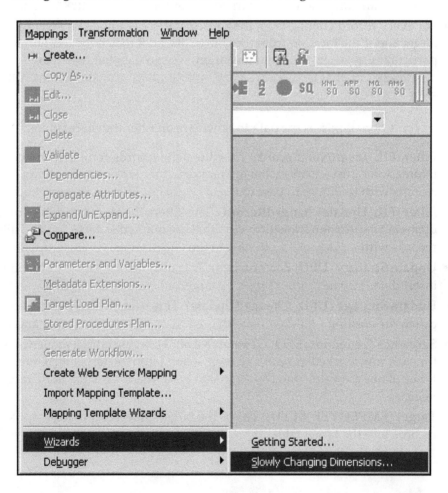

2. A new window will pop up asking the name of the new SCD mapping
   (m_SCD2_VERSION_NUMBER). Also, select the Type of SCD you wish to
   implement. Select **Type 2 Dimension - keep a full history of the changes in the
   target** as we are implementing SCD2 using version number. Click on **Next:**

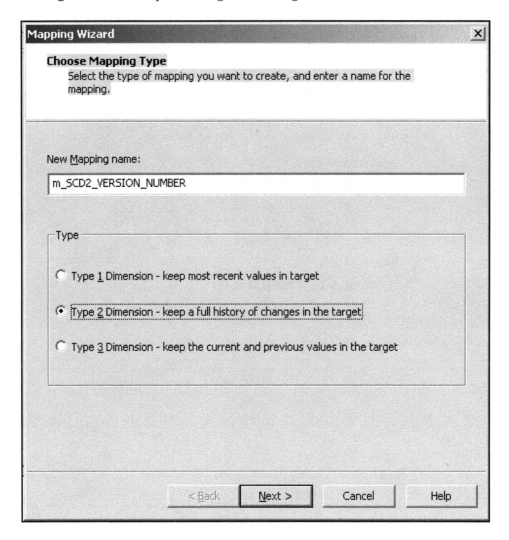

3. The next screen will ask you to select the source. Select a source from the drop-down. We are using EMP_FILE.txt as the source file for our reference. Also, specify the name of the target you wish to create. We will name the target EMPLOYEE_SCD2_VERSION_NUMBER for our reference in this book. Click on **Next**:

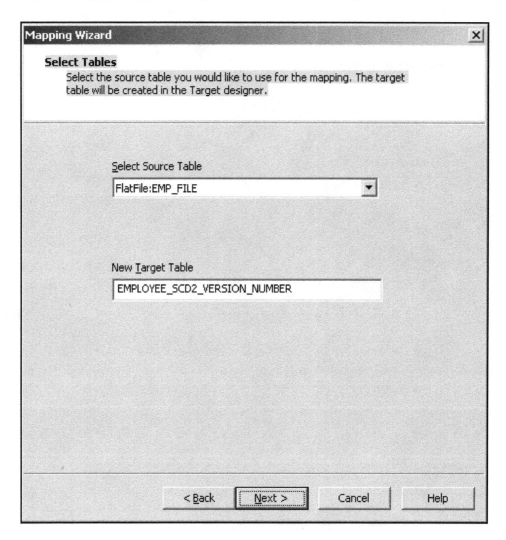

4. In the next window, select **EMPLOYEE_ID** as **Logical Key Field**. Also, add LOCATION under **Fields to compare for changes**. Click on **Next**:

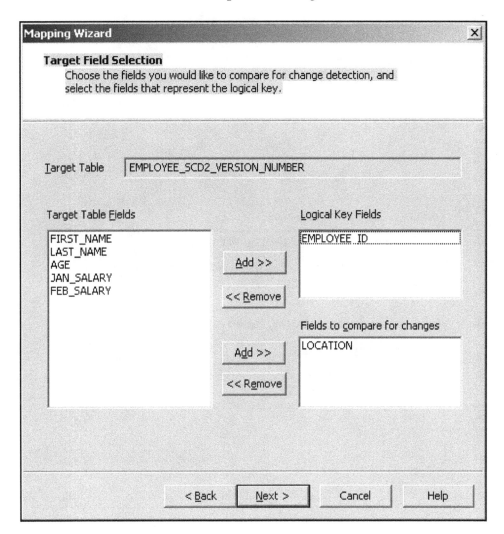

5. The next screen asks you to choose the option to maintain history in the target. Select **Keep the 'version' number in separate column**, and click on **Finish**:

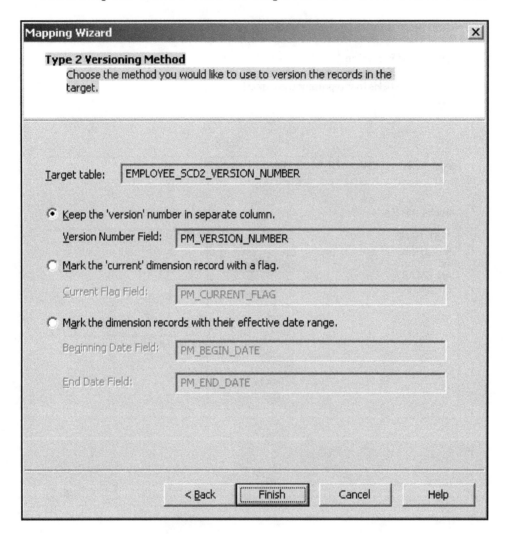

The wizard creates a complete mapping in your mapping designer workspace. Make the necessary changes into the mapping if required:

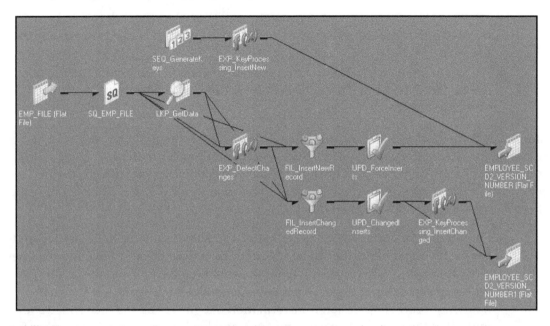

Change the target data type from flat file to Oracle table as shown in the following figure:

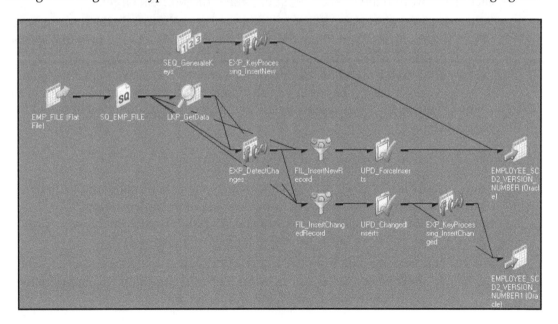

When we create an SCD2 mapping using a version number, the wizard creates two additional columns in the target table:

- PM_PRIMARY_KEY: The wizard generates a primary key for each row to be inserted into the target. Note that EMPLOYEE_ID will not be the primary key in the table.
- PM_VERSION_NUMBER: The wizard generates a version number for each row inserted into the table. This will allow us to differentiate between current and historical records.

Informatica PowerCenter SCD2 mapping uses lookup transformation LKP_GetData to lookup on the data in the target table and uses expression transformation EXP_Detect_Changes to compare the target data with the source data. Based on the comparison, expression transformation marks a record as NewFlag or ChangedFlag using a flag. The mapping divides into two flows:

- Filter transformation FIL_InsertNewRecord allows only the NewFlag record to pass further and filters the ChangedFlag record from the first flow. It passes new records to UPD_ForceInserts, which inserts these records into the target. The sequence generator SEQ_generateKeys generates aq primary key for each NewFlag record. Expression transformation EXP_KeyProcessing_InsertNew multiplies the primary key value by 1000 and loads 0 as the version number for each new row into the EMPLOYEE_SCD2_VERSION_NUMBER target.
- Filter transformation FIL_InsertChangedRecord allows only the ChangedFlag record to pass further and filters the records marked as NewFlag from the second flow. It passes changed records to UPD_ChangedUpdate, which replaces the existing rows in the target to reflect the latest changes. Expression transformation EXP_KeyProcessing_InsertChanged increments both the primary key and the version number by 1 and loads into the EMPLOYEE_SCD2_VERSION_NUMBER1 target instance.

Let's understand each transformation used in the SCD2 mapping:

- **Source Qualifier** (SQ_EMP_FILE): This extracts the data from the file/table you used as the source in the mapping. It passes data to the downstream transformations, that is, lookup, expression, and filter transformations.
- **Lookup** (LKP_GetData): This is used to lookup on the target table.
- It caches the existing data from EMPLOYEE_SCD2_VERSION_NUMBER.
    - The EMPLOYEE_ID=IN_EMPLOYEE_ID condition will compare the data with the source table and target table.

- It passes the data based on the comparison to Expression transformation.
- **Expression** (`EXP_DetectChanges`): This receives the data from the upstream transformation and based on that, creates two flags: `NewFlag` and `ChangedFlag`.
- The condition for `NewFlag` is `IIF(ISNULL(PM_PRIMARYKEY), TRUE, FALSE)`.
- The condition for `ChangedFlag` is `IIF(NOT ISNULL(PM_PRIMARYKEY) AND (DECODE(LOCATION,PM_PREV_LOCATION,1,0)=0), TRUE, FALSE)`.
- It passes the data to the downstream filter transformations.
- **Filter** (`FIL_InsertNewRecord`): This filters the records coming from the upstream Expression transformation that are marked as `ChangedFlag` and allows only records with NewFlag to pass to the `UPD_ForceInserts` update strategy.
- **Filter** (`FIL_UpdateChangedRecord`): This filters the records coming from the upstream Expression transformation that are marked as `NewFlag` and allows only records with `ChangedFlag` to pass to the `UPD_ChangedInserts` update strategy.
- **Update Strategy** (`UPD_ForceInserts`): This uses the `DD_INSERT` condition to insert data into the `EMPLOYEE_SCD2_VERSION_NUMBER` target.
- **Update Strategy** (`UPD_ChangedInserts`):This uses the `DD_UPDATE` condition to overwrite existing `LOCATION` into the `EMPLOYEE_SCD2_VERSION_NUMBER1` target instance.
- **Sequence Generator** (`SEQ_GenerateKeys`): This generates a sequence of values for each new row marked as `NewFlag` coming into the target incrementing by 1. It populates the value into the `PM_PRIMARYKEY` column in the `EMPLOYEE_SCD2_VERSION_NUMBER` target.
- **Expression** (`EXP_KeyProcessing_InsertNew`): This multiplies the `Nextval` generated by the sequence generator by 1000, using the `NEXTVAL*1000` condition. Note thatyou can change this number as per your requirement. Using 1000 here means we can maintain 1000 history entries of a particular record.
- **Expression** (`EXP_KeyProcessing_InsertChanged`): This is used to increment the primary key and the `Version` number by 1 each for every changed record.
- **Target** (`EMPLOYEE_SCD2_VERSION_NUMBER`): This is the target table instance to accept new records into the target table.
- **Target** (`EMPLOYEE_SCD2_VERSION_NUMBER1`): This is the target table instance to accept changed records into the target table.

# SCD2 (flag) - flag the history

To implement SCD2 by maintaining a flag, follow these steps:

1. In the **Designer**, go to **Tools** | **Mapping Designer** | **Mapping** | **Wizard** | **Slowly Changing Dimensions** as shown in the following screenshot:

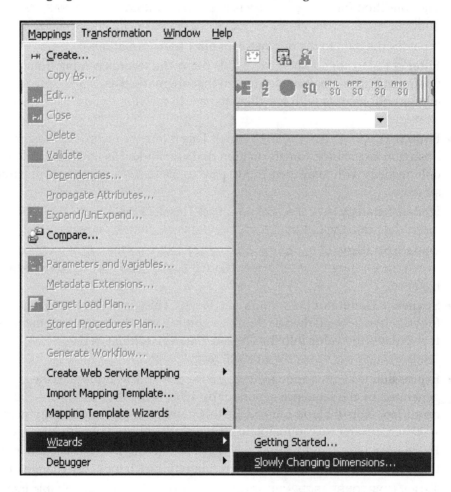

- A new window will pop up asking the name (m_SCD2_FLAG) of the new SCD2 mapping. Select **Type 2 Dimension - keep a full history of the changes** as we are implementing SCD2, and click on **Next**:

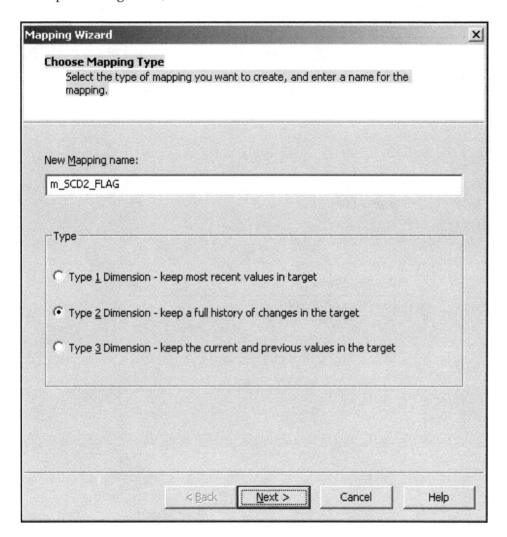

- The next screen will ask you to select the source. Select a source from the drop-down. We are using EMP_FILE.txt as the source file for our reference. Also, specify the name of the target you wish to create. We will name the target EMPLOYEE_SCD2_FLAG for our reference in this book. Click on **Next**:

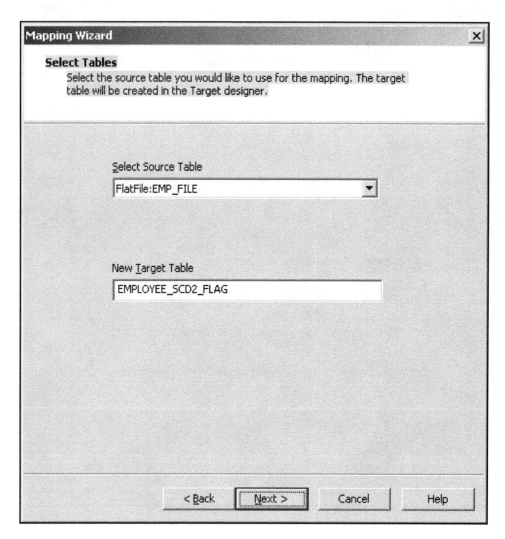

- In the next window, select EMPLOYEE_ID as Logical Key Field. Also, add
  LOCATION under **Fields to compare for changes,** and click on **Next:**

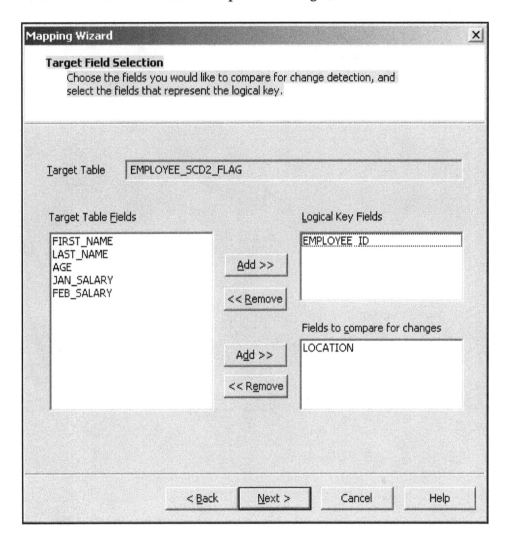

- The next screen asks you to choose the option to maintain the history in the target. Select **Mark the 'current' dimension record with a flag,** and click on **Finish**:

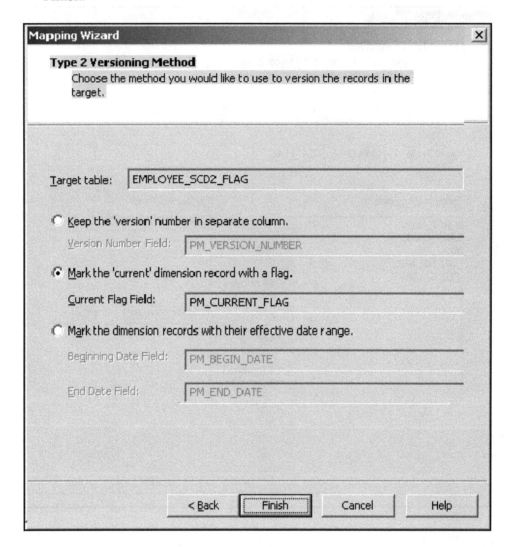

The wizard generates a complete mapping in your mapping designer workspace. Make the necessary changes into the mapping if required:

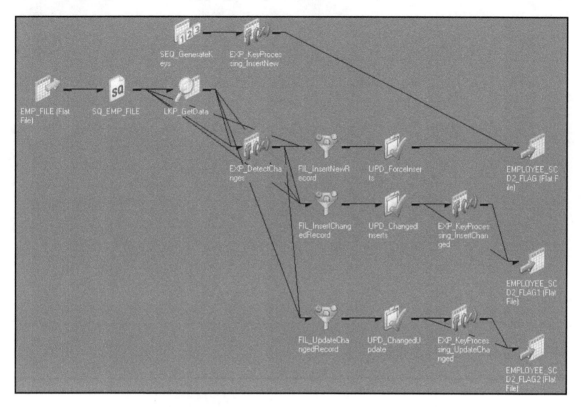

Change the target data type from flat file to Oracle table as shown in the following figure:

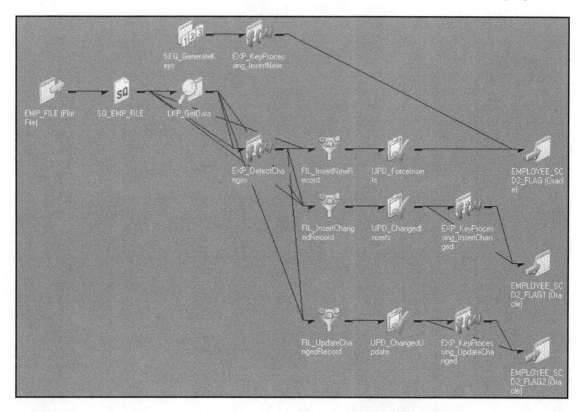

When we create mapping using the flag option, the wizard creates two additional columns in the target table:

- PM_PRIMARY_KEY: The wizard generates a primary key for each row to be inserted into the target. Note that EMPLOYEE_ID will not be the primary key in the table.
- PM_CURRENT_FLAG: The wizard loads 1 for each new record inserted into the table and marks all history records as 0. This allows us to differentiate between current and historical records.

Informatica PowerCenter SCD2 mapping uses lookup transformation LKP_GetData to lookup on the data in the target table and uses expression transformation EXP_DetectChanges to compare the data with the source data. Based on the comparison, expression transformation marks a record as NewFlag or ChangedFlag. The mapping divides into three flows:

- Filter transformation FIL_InsertNewRecord allows only the NewFlag record to pass further and filter the ChangedFlag record from the first flow. It passes new records to UPD_ForceInserts, which inserts these records into the target. The sequence generator SEQ_GenerateKeys generates a primary key for each NewFlag record. Expression transformation EXP_KeyProcessing_InsertNew multiplies the Next Val value by 1000 and loads 1 as the current flag for each new row.
- Filter transformation FIL_InsertChangedRecord allows only the ChangedFlag record to pass to UPD_ChangedInserts, which inserts changed records in the EMPLOYEE_SCD2_FLAG1 target. Expression transformation EXP_KeyProcessing_InsertChanged increments the primary key by 1 and loads the current flag as 1 to indicate that the updated row contains the current data.
- The third filter transformation FIL_UpdateChangedRecord passes the primary key of the previous value for every ChangedFlag record to UPD_ChangedUpdate, which updates changed records in the EMPLOYEE_SCD2_FLAG2 target. Expression transformation EXP_KeyProcessing_UpdateChanged changes the current flag to 0 to indicate the row now no more contains the current data.

Let's understand each transformation used in the SCD2 mapping:

- **Source Qualifier** (SQ_EMP_FILE): This extracts the data from the file/table you used as source in the mapping. It passes data to the downstream transformations, that is, lookup, expression, and filter transformation.
- **Lookup** (LKP_GetData): This is used to lookup on the target table. It caches the existing data from the EMPLOYEE_SCD2_FLAG.
- The EMPLOYEE_ID=IN_EMPLOYEE_ID condition will compare the data with the source and target tables.
- It passes the data based on the comparison to Expression transformation.
- **Expression** (EXP_DetectChanges): This receives the data from the upstream transformation and, based on that, create two flags: NewFlag and ChangedFlag.
- The condition for NewFlag is IIF(ISNULL(PM_PRIMARYKEY), TRUE, FALSE).
- The condition for ChangedFlag is IIF(NOT ISNULL(PM_PRIMARYKEY) AND (DECODE(LOCATION,PM_PREV_LOCATION,1,0)=0), TRUE, FALSE).

Based on the condition, it passes the data to downstream filter transformations.

- **Filter (FIL_InsertNewRecord):** This filters the records coming from the upstream Expression transformation that are marked as ChangedFlag and allows only records as NewFlag to pass to the *UPD_ForceInserts* update strategy.
- **Filter (FIL_InsertChangedRecord):** This filters the records coming from the upstream Expression transformation that are marked as NewFlag and allows only records as ChangedFlag to pass to the Update Strategy *UPD_ChangedInserts* update strategy.
- **Filter (FIL_UpdateChangedRecord):** This filters the records coming from the upstream Expression transformation that are marked as NewFlag and allows only records as ChangedFlag to pass. For every record marked as ChangedFlag, Filter passes the primary key of the previous version to the *UPD_ChangedUpdate* update strategy.
- **Update Strategy (UPD_ForceInserts):** This uses the *DD_INSERT* condition to insert data into the *EMPLOYEE_SCD2_FLAG* target instance.

- **Update Strategy (UPD_ChangedInserts):** This uses the *DD_INSERT* condition to insert data into the *EMPLOYEE_SCD2_FLAG1* target instance.
- **Update Strategy (UPD_ChangedUpdate):** This uses the *DD_UPDATE* condition to overwrite the existing *LOCATION* value into the *EMPLOYEE_SCD2_FLAG2* target.
- **Sequence Generator (SEQ_GenerateKeys):** This generates a sequence of values for *PM_PRIMARYKEY* for each row marked as NewFlag into the target, incrementing the value by 1.
- **Expression (EXP_KeyProcessing_InsertNew):** This multiplies the Nextval generated by the sequence generator by 1000 using the *NEXTVAL*1000* condition. Note you can change this number as per your requirement. Using 1000 here means we can maintain 1000 history entries of a particular record. It creates a current flag of 1 for each NewFlag record to load into the *PM_CURRENT_FLAG* column in the target.
- **Expression (EXP_KeyProcessing_InsertChanged):** This is used to increment the primary key by 1 by using the *PM_PRIMARYKEY + 1* condition. It also creates a current flag of 1 for each NewFlag record to load the *PM_CURRENT_FLAG* column in the target.
- **Expression (EXP_KeyProcessing_UpdateChanged):** This is used to set *PM_CURRENT_FLAG* to 0 for the record marked as changed, indicating the record is no more current.
- **Target (EMPLOYEE_SCD2_FLAG):** This is the target table instance to accept new records into the target table.
- **Target (EMPLOYEE_SCD2_FLAG1):** This is the target table instance to accept changed records into the target table.
- **Target (EMPLOYEE_SCD2_FLAG2):** This is the target table instance to allow updates to existing records into the target table.

# SCD2 (date range) - marking the dates

To implement SCD2 by maintaining a flag, follow these steps:

1. In the **Designer**, go to **Tools** | **Mapping Designer** | **Mapping** | **Wizard** | **Slowly Changing Dimensions** as shown in the following screenshot:

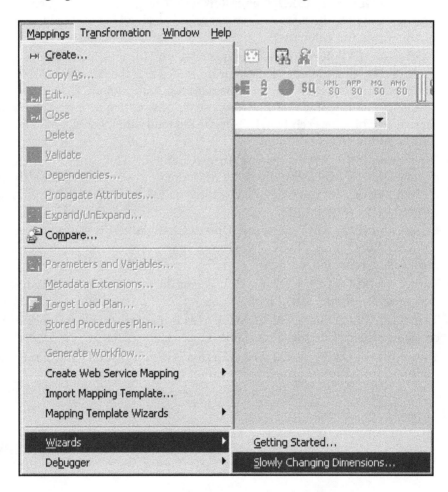

2. A new window will pop up asking the name (m_SCD2_DATE_RANGE) of the new SCD mapping. Select **Type 2 Dimension - keep a full history of the changes**as we are implementing SCD2, and click on **Next**:

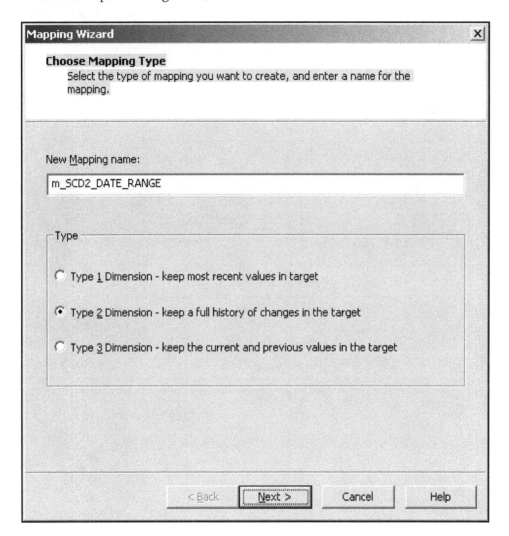

3. The next screen will ask you to select the source. Select a source from the drop-down. We are using `EMP_FILE.txt` as the source file for our reference. Also, specify the name of the target you wish to create. We will name the target `EMPLOYEE_SCD2_DATE_RANGE` for our reference in this book. Click on **Next**:

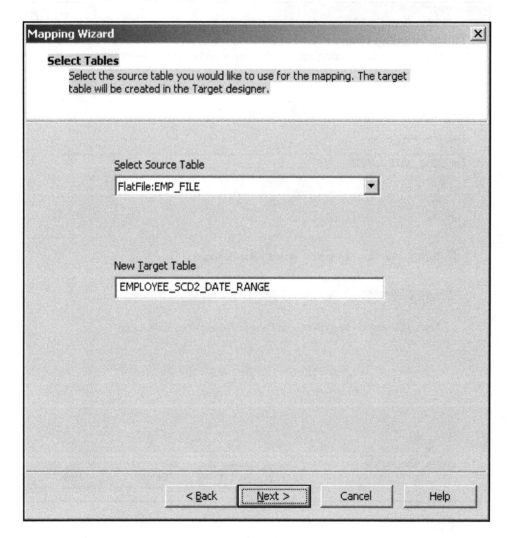

4. In the next window, select EMPLOYEE_ID as Logical Key Field. Also, add
   LOCATION under **Fields to compare for changes,** and click on **Next**:

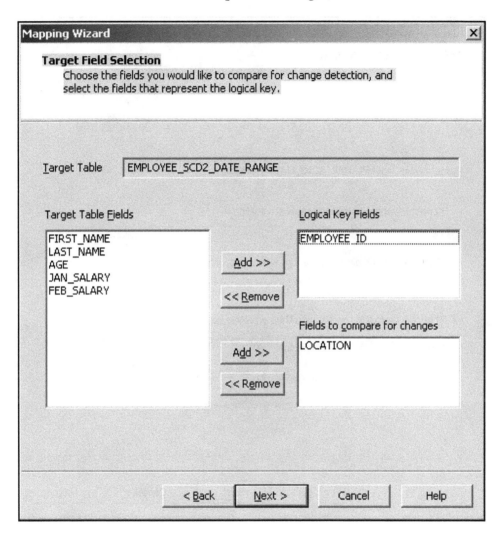

5. The next screen asks you to choose the option to maintain history in target. Select **Mark the dimension records with their effective date range,** and click on **Finish**:

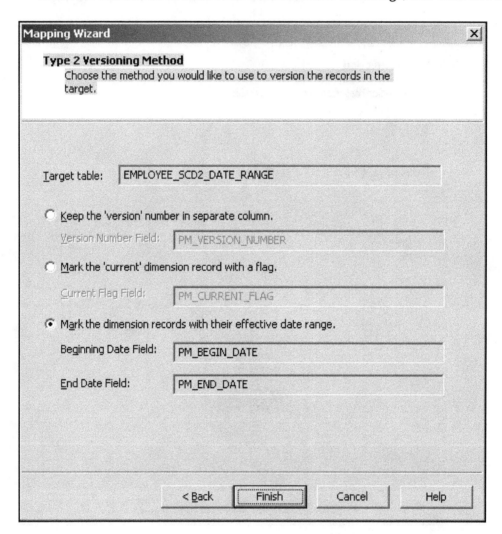

6. The wizard generates a complete mapping in your mapping designer workspace. Make the necessary changes into the mapping if required:

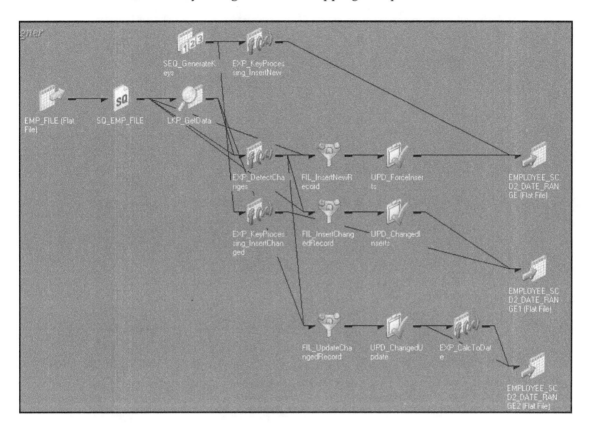

7. Change the target data type from flat file to Oracle table as shown in the
   following figure:

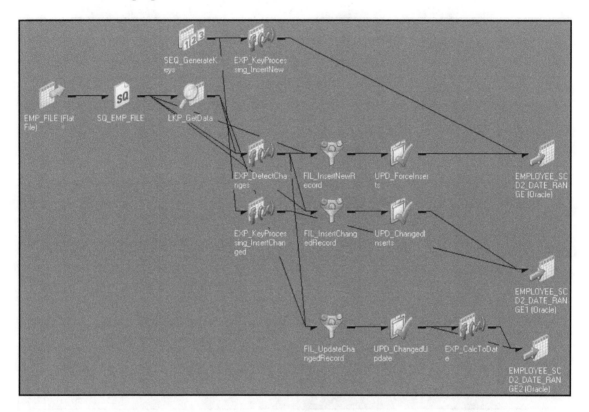

When we create mapping using this option, the wizard creates three additional columns in the target table:

- **PM_PRIMARY_KEY:** The wizard generates a primary key for each row to be inserted into the target. Note that *EMPLOYEE_ID* will not be a primary key in the table.
- **PM_BEGIN_DATE:** The wizard loads *SYSTEM DATE* for each NewFlag and ChangeFlag record inserted into the table.
- **PM_END_DATE:** The wizard loads *SYSTEM DATE* for each updated record inserted into the table indicating the end date of the record.

Informatica PowerCenter SCD2 mapping uses lookup transformation LKP_GetData to lookup on the data in the target table and uses expression transformation EXP_DetectChanges to compare the data with the source data. Based on the comparison, Expression transformation marks a record as NewFlag or ChangedFlag. The mapping divides into three flows.

- Filter transformation *FIL_InsertNewRecord* allows only the NewFlag records to pass further and filter the ChangedFlag records from the first flow. It passes the NewFlag records to *UPD_ForceInserts*, which inserts these records into the *EMPLOYEE_SCD2_DATE_RANGE* target instance. The sequence generator *SEQ_GenerateKeys* generates primary key for each NewFlag record. The expression transformation *EXP_KeyProcessing_InsertNew* loads *SYSTEMDATE* into the *PM_BEGIN_DATE* column and leaves *PM_END_DATE* as null. This indicates the new record has been added from the date loaded in *PM_BEGIN_DATE*.
- Filter transformation *FIL_InsertChangedRecord* allows only the ChangedFlag record to pass to *UPD_ChangedInserts*, which inserts changed records in the target instance *EMPLOYEE_SCD2_DATE_RANGE1*. For every ChangedFlag record, Expression transformation *EXP_KeyProcessing_InsertChanged* loads *SYSTEMDATE* into the *PM_BEGIN_DATE* column and leaves *PM_END_DATE* as null. This indicates the changed record has been added and the changed row now contains current data.
- The third Filter transformation FIL_UpdateChangedRecord passes the primary key of the previous value for every ChangedFlag record to UPD_ChangedUpdate, which inserts changed records in the EMPLOYEE_SCD2_DATE_RANGE2 target. Expression transformation EXP_CalcToDate loads SYSTEMDATE into PM_END_DATE to indicate the row now contains the historical data.

Let's understand each transformation used in the SCD2 mapping:

- **Source Qualifier (SQ_EMP_FILE):** This extracts the data from the file/table you used as source in the mapping. It passes data to the downstream transformations, that is, lookup, expression, and filter transformations.
- **Lookup (LKP_GetData):** This is used to lookup on the target table. It caches the existing data from the *EMPLOYEE_SCD2_DATE_RANGE*.
  - The `EMPLOYEE_ID=IN_EMPLOYEE_ID` condition will compare the data with the source table and target table.
  - It passes the data based on the comparison to Expression transformation.
- **Expression (EXP_DetectChanges):** This receives the data from the upstream transformation and, based on that, creates two flags: **NewFlag** and **ChangedFlag**.
  - The condition for NewFlag is IIF(ISNULL(PM_PRIMARYKEY), TRUE, FALSE).
  - The condition for ChangedFlag is IIF(NOT ISNULL(PM_PRIMARYKEY) AND (DECODE(LOCATION,PM_PREV_LOCATION,1,0)=0), TRUE, FALSE).

Based on the condition, it passes the data to downstream filter transformations.

- **Filter (FIL_InsertNewRecord):** This filters the records coming from the upstream Expression transformation that are marked as ChangedFlag and allows records with NewFlag to pass to the *UPD_ForceInserts* update strategy.
- **Filter (FIL_InsertChangedRecord):** This filters the records coming from the upstream Expression transformation that are marked as NewFlag and allows records with ChangedFlag to pass to the *UPD_ForceInserts* update strategy.
- **Filter (FIL_UpdateChangedRecord):** This filters the records coming from the upstream Expression transformation that are marked as NewFlag and allows records with ChangedFlag to pass to the *UPD_ChangedUpdate* update strategy. For each row marked as ChangedFlag, it passes the primary key of the previous version to *UPD_ChangedUpdate*.
- **Update Strategy (UPD_ForceInserts):** This uses the *DD_INSERT* condition to insert data into the *EMPLOYEE_SCD2_DATE_RANGE* target instance.

- **Update Strategy (UPD_ChangedInserts):** This uses the *DD_INSERT* condition to insert data into the *EMPLOYEE_SCD2_DATE_RANGE1* target instance.
- **Update Strategy (UPD_ChangedUpdate):** This uses the *DD_UPDATE* condition to overwrite existing LOCATION into the *EMPLOYEE_SCD2_DATE_RANGE2* target instance.
- **Sequence Generator (SEQ_GenerateKeys):** This generates a sequence of values for each new row marked as NewFlag coming into the target, incrementing by 1. It passes the value to *EXP_KeyProcessing_InsertNew*.
- **Expression (EXP_KeyProcessing_InsertNew):** This loads the generated value in the *PM_PRIMARYKEY* column in the *EMPLOYEE_SCD2_DATE_RANGE* target instance. It loads *SYSTEMDATE* into the *PM_BEGIN_DATE* column in the target, marking the start of the record.
- **Expression (EXP_KeyProcessing_InsertChanged):** This loads the generated value in the *PM_PRIMARYKEY* column in the *EMPLOYEE_SCD2_DATE_RANGE1* target instance. It loads *SYSTEMDATE* into the *PM_BEGIN_DATE* column in the target, marking the start of the record in the *EMPLOYEE_SCD2_DATE_RANGE1* target instance.
- **Expression (EXP_CalcToDate):** This uses *SYSTEMDATE* to update the *PM_END_DATE* column in the *EMPLOYEE_SCD2_DATE_RANGE2* target instance in an existing record, indicating the record is no more current.
- **Target (EMPLOYEE_SCD2_DATE_RANGE):** This is the target table instance to accept New records into the target table.
- **Target (EMPLOYEE_SCD2_DATE_RANGE1):** This is the target table instance to accept changed records into the target table.
- **Target (EMPLOYEE_SCD2_DATE_RANGE2):** This is the target table instance to allow updates to existing records into the target table.

# SCD3 - store something if not everything

To implement SCD3 using wizard, please follow the steps mentioned here:

1. In the Designer, go to **Tools | Mapping Designer | Mapping | Wizard | Slowly Changing Dimensions** as shown in the following screenshot:

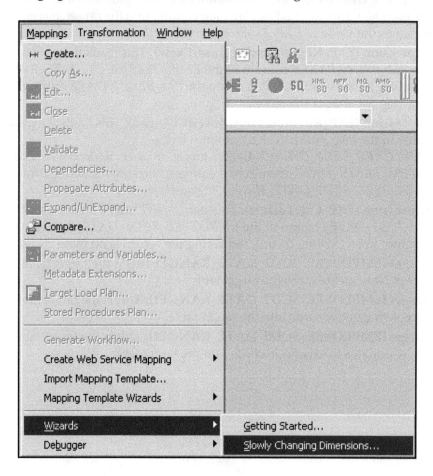

2. A new window will pop up asking the name (m_SCD3) of the new SCD mapping. Also select the type of SCD you wish to implement. Select **Type 3 Dimension - keep the current and previous value in the target** as we are implementing SCD3, and click on **Next:**

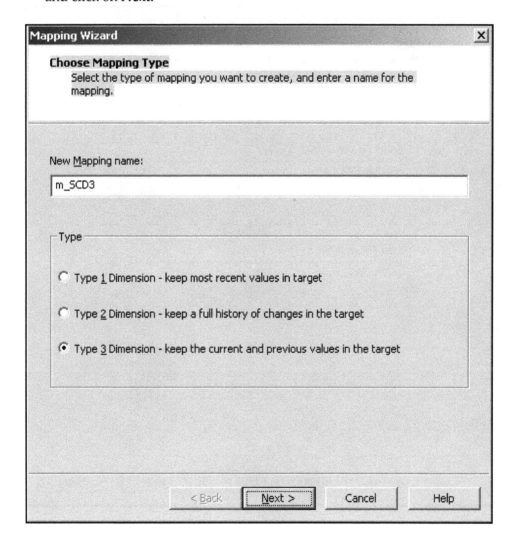

3. The next screen will ask you to select the source. Select a source from the drop-down. We are using EMP_FILE.txt as the source file for our reference. We will name the target EMPLOYEE_SCD3 for our reference in this book. Click on **Next**:

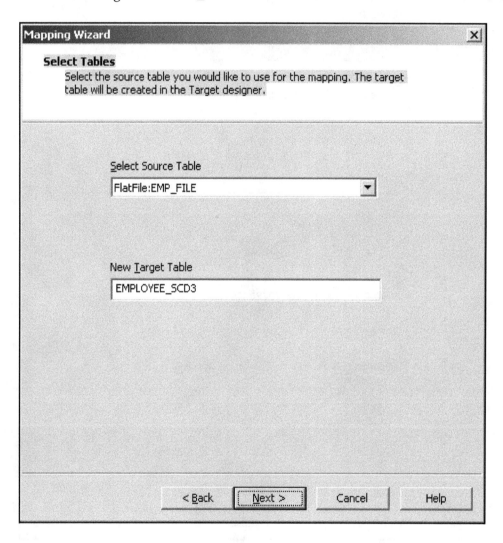

4.  In the next window, select EMPLOYEE_ID as Logical Key Field. Also, add LOCATION under **Fields to compare for changes,** and click on **Next**:

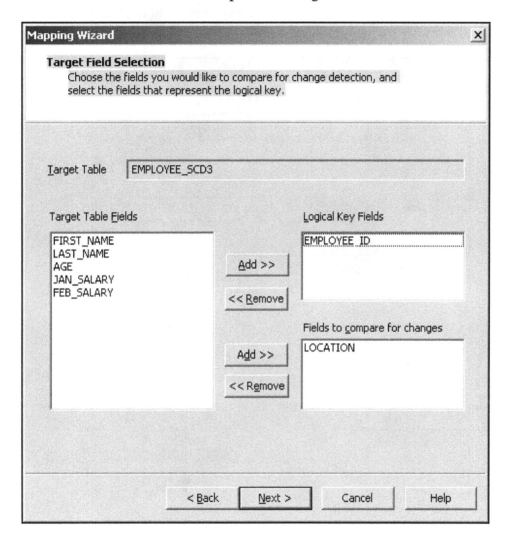

5. In the next window, select the target columns you wish to compare to detect changes. In our case, the LOCATION column in the target will be compared to PM_PREV_LOCATION. You can select an optional field PM_EFFECT_DATE to understand the loading of new or changed records. Click on **Finish**:

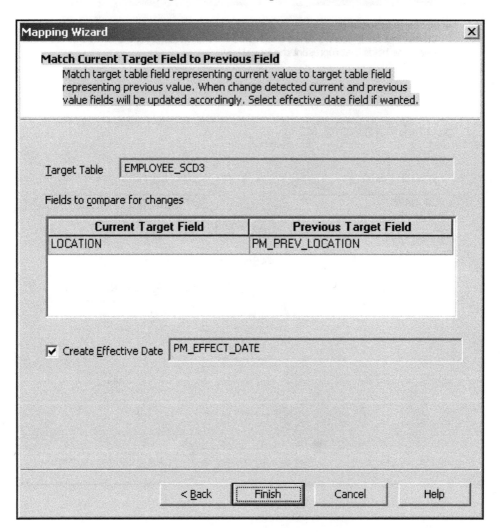

The wizard generates a complete mapping in your mapping designer workspace. Make the necessary changes into the mapping if required:

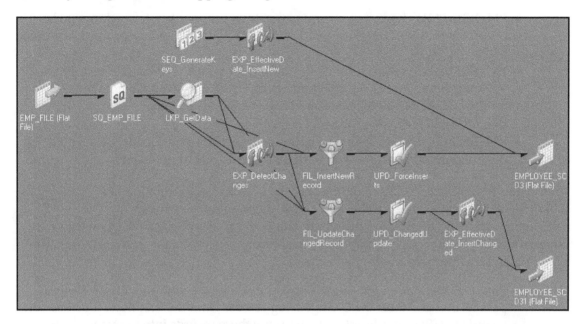

Change the target data type from Flat File to Oracle table as shown in the following figure:

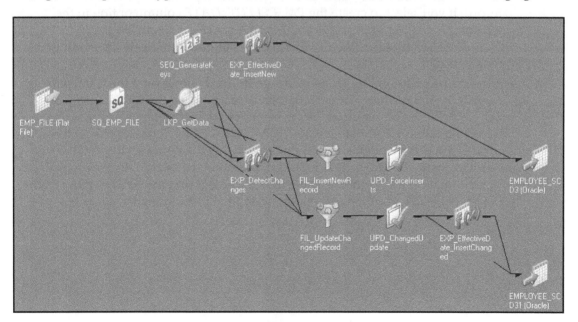

When we create mapping using this option, the wizard creates three additional columns into the target table:

- **PM_PRIMARY_KEY:** The wizard generates a primary key for each row to be inserted into the target. Note that *EMPLOYEE_ID* will not be a primary key in the table.
- **PM_PREV_***columnName*: For every column for which we maintain history, the wizard generates a previous column. In our case, we wish to maintain the history for the *LOCATION* field, so wizard creates another column *PM_PREV_LOCATION*.
- **PM_EFFECT_DATE:** This is an optional field. The wizard loads SYSTEMDATE in this column to indicate inserts or updates to the record in the table.

Informatica PowerCenter SCD2 mapping uses the Lookup transformation LKP_GetData to lookup on the data in the target table and uses expression transformation EXP_DetectChanges to compare the target data with the source data. Based on the comparison, Expression transformation marks a record as NewFlag or ChangedFlag. The mapping divides into two flows:

- Filter transformation *FIL_InsertNewRecord* allows only the NewFlag records to pass further and filter the ChangedFlag records from the first flow. It passes new records to *UPD_ForceInserts*, which inserts these records into the target. The sequence generator *SEQ_GenerateKeys* generates a primary key for each NewFlag record. If you select to create the *PM_EFFECT_DATE* column option in the wizard, Expression Transformation *EXP_EffectiveDate_InsertNew* loads *SYSTEMDATE* into the *PM_EFFECT_DATE* column to indicate the loading of new records.
- Filter transformation FIL_UpdateChangedRecord allows only the ChangedFlag records to pass further. The current data is passed from the source qualifier SQ_EMP_FILE, and previous data is taken from the target by using lookup transformation to load data in PM_PREV_LOCATION. It passes changed records to UPD_ChangedUpdates, which updates changed records in the target. If you select to create the PM_EFFECT_DATE column in the wizard, Expression Transformation EXP_EffectiveDate_InsertChanged updates SYSTEMDATE into the PM_EFFECT_DATE column to indicate the update of new records.

Let's understand each transformation used in the SCD2 mapping:

- **Source Qualifier** (**SQ_EMP_FILE**): This extracts the data from the file/table you used as source in the mapping. It passes data to the downstream transformations, that is lookup, expression, and filter transformations.
- **Lookup (LKP_GetData):** This is used to lookup on the target table. It caches the existing data from *EMPLOYEE_SCD3*.
  - The `EMPLOYEE_ID=IN_EMPLOYEE_ID` condition will compare the data with the source table and target table.
  - It passes the data based on the comparison to Expression transformation.
- **Expression (EXP_DetectChanges):** This receives the data from the upstream transformation and, based on that, creates two flags: **NewFlag** and **ChangedFlag**.
  - The condition for NewFlag is IIF(ISNULL(PM_PRIMARYKEY), TRUE, FALSE).
  - The condition for `ChangedFlag` is `IIF(NOT ISNULL(PM_PRIMARYKEY) AND (DECODE(LOCATION,PM_PREV_LOCATION,1,0)=0), TRUE, FALSE).`

Based on the condition, it passes the data to downstream filter transformations.

- **Filter (FIL_InsertNewRecord):** This filters the records coming from the upstream Expression transformation that are marked as ChangedFlag and allows records with NewFlag to pass to the *UPD_ForceInserts* update strategy.
- **Filter (FIL_UpdateChangedRecord):** This filters the records coming from the upstream Expression transformation that are marked as NewFlag and allows records with ChangedFlag to pass to the *UPD_ChangedUpdate* update strategy. It uses the value of the *LOCATION* field returned from *LKP_GetData* to load *PM_PREV_LOCATION*.
- **Update Strategy (UPD_ForceInserts):** This uses the *DD_INSERT* condition to insert data into the *EMPLOYEE_SCD3* target instance.
- **Update Strategy (UPD_ChangedUpdate):** This uses the *DD_UPDATE* condition to overwrite existing *LOCATION* into the *EMPLOYEE_SCD3* target instance. It passes data to *EXP_EffectiveDate_insertChanged* to load *PM_PREV_LOCATION* in target.
- **Sequence Generator (SEQ_GenerateKeys):** This generates a sequence of values for each new row marked as NewFlag coming into target, incrementing by 1. It passes the generated value to *EXP_KeyProcessing_InsertNew*.

- **Expression (EXP_EffectiveDate_InsertNew):** This transformation is created by the wizard only if you selected to load the *PM_EFFECT_DATE* option in the wizard. It loads the generated value in the *PM_PRIMARYKEY* column in the *EMPLOYEE_SCD3* target. It loads *SYSTEMDATE* into the *PM_EFFECT_DATE* column in the target, marking the start of the record.
- **Expression (EXP_EffectiveDate_InsertChanged):** This transformation is created by the wizard only if you selected to load the *PM_EFFECT_DATE* option in the wizard. It loads the generated value in the *PM_PRIMARYKEY* column in the *EMPLOYEE_SCD32* target instance. It loads *SYSTEMDATE* into the *PM_EFFECT_DATE* column in the target to indicate the record has been updated.
- **Target (EMPLOYEE_SCD3):** This is the target table instance to accept new records into the target table instance.
- **Target (EMPLOYEE_SCD31):** This is the target table instance to accept updates to the existing row in the target table instance.

With this, we have seen in detail how to implement different types of SCDs. You have learned to implement SCD using the wizard. You can also manually create the mapping to get better practice and better hands-on experience.

# Summary

In this chapter, we specifically concentrated on a very important feature slowly changing dimension. We talked about different types of SCDs, that is, SCD1, SCD2, and SCD3. We saw in detail how we use different transformations to achieve the SCD functionality. In the beginning of the chapter, we took an example to understand different types of SCDs. You learned how to maintain only current data in SCD1. We checked different forms of SCD2 mapping possible, that is, using version number, using flag, and using date range. We checked how SCD3 maintains partial data and how the wizard creates different columns in different types of SCD mapping.

In the next chapter, we will talk about another client screen called Informatica PowerCenter Workflow Manager. You will learn how to create workflows to execute mappings and how to add tasks. We will also have a discussion about adding the connection objects in workflow.

# 7

# Using the Workflow Manager Screen

In the previous chapters, we have discussed about the Informatica PowerCenter Designer Screen, various transformations, and SCDs. This chapter marks the beginning of another client tool called the Workflow Manager. The Informatica PowerCenter Workflow Manager lets you execute Informatica code. By now, you must be clear that we can create a skeleton of the data flow in mapping, which contains the source to the target flow. The Workflow Manager allows us to execute the mapping; in other words, we actually make the data flow from source to target when we execute a process called Workflow in the Workflow Manager.

Basically, the Workflow Manager contains a set of instructions that we define as Workflow. The basic building blocks of a Workflow are Tasks. As we have multiple transformations in the designer screen, we have multiple tasks in the Workflow Manager screen. When you create a workflow, you add tasks to it as per your requirement and execute the workflow to see the status in the monitor.

## Using the Workflow Manager

As we have already discussed in Chapter 3, *Understanding Designer Screen and its components*, the Designer client screen is divided into five sections. Similarly, the Workflow Manager screen is also divided into five sections: Navigator, Toolbar, Workspace, Output Panel, and Status bar. Refer to Chapter 3, *Understanding Designer Screen and its components*, for a detailed description.

The Informatica PowerCenter Workflow Manager has the following tools that you can use to create and execute Workflows and Tasks:

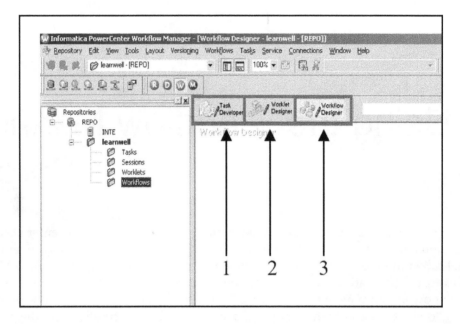

The tools are as follows:

- **Task Developer**: Using this component, you can create different types of tasks that you wish to add to your Workflow. The tasks created in **Task Developer** are reusable tasks.
- **Worklet Designer**: A group of reusable tasks is defined as Worklet. You can create a Worklet in **Worklet Designer**.
- **Workflow Designer**: Workflows can be created in **Workflow Designer**. Add different tasks to the workflow by connecting with Links.

# Creating a workflow

A workflow is a combination of multiple tasks connected with links that trigger the proper sequence to execute a process. Every workflow contains a Start task along with other tasks. When you execute the workflow, you actually trigger a Start task, which in turn, triggers other tasks connected in the flow.

The following figure shows a sample workflow:

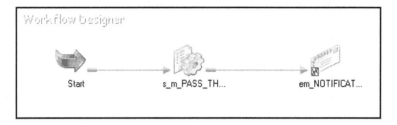

Informatica PowerCenter provides options to create workflows manually and automatically, which are discussed in the following sections.

# Creating a workflow manually

To create a workflow manually, perform the following steps:

1. In the Workflow Manager, navigate to **Workflows** | **Create:**

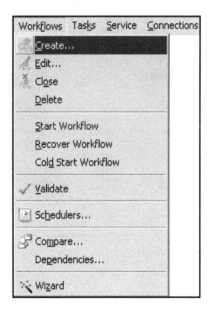

2. Specify the name of the workflow. Read the naming conventions to be followed while working on the PowerCenter tool. Use the link, `http://www.dw-learnwell .com/informatica/naming_conventions.pdf`, to download the Naming Convention document. The name of the workflow should be `wf_WORKFLOWNAME` and click on **OK**. We are using `wf_PASS_THROUGH` as the workflow name for our reference:

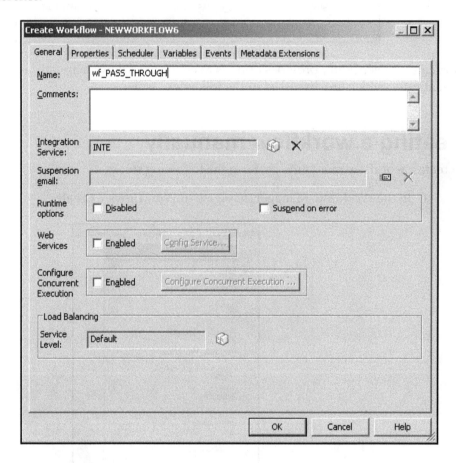

3. A start symbol appears on the screen in Workflow Manager. Additionally,the
   `wf_PASS_THROUGH` workflow appears under Navigator, as shown in the
   following screenshot:

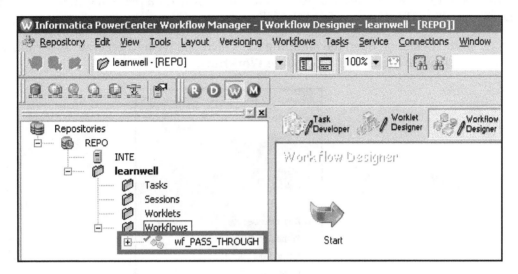

With this, you have learned how to add the Start task as the first step toward creating the
workflow. In the next section, we will create the workflow directly from the Designer
screen.

# Creating a workflow automatically

Informatica PowerCenter provides you with a utility to create a workflow directly from the Designer client tool. This feature lets you create a workflow for a particular mapping from the Designer screen. To do so, perform the following steps:

1. In the Designer, open the mapping for which you wish to generate a workflow. Navigate to **Mappings** | **Generate Workflow**:

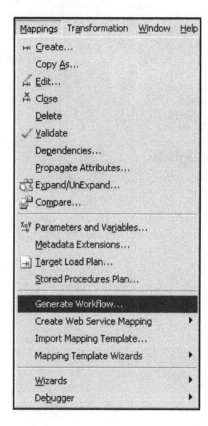

2. In the next screen, select the appropriate option for your session task that will be created. By default, you create **Workflows with a non-reusable session**:

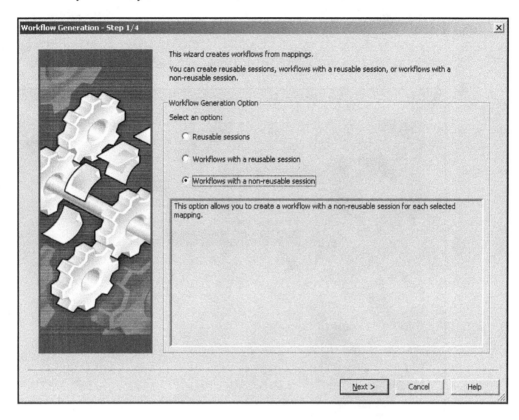

3. In the next screen, select the **Integration Service** (if you have multiple Services available) from the drop-down list. Specify **Connection Object**. We have selected Oracle for our reference as our Source and Target in the mapping to the Oracle Database. Specify the name of the workflow and session task. We are using wf_PASS_THROUGH_EMPLOYEE and s_m_PASS_THROUGH_EMPLOYEE as our workflow and session task names. Click on **Next**:

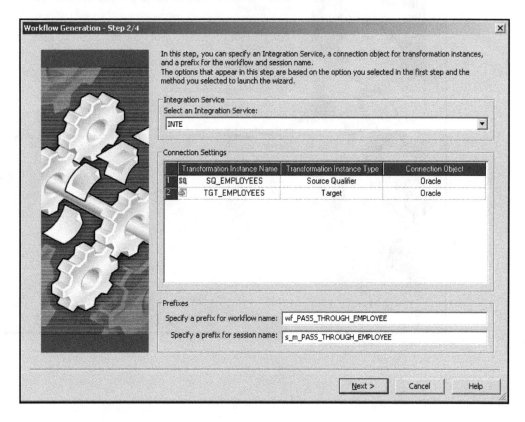

4. In the next screen, you can modify the workflow and session task details. Usually, you need not change anything unless you see any conflict. Click on **Next**:

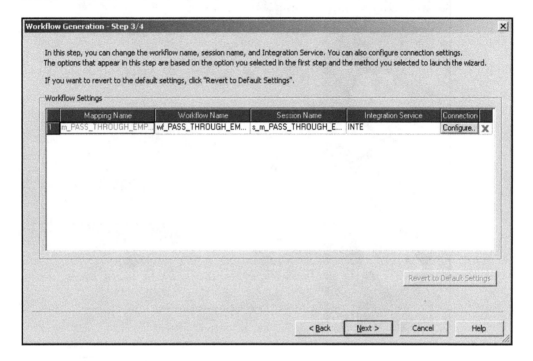

5. The next window gives you a confirmation that the workflow has been created successfully. Click on **Finish**:

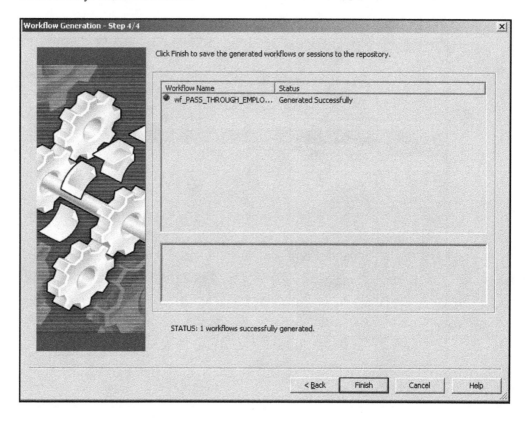

PowerCenter will generate a workflow with a Start task and Session task in Workflow Manager. Open the Workflow Manager screen to check the workflow. If you are already connected to Workflow Manager, disconnect the repository and connect again to see the workflow under Navigator.

# Adding a task to the workflow

Once you have created a workflow, you can add multiple tasks to the workflow. You can directly add the tasks by creating them in Workflow Manager or you can create them in Task Developer and use them in the workflow.

# Adding tasks to the workflow directly

To add a task to the workflow, perform the following steps:

1.  In the Workflow Manager, navigate to **Tasks** | **Create**:

2.  Select the type of task from the drop-down list that you wish to add to the workflow and specify the name of the task. The selected task will appear on the screen. Read the naming convention. For our reference, we are creating a **Session** task. The name of the **Session** task should be s_mappingname. Click on **OK**:

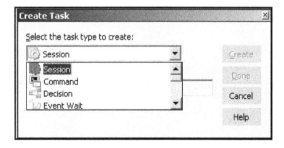

Note that we will discuss in detail about all the tasks in the next chapter.

3. If you create a **Session** task, another window will pop up, asking you to select the mapping that you wish to associate in Session. The window displays a list of all the valid mappings present in you repository. Select the appropriate mapping and click on **OK**.

    We are selecting m_PASS_THROUGH_EMPLOYEES for our reference:

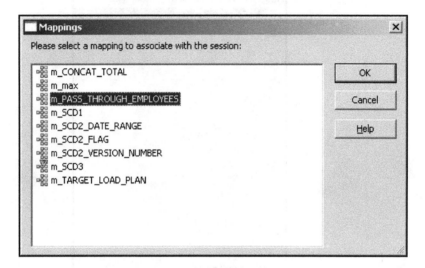

    The session task appears in the Workspace, as shown in the following screenshot:

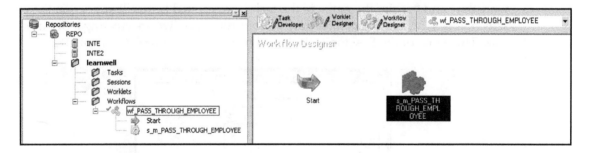

    As you can see in this screenshot, s_m_PASS_THROUGH_EMPLOYEE has been added to Navigator.

Note that every task will have a different appearance; based on the task that you select to create, the icon will appear in the Workspace.

You can associate only one mapping in one session. You cannot change the mapping once you associate the mapping to the session. If you associate a wrong mapping, delete the Session task, create a new one, and assign the correct mapping.

# Adding tasks to the workflow by task developer

We have seen in the previous section how to create non-reusable tasks in Workflow Manager. We can create reusable tasks in Task Developer. Follow these steps to create tasks in Task Developer:

1. In the Workflow Manager, click on **Task Developer**:

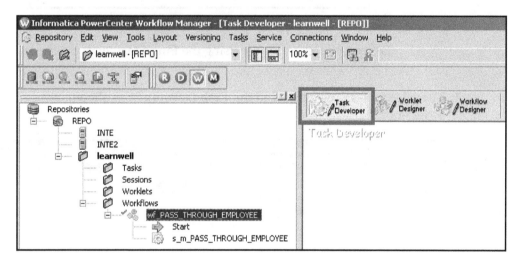

2. In the Task Developer, navigate to **Tasks** | **Create**:

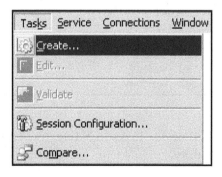

3. Select the required task from the drop-down list, provide the name of the task, and click on **Create** | **Done**:

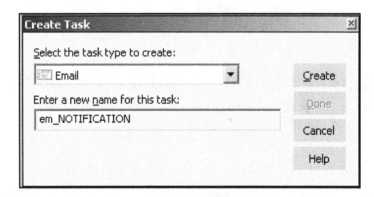

For our reference, we are using the **Email** task with the name, em_NOTIFICATION.

4. The selected task will appear in the **Task Developer**, as shown in the following screenshot:

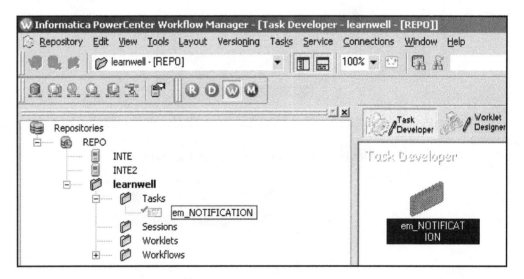

The task will also get added under Tasks in Navigator. This indicates that a reusable task has been created in Repository.

# Adding tasks to the workflow by task developer

If you have created tasks earlier in the Task Developer, you can use those tasks in the Workflow Manager. Open the Navigator and drag the appropriate task to the Workspace where your workflow is already open; the task will appear in the Workspace.

To add the reusable task created in the previous step to the workflow, drag the **em_NOTIFICATION** task to the workspace. The task will appear in the workflow, as shown in the following screenshot:

A small icon under **em_NOTIFICATION** represents that it is a reusable task.

The tasks created in Workflow Manager are non-reusable and tasks created in Task developer are reusable; that is, you can use those tasks in multiple workflows.

# Working with the Session task and basic properties

Before we can execute the workflow and make the data flow from Source to Target in mapping, we need to configure some basic properties in the Session task. These properties enable the Session task to pick the data from the source and load the data in the target.

Mapping is only a structural representation of the source and target requirement, the actual data movement happens with the properties that we define in the Session task.

To define the properties, perform the following steps:

1. In the Workflow Manager, open the workflow containing the Session task. Double-click on the Session task, click on **Mapping**, and click on Source:

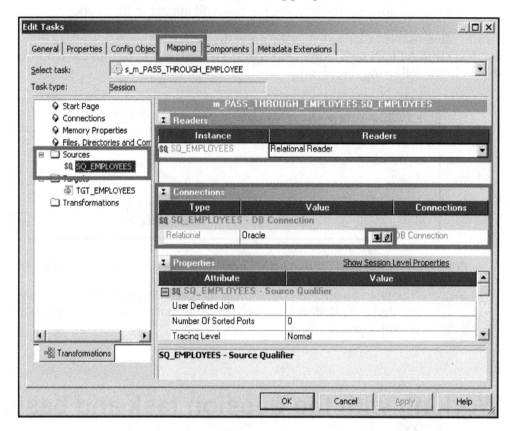

- The **Mapping** tab of the Session task lets you define the properties for Sources and Targets.
- Let's discuss the options in detail:
- **Readers**: As we are using the Oracle table as our source, the property is mentioned as **Relational Reader**. It signifies that our source is Table from where we extract the data. If our source is Flat File, the property will change to **File Reader**.

- **Connections**: Assign the Connection for the database, as shown in the previous screenshot. In case your source is file, the **Connections** option will be disabled as we need not define Connections for files. Note that we will be discussing adding Connection objects later in this chapter.

- **Properties**: Scroll through the properties and make changes, if required. In case we are using File as a source, we need to define the location of the file in your system under **Source file directory**. Also specify the name of the file under **Source filename** if you use flat file as a source, as shown in the following screenshot:

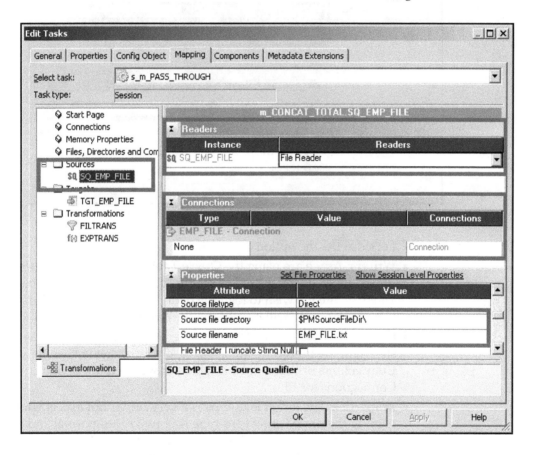

2. Click on Targets:

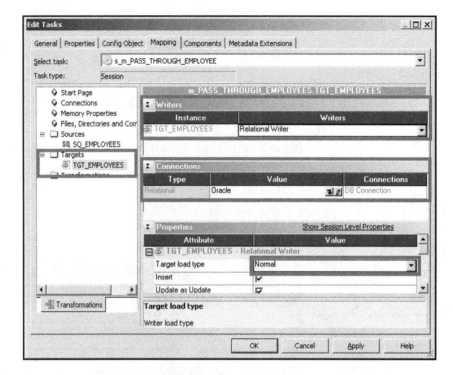

- Let's discuss the options in detail:
- **Writers**: As we are using the Oracle Table as a target, the property is mentioned as **Relational Writer**. It signifies that our target is Table, where we wish to load the data. If we use the target as Flat File, the property will change to **File Writer**.
- **Connection**: Assign the target Connection for the database, as shown in the preceding image. In case your target is File, the **Connections** option will be disabled as we need not define Connections for files.
- **Properties**: The target load type is a very important aspect while loading the data. Target load type is of two types-normal and bulk. Selecting the property as bulk allows faster loading in the target. You cannot use the property as bulk if you have a primary key or other constraints in your target table. As our target table has keys defined, we are using the property as normal.

- Scroll through the properties and make changes, if required. In case you use File as the target, you need to define the location of the file in your system under **Output file directory**. Also, specify the name of the file under **Output filename** if you use Flat File as the target, as shown in the following screenshot:

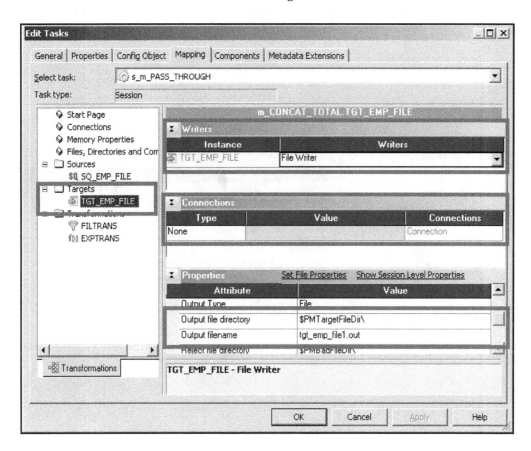

3. If you use Lookup Transformation in your mapping, you will need to define the file path/table connection for the lookup. Click on **Lookup** under Transformations and define the Connection details, as shown in the following screenshot.

4. Lookup Sql Override, as indicated in the following screenshot, is a property available if you are using lookup transformation to look up on a table. When you use lookup transformation to look up on a table, lookup transformation generates a default query to extract the data from the table and bring in Informatica PowerCenter. You can modify the default query generated by lookup transformation and is referred as Lookup SQL override. Using this property, you can save time by eliminating unwanted records while extracting itself:

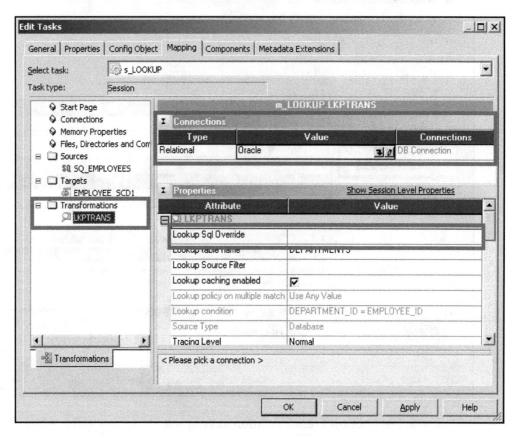

5. If you use Lookup Transformation to look up on a file, you will need to define **LookupFileDirectory** and **LookupFileName**, as shown in the following screenshot:

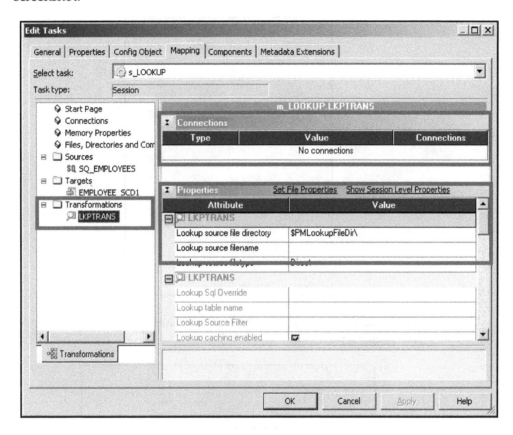

We will discuss the other properties of the Session task in detail in the next chapter.

At this point, you have learned how to create a workflow and add reusable and non-reusable tasks. Before you execute the workflow, you need to connect the Start task to other tasks present in the workflow. We use the Link task to connect. The Link task is also used to define the condition if you have multiple branches in the workflow. Links control the flow of the workflow if you have multiple branches.

To use the Link, perform the following steps:

1. Open Workflow Manager, and click on **Tasks** | **Link task**:

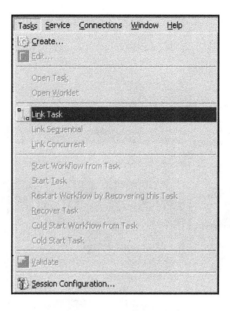

Alternatively, you can use the icon to create the link, as shown in the following screenshot:

2. In the Workflow Manager workspace, click on the **Start** task and drag to the task that you wish to connect:

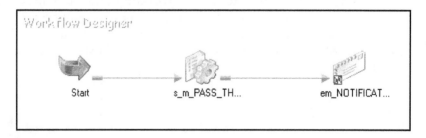

This results in a link between the tasks, as shown in preceding screenshot.

Note that you can connect any two tasks using the Link task.

# Assigning the integration service to the workflow

When you create a workflow, Informatica assigns an integration service to the workflow to enable data movement from the source to target. If you have created multiple integration services under the repository, you can change the integration service assigned to a particular workflow. You may require changing the integration service if the assigned integration service is not available due to certain reasons. Follow the steps to assign an integration service:

1. In the Workflow Manager, open the workflow for which you wish to assign an integration service.
2. Navigate to **Workflows** | **Edit**:

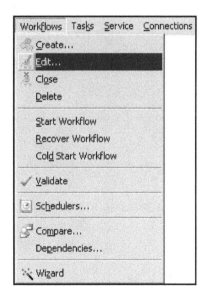

3. A new window will pop up, as shown in the following screenshot. Click on the icon that allows you to select the Integration Service:

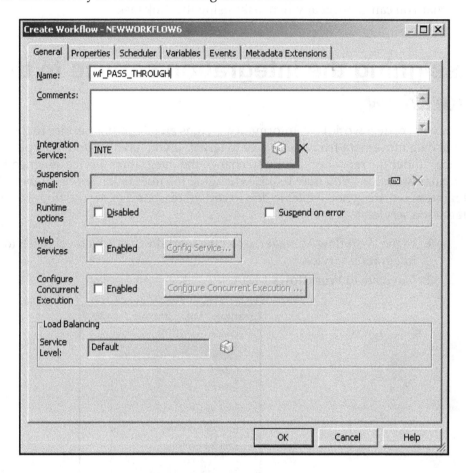

A window with a list of all the integration services will appear.

4. Select the integration service and click on **OK**. Again, click on **Ok.** The new service will be assigned to the workflow:

# Deleting a workflow

We may need to discard some of the workflows that are no longer required. Make sure that you check the usability or dependability of the workflow you are deleting. There are various ways in which you can delete a workflow:

- To delete a workflow, select the workflow in Navigator and press the **Delete** button.

- To delete a workflow currently opened in Workspace, click on **Workflows | Delete**, as shown in the following screenshot:

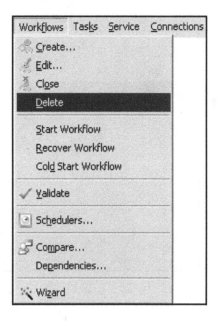

When you delete a workflow, all the associated non-reusable tasks are deleted from the repository. Reusable tasks remain in the repository.

# Trigger - starting a workflow

Before you start a workflow, make sure that the workflow is valid. Note that you can either make a complete workflow to execute or a part of the workflow.

# Running a complete workflow

To run Workflow Manager, perform the following steps:

1. In the Workflow Manager, open the workflow that you wish to execute in the Workspace.
2. Click on **Workflows** | **Start Workflow**:

The workflow will start the execution and the status can be checked in Workflow Manager.

# Running a part of the workflow

If you wish to execute only a part of the workflow, select the task from which you wish to execute the workflow. Right-click on the task and click on**Start Workflow From Task**, as shown in the following screenshot:

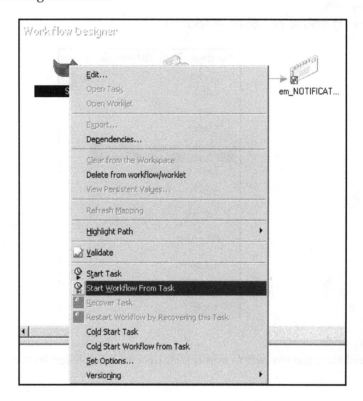

# Running a task

Apart from the running workflow, Informatica PowerCenter allows you to run only a particular task. This feature is specifically important when you are in the development phase of your project and you wish to check each component before running the complete workflow. To run a task, perform the following steps:

1. In Workflow Manager, open the workflow containing the task.

2. Right-click on the task that you wish to execute and click on **Start Task**:

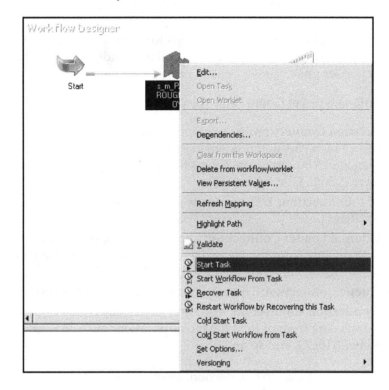

You can check the status of the task in Workflow Monitor. You will notice that only the selected task has been executed.

# Working with Connection objects

At this stage, you must be aware that we will need to define database connections in Workflow Manager before we can define the connections in the workflow. Defining connections is necessary in order to make the data flow from the actual database table to Informatica.

If we use File for a source or target, we need to define the path location for the source or file. If we are using a database table as our Source, Target, or Lookup Transformation, we need to define the database connections, as we discussed in the Working with the Session task section. Before you can assign the connections to the Session task, you need to configure the Connection object in the workflow. This is similar to adding the Database Connection object in PowerCenter Designer.

There are various types of Connection objects that Informatica PowerCenter supports:

- **Relation Connection:** As mentioned earlier, before you can define connection values in the Session task, you need to add connections under Workflow Manager. You can create connections for any type of relation database such as Oracle, SQL, DB2, and so on.
- **FTP Connection:** You can create a File Transfer Protocol connection to transfer the files.
- **External Loader Connection:** Informatica supports External Loader to load the data directly from the file to database tables. External Loader eliminates the need to run SQL commands to insert data into the table.
- **Queue Connection:** These connections enable the processing of message queues.
- **Application Connection:** You can create connections to enable the Session task to extract data from or load data to applications such as Salesforce, PeopleSoft, Siebel, TIBCO, and so on.

Note that, apart from Relation Connection, all other connection objects are rarely required based on your project requirements. So you may be more interested in learning Relational Database first.

# Creating a Connection object

To create a new Connection object in Workflow Manager, click on **Connections** in Workflow Manager and select the type of connection that you wish to create:

# Configuring the Relational Database

To create a new Relational Database connection, perform the following steps:

1. In Workflow Manager, navigate to **Connections** | **Relational**, as shown in the preceding screenshot.
2. In the next screen, click on **New** to add a new connection:

2. Select the Database subtype and click on **OK**. For our reference, we are selecting **Oracle**:

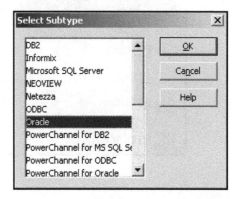

4. In the next screen, you can define all the properties. Define the properties and click on **OK** and **Close** to get the connection added to your repository.

Note that you need to have all the details available with you before you can configure a Relation Database Connection object.

The following is a list of details that are to be filled in while creating a database connection object:

- **Database Name:** Specify the name of the database, for example, Oracle, SQL Server, and so on. In our case, we are using *Oracle*.
- **Database Type:** Specify the type of the database, for example, Oracle, SQL Server, and so on. In our case, we are using *Oracle*.
- **Database User Name:** Mention the name of the database user that has proper authentication to read from and write to the database table. We are using *HR* as a username for our reference.
- **Password:** Mention the password for the user that you mentioned under Database User Name. We are using *HR* as the password for our reference.
- **Connect String:** Mention the connection string to transfer data to the table. For our reference, we are using *XE* as the connection string.
- **Database Code Page:** Select the associated code page with your database.

The details required to be filled in are shown in the following screenshot:

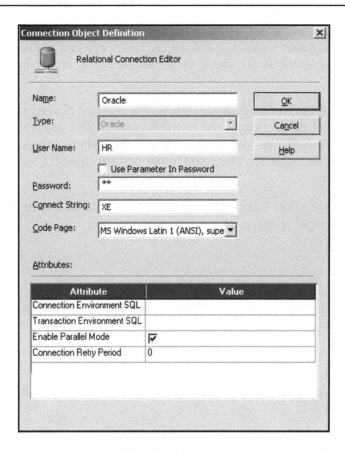

This will add the connection to your Workflow Manager screen under therepository. Now you can use the connection in your Session task.

# Summary

We can summarize this chapter by saying that we have covered the complete development of Informatica; that is, the Designer screen and Workflow Manager screen. By now, you should be able to create mapping and workflows.

In this chapter, you learned about working in the Workflow Manager screen. We covered creating a workflow, adding tasks, and linking the tasks. We saw various options to create a workflow and tasks. We discussed how to create reusable and non-reusable tasks in Task Developer.

Later, we discussed about running the workflow. We checked how to run a complete workflow and a part of the workflow and individual tasks. The last section of the chapter explains the Connection objects. We discussed about the different types of Connection objects present in Informatica. We discussed in detail the frequently used connection, that is, relation connection.

In the next chapter, we will talk about the various types of tasks and high-level properties of the Workflow Manager screen.

# 8
# Learning Various Tasks in Workflow Manager screen

In the previous chapter, we discussed the basics of Workflow Manager screen. In this chapter, we will take the words of the previous chapter forward and talk about the advanced topics of Workflow Manager Screen. We will start the chapter with a discussion on various tasks. As mentioned in the previous chapter, tasks are the basic building blocks of Workflow Manager.

## Working with tasks

As mentioned in the previous chapter, tasks are the basic building blocks of Workflows. Every task has a different functionality as every transformation has a different functionality. We need to use tasks as per our requirement in the workflow or worklet. Tasks can be created as reusable or non-reusable.

You can create reusable tasks in Task Developer and non-reusable tasks in Workflow Manager.

Before we talk in detail about each task, let's have a brief understanding of the different tasks we have:

| Name of task | Details |
| --- | --- |
| Session task | This is used to execute a mapping. |
| Email task | This is used to send success or failure email notifications. |
| Command task | This is used to execute Unix/Perl scripts or commands. It can also be used to execute DOS commands in Windows. |
| Timer task | This is used to add some time gap or delay between two tasks. |
| Assignment task | This is used to assign a value to Workflow variables. |
| Control task | This is used to control the flow of the workflow by stopping or aborting the Workflow in case on some error. |
| Decision task | This is used to check the status of multiple tasks and hence control the execution of the workflow based on the condition defined in the decision task. |
| Event-wait task | This is used to wait for a particular event to occur. Usually, it is called the File Watcher Task. |
| Event-raise task | This is used to trigger user-defined events. |
| Link task | This is used to link tasks to each other. You can also define conditions in the link to control the execution of the workflow. |

Before we move into the chapter, let's talk about an important topic. Consider we have two Workflows, *wf_WORKFLOW1* and *wf_WORKFLOW2*. *Wf_WORKFLOW1* contains session task and command task. We have a requirement in which *wf_WORKFLOW1* upon successful completion triggers *wf_WORKFLOW2*.

For session task and command task, *wf_WORKFLOW1* will be called the **parent workflow**.

For *wf_WORKFLOW2*,*wf_WORKFLOW1* will be called the **Top-level workflow** because *wf_WORKFLOW1* triggers *wf_WORKFLOW2*.

# Configuring a task

In the previous chapter, we discussed the creation of tasks in Workflow Manager and Task Developer. After we create a task, we can configure the options on the **General** tab of every task as shown in the following screenshot:

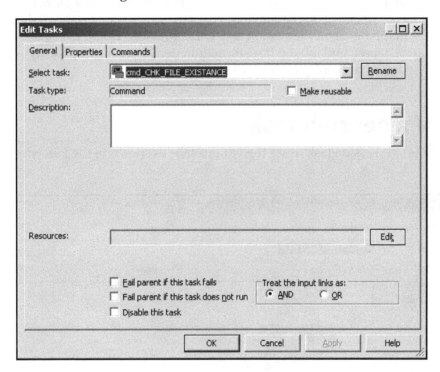

Every task has similar properties related to controlling Workflow in the **General** tab. Following options are available in **General** Tab.

- **Fail parent if this task fails**: When you check this option, the workflow or worklet will fail if the task in that workflow or worklet fails
- **Fail parent if this task does not run**: When you check this option, the workflow or worklet will fail if the task in that workflow or worklet does not run
- **Disable this task**: When you check this option, the task in the workflow or worklet will become invisible and it will not run in the sequence
- **Treat input link as AND or OR**: When you check this option, Informatica PowerCenter will run the task if all or one of the input link conditions becomes true

# Session task

In the previous chapter, we discussed the basic properties of the session task.

Session task is used to execute a mapping. It is the most widely used task among the tasks in Workflow Manager. As you must have seen earlier, there are lots of properties that we can define in the session task. In the previous chapter, we discussed some of the properties along with the mapping tab of the session task in the previous chapter. You learned about providing source, target, and lookup transformation details for moving the data. We will discuss the remaining properties in this chapter.

# Tabs of a session task

Double-click on the session task to see the various tabs as shown in the following screenshot:

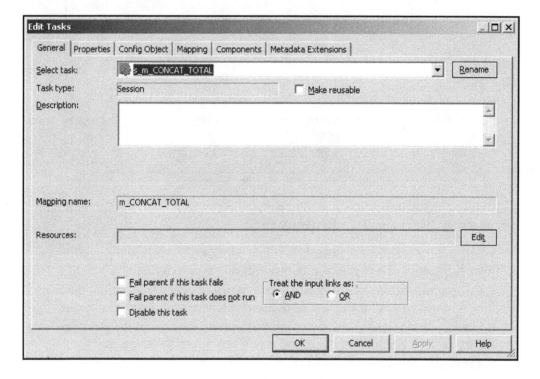

The various tabs of session task are mentioned as follows:

- **General**: As discussed in the previous section, you can define a session name, rename the session name, mention the description and other task-related properties as shown in the previous screenshot.
- **Properties**: You can define the session log file name, commit interval, test load setting, recovery settings, and other performance-related properties. The following screenshot shows the **General Options** properties that can be defined under the **Properties** tab:

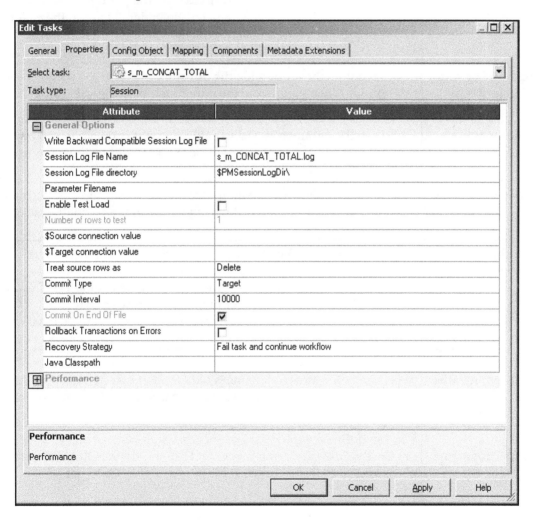

- The description of the properties shown in this screenshot is as follows:

| Property | Description |
|---|---|
| **Write Backward Compatible Session Log File** | You can select this option if you wish to write the generated session logs to a file. If you select this option, Informatica Power Center creates a log file, else it generates normal session log file. |
| **Session Log File Name** | You define the session log file name. The default session log file name is SESSION_NAME.log. You can also define the parameter in this option. We will discuss the parameter file in detail later in the chapter. When you define the parameter, pass the value from the parameter file. |
| **Session Log File Directory** | You can define the session log file directory and also the parameter in this option. When you define the parameter, pass the value from the parameter file. |
| **Parameter Filename** | If you use the parameters and variables in your code, you need to pass the value from the parameter file. You can define the parameter file name and path here. |
| **Enable Test Load** | You can select this option to allow only a few records to pass through mapping. This option is useful when you are in the testing phase of your project. |
| **Number of rows to test** | When you select the Enable Test Load option, you can define the number of records you wish to flow from the mapping. Suppose you have 10,000 records to process. You can check the Enable Test Load option and mention the number of records you wish to test. So, if you define 100, Informatica will only process 100 records out of 10,000 records. |
| **$Source connection value** | You can define the database connection value here. Consider that your database connection name is ORACLE. If you define ORACLE at this place, you can select $Source in the **Mapping** tab for the source connection. |
| **$Target connection value** | You can define the database connection value here. Consider your database connection name is ORACLE. If you define ORACLE at this place, you can select $Target in **Mapping** tab for the target connection. |

| Treat source rows as | This property allows you to treat records as INSERT, UPDATE, DELETE, or DATA DRIVEN for the records coming from the source. The default property is INSERT, which indicates all the records coming from the source will be INSERTED into the target. The DATA DRIVEN property is selected when you use Update Strategy transformation in mapping. |
|---|---|
| **Commit Type** | You can select either source-based or target-based commit type. The default property is target-based commit type. If you select source-based commit type, Informatica commits the data into the target based on the commit interval and flush latency interval. Flush latency is the time interval you wish data to commit. If you define flush latency as 5 seconds and commit interval as 10,000, Informatica will commit the data to the target based on whichever interval in reached first. Flush latency is the property defined by the Informatica Power Center administrator. So you need not worry about setting up this property. In most cases, data is committed based on the commit interval, so we don't frequently use the flush latency property. If you select target-based commit type, Informatica commits the data based on the commit interval. |
| **Commit On End Of File** | This is a default option selected. This property indicates that the records will be committed to the target if the file contains fewer number of records than the commit interval defined. |
| **Rollback Transactions on Errors** | When you select this option, Informatica will roll back the records at the next commit interval. This only happens if there is any non-fatal error. |
| **Recovery Strategy** | Using this property, you can recover the session task if the session happens to fail. Various options are available in this property, which you can select based on your requirement. Fail session and continue the workflow: If you select this option, you cannot recover your session task. The session will fail if it encounters an error, but it will continue the workflow. Restart task: If you select this option, the session task restarts when the workflow is recovered after a failure. Resume from the last checkpoint: If you select this option, Informatica saves the start of the session task and resumes the session from the last checkpoint. |

| Java Classpath | Use this option if you wish to use different types of Java packages in Java transformation. |
|---|---|

- The following screenshot shows the **Performance** properties that can be defined under the **Properties** tab:

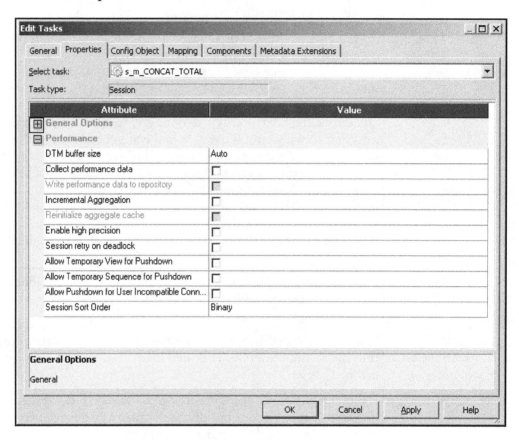

- The description of the property shown in this screenshot is as follows:

| Property | Description |
|---|---|
| DTM buffer size | This indicates how much memory you wish to assign for the DTM processes. When you create a session, Informatica assigns a specific value for the DTM. You can set the value as **Auto** so Informatica keeps on increasing the value automatically if needed. |
| Collect performance data | If you select this option, Informatica collects the performance data as it runs the session. Usually, you do not select this option unless you really need to find the performance. This option can actually hamper your performance in some way because it takes some time to collect the performance details. So unless very important, do not check this option. |
| Write performance data to repository | You can save the performance collected for the session run to the repository so that you can check the details later. This again hampers the performance, so unless needed, do not check this option. |
| Incremental Aggregation | If you wish to make use of Incremental Aggregation, check this option.<br>We will discuss this in more detail later in the chapter. |
| Reinitialize aggregate cache | If you are using Incremental Aggregation, you can use this option. When you use Incremental Aggregation, Informatica stores the data of the previous run in cache memory. If you wish to reinitialize the value, select this option.<br>We will discuss this in more detail later in the chapter. |
| Enable high precision | If you select this option, Informatica processes the decimal data to the precision of 28. Usually, you leave this option unchecked. |
| Session retry on deadlock | If you select this option, Informatica tries to load the data in the target if it finds the deadlock. So instead of giving an error, it tries to load the data again.<br>This option is available only for normal load, not bulk load setting. |
| Allow temporary view for pushdown | If you select this option, Informatica creates a temporary view in the database when you use the pushdown feature.<br>Pushdown optimization is a feature that we will discuss with the performance in Chapter 11, *The Deployment Phase - Using Repository Manager*. |

| Allow temporary sequence for pushdown | If you select this option, Informatica creates a temporary sequence in the database when you use the pushdown feature. |
|---|---|
| Allow pushdown for user incompatible connections | This property indicates that the user through which you are accessing the database used in the session has read permission. If the user does not have the read permission, the session task fails. |
| Session sort order | You can select the sort order for your session. The default sort order is binary. |

- The **Config Object** tab: You can select the **Advanced** setting, the **Log Options**, **Error handling** properties, and **Partitioning Options** under this tab.
- The **Advanced** setting under Config (Configuration) Object tab is shown in the following screenshot:

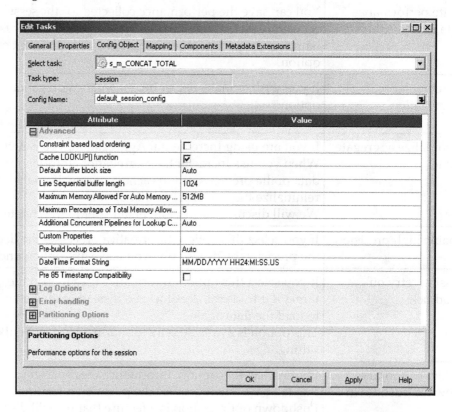

- The description of the property shown in this screenshot is as follows:

| Property | Description |
|---|---|
| **Constraint based load ordering** | If you check this option, the data is loaded into the target based on the primary key-foreign key relationship, wherever possible. |
| **Cache LOOKUP() function** | This property is related to the Lookup transformation functionality. By default, lookup transformation performs row-by-row operations. If you check this option, Informatica overrides mapping-level Lookup settings. |
| **Default buffer block size** | This option specifies the size of the buffer block you wish to assign for the data cache and index cache movement from the source to the target. By default, it is set to **Auto**, so the size is automatically increased as required. |
| **Line Sequential buffer length** | This property is related to the number of bytes in an individual record in a flat file. The default value for this property is set as 1,024 bytes. If your records have a larger byte length, increase the value as per requirement. |
| **Maximum Memory Allowed For Auto Memory Attributes** | This setting is related to the amount of memory allocated to the session cache at run time. |
| **Maximum Percentage of Total Memory Allowed for Auto Memory Attributes** | This setting is related to the percentage of memory allocated to the session cache at run time. |
| **Additional Concurrent Pipelines for Lookup Cache Creation** | This setting is related to the creation of concurrent cache by creating additional pipelines for Lookup transformation. By default, the value is set to Auto, which indicates the value will be decided at run time. Informatica caches the data either concurrently or sequentially. If you set this property to 0, Informatica processes the lookup cache sequentially. |
| **Custom Properties** | You can customize some of the default properties for session. Usually, we need not change the settings. |

- The **Log Options** setting under the **Config Object** tab is shown in the following screenshot:

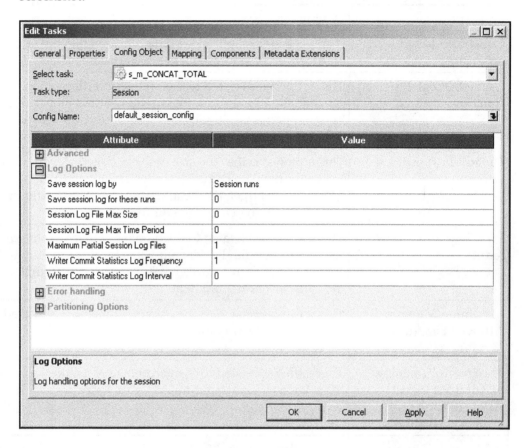

- The description of the property shown in this screenshot is as follows:

| Property | Description |
|---|---|
| **Save session log by** | You have the option of saving the session log file by either Session Runs or Timestamp.<br>When you set the option as Session run, Informatica saves a specific number of Session log files. You can set the number of log files to save in the Save Session Log for These Runs.<br>When you set the option as Timestamp, Informatica saves the session log file by appending the timestamp to the log file name.<br>When you save the history of the Session log files, you can use the files to compare them in case of some errors. |
| **Save session log for these runs** | This option allows you to define the number of Session log files you wish to save to maintain the history of log files. By default, the session log files are over-written. The maximum number of history entries you can maintain is 2,147,483,647. |
| **Session Log File Max Size** | You can define the maximum size of the session log file. If the log file size exceeds the value defined in this property, a new log file is created. The default value is 0. |
| **Session Log File Max Time Period** | You can define the maximum number of hours for which the information is written in a session log file. If the maximum time exceeds the value defined in this property, a new log file is created. The default value is 0. |
| **Maximum Partial Session Log Files** | You can define the maximum number of log files to save. If the number of files exceeds the value defined in this property, the oldest file is over-written. |
| **Writer Commit Statistics Log Frequency** | You can define the frequency at which the commit statistics are written to the Session log. The default value is 1. |
| **Writer Commit Statistics Log Interval** | You can define the time interval at which the commit statistics are written to the session log. The time is defined in minutes. |

- The **Error handling** properties under the **Config Object** tab is shown in the following screenshot:

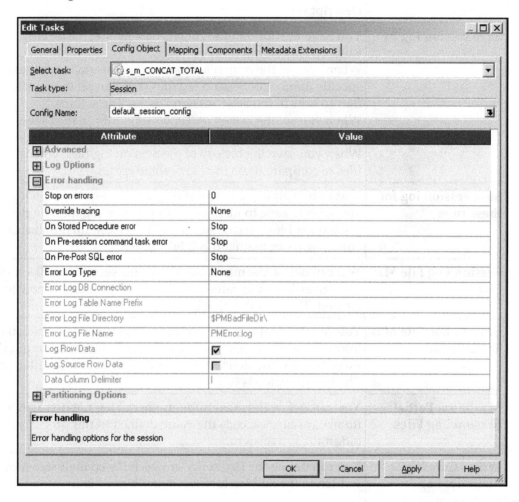

- The description of the property shown in this screenshot is as follows:

| Property | Description |
| --- | --- |
| **Stop on errors** | This option defines till how many errors you do not wish to fail the Workflow. If you set this as 5, Informatica will keep on running till it encounters five error rows. On the sixth error record, Informatica will fail the Workflow. |
| **Override tracing** | You can override the tracing level set in the Mapping. If you defined tracing level as Terse in Mapping and selected Normal Tracing level in Session, Informatica will take the Tracing level as Normal and reject the setting on Mapping. The various options available are None, Terse, Normal, Verbose Initialization, and Verbose Data. |
| **On Stored Procedure error** | You can select this option to define what should happen if there is any pre-session or post-session Stored procedure error. If you select the Stop option, the Session will fail if it encounters an error in the Stored Procedure. If you select the Continue option, the session will continue even if it encounters an error in the Stored Procedure. |
| **On Pre-session command task error** | You use this option when you use the pre-session Command task in the Session task. If you select the Stop option, the Session will fail if it encounters an error in the pre-session command. If you select the Continue option, the session will continue even if it encounters an error in the pre-session command. |
| **On Pre-Post SQL error** | You use this option when you use pre-SQL or post-SQL command in Session task. If you select the Stop option, the Session will fail if it encounters an error in pre-SQL or post-SQL. If you select the Continue option, the session will continue even if it encounters an error in pre-SQL or post-SQL. |
| **Error Log Type** | You can use this option to define the type of error log to be generated. The available options are Flat File, Relational Database, or None. The default setting is set to None. |
| **Error Log DB Connection** | If you select Relational Database as the Error Log Type, this option gets enabled. You can specify the database connection details for the Error Log. |

| Error Log Table Name Prefix | Mention the table name you created for storing Error logs. |
|---|---|
| Error Log File Directory | If you select Flat File as the Error Log Type, this option gets enabled. You can specify the File Directory details for the Error Log. |
| Error Log File Name | Mention the name of the Error log file. |
| Log Row Data | If you select this option, you can save the row-level transformation data into the log. |
| Log Source Row Data | If you select this option, you can save the Source row-level data into log. By default, the data is not saved. |
| Data Column Delimiter | You can define the delimiter to be used when saving row data and source row data. The default delimiter is (|) pipeline. |

- The **Partitioning Options** properties under the **Config Object** tab are shown in the following screenshot:

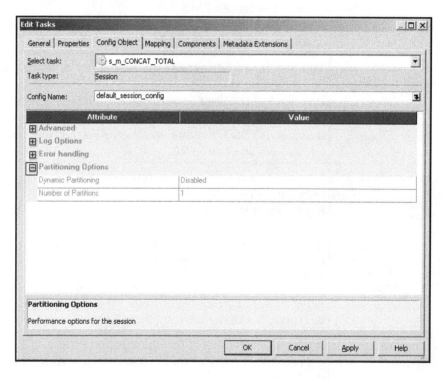

- The description of the property shown in this screenshot is as follows:

| Property | Description |
|---|---|
| **Dynamic Partitioning** | You can enable the partitioning option for which you run the process. The default setting is disabled. This is available only if you have the partitioning license available. The various options available are Based on Number of Partitions, Based on Number of nodes in grid, Based on source partitioning, and Based on Number of CPUs. |
| **Number of Partitions** | You can define the number of partitions you wish to set. |

- The **Mapping** tab: You define the session, Target, and Lookup Transformation path or Connection. We discussed this tab in the previous chapter.
- The **Components** tab: You can define pre or post command and email tasks. This acts as replacement of the command and email task.
- The **Components** tab is shown in the following screenshot:

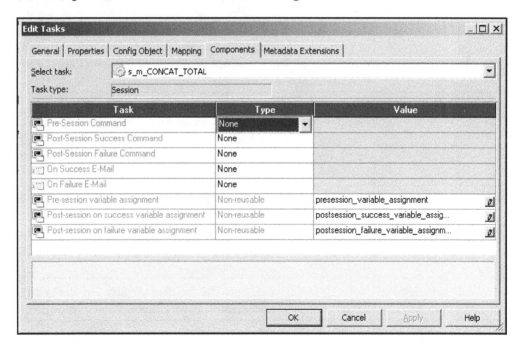

- The description of the property shown in this screenshot is as follows:

| Property | Description |
|---|---|
| **Pre-Session Command** | You can use this option as a replacement of the command task used before the session task. You can define reusable or non-reusable type. Define the shell command you wish to mention in the command task. Informatica executes the pre-session command before it executes the session task.<br>We will talk about command tasks in detail under the *Command Task* section.. |
| **Post-Session Success Command** | You can use this option as a replacement of the post-session success command task used after the session task. You can define reusable or non-reusable type. Define the shell command you wish to mention in the command task. Informatica executes the post-session command after successful completion of the session task. You need not define any condition in the link. |
| **Post-Session Failure Command** | You can use this option as a replacement of the post-session failure command task used after the session task. You can define reusable or non-reusable type. Define the shell command you wish to mention in the command task. Informatica executes the post-session command if the session task fails. |
| **On Success Email** | You can use this option as a replacement of the post-session success email task used after the Session task. You can define reusable or non-reusable type. Define the email properties you wish to mention in the email task. Informatica executes the post-session email after successful execution of the session task. |
| **On Failure Email** | You can use this option as a replacement of the post-session failure email task used after session task. You can define reusable or non-reusable type. Define the email property you wish to mention in the email task. Informatica executes the post-session email if the session task fails. |
| **Pre-session variable assignment** | You can assign values to the various parameters and variables used in the mapping and session before the session executes. |
| **Post-session on success variable assignment** | You can assign values to the various parameters and variables used in the workflow and worklet after the session executes successfully. |

| Post-session on failure variable assignment | You can assign values to the various parameters and variables used in the workflow and worklet if the session task fails. |
|---|---|

- The **Metadata Extensions** tab: You can define Metadata extension-related properties. We usually don't use this tab. This is used to define general information related to the workflow or to define project-level information that can be used in the future for reference purposes.

# Creating a Session Task

To create a Session Task in Workflow Manager or Task Developer, perform the following steps:

1. In the Workflow Manager or Task Developer, go to **Tasks | Create**:

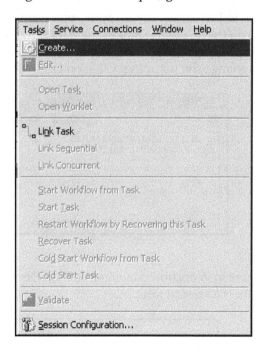

This step is the first step to be performed while creating any task.

2. From the list of tasks, select Session task, and specify the name of the Session task, s_TASK_NAME. For our reference, we are using s_CONCAT_TOTAL as the Session Task name. Click on **Create**:

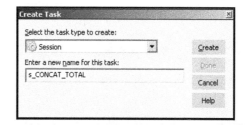

3. In the next window, select the mapping you wish to associate in the session. When you run the session, it makes the data flow from the source to the target in the mapping you selected. Note that once you associate a mapping to a session, you cannot change the mapping. Click on **OK** and then on **Done**:

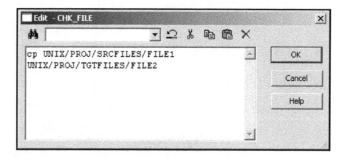

The Session task appears in Workflow Manager or Task Developer. Use the Link Task to connect the Start task to the session task:

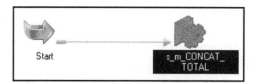

# Command task

Command task is used to execute Shell scripts or standalone shell commands. You can define one or more commands or scripts in a command task. If you define multiple command or scripts in the same command task, the task executes the commands in a sequence.

You can define Unix/Perl commands for Unix servers or DOS command for Windows servers. If your Informatica server is installed on Unix Operating system, you will be able to execute Unix commands. If the Informatica server is installed in Windows, then you can use DOS commands.

## Creating a Command task

To create a command task in Workflow Manager or Task Developer, follow these steps:

1. In Workflow Manager or Task Developer, go to **Tasks | Create** (refer to the screenshot shown in the *Creating Session Task* section).
2. From the list of tasks, select Command task, and specify the name of the command task, cmd_TASK_NAME. For our reference, we are using cmd_COPY_FILE as the command task name. Click on **Create** and then on **Done**:

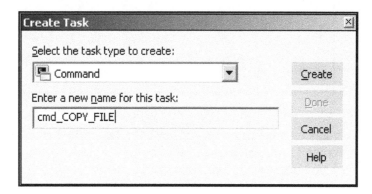

3. The task appears in Workflow Manager or Task Developer. Use the Link task to connect the Start task to the command task:

4. Double-click on the command task to open the task in the edit view. Click on **Commands**:

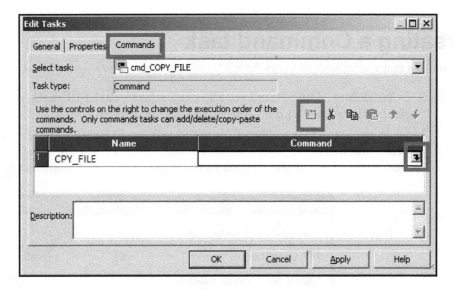

Add a new command by clicking on the Add a new Command option as shown in the previous screenshot. In the **Name** column, enter the name of the command. For our reference, we are using CPY_FILE as the command name.

5. Click on the edit button to open the Command Editor, and write the command that you wish to execute. If you wish to execute Unix scripts, write the Unix script path and name, else simply define the Unix command. Click on **OK** to close the edit view:

A sample windows command is indicated in the following screenshot:

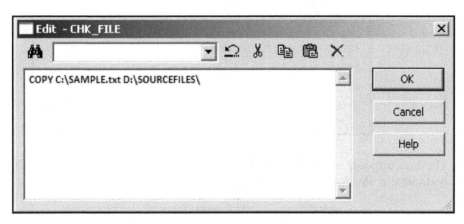

# Email Task

Email task is used to send success or failure email notification. You can use the email task to send an email notification to inform about the success or failure of a particular part of the workflow. You can use your mail server to send the email notification. Your admin team will configure the mail server with Informatica to send the email notification. Once you configure your mail server with Informatica, when the email task gets triggered, the email is sent directly from your mail box.

You can configure the email task to send an email notification, or you can also configure the session task to send an email notification. We discussed the latter option in the session task section.

# Creating an Email Task

To create an Email Task in Workflow Manager or Task Developer, follow these steps:

1. In Workflow Manager or Task Developer, go to **Tasks | Create**.

2. From the list of tasks, select Email task, and specify the name of the email task, em_TASK_NAME. For our reference, we are using em_FAILURE_NOTIFICATION as the email task name. Click on **Create** and then on **Done**:

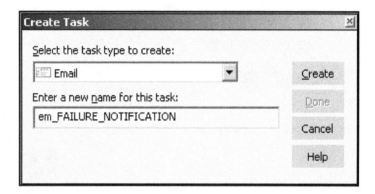

3. The task appears in Workflow Manager or Task Developer. Use the Link Task to connect the Start task to the email task:

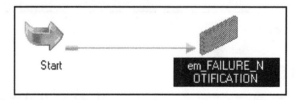

4. Double-click on the email task to open the task in the edit view. Click on **Properties**:

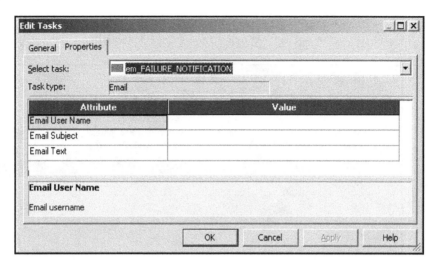

5. Click on **OK** to close the edit view.
6. Add the details in the Email task mentioned as follows:

   - **Email user name:** Mention the name of the email to which you wish to send the email notification. If you wish to send the email to multiple users, separate the email IDs by comma.
   - **Subject:** Enter the subject of the email you wish to send.
   - **Text:** Click to open the email editor to enter the text that you wish to send in the email. You can attach the log file, workflow name, repository name, and so on using the variables available in the email task editor.

# Assignment Task

Assignment task is used to assign a value to user-defined variables in workflow Manager.

Before you can define a variable in assignment task, you need to add the variable in Workflow Manager. To add a variable to the workflow, perform the following steps:

1. In Workflow Manager, open the workflow for which you wish to define the user-defined variable. Go to **Workflow** | **Edit** | **Variables**:

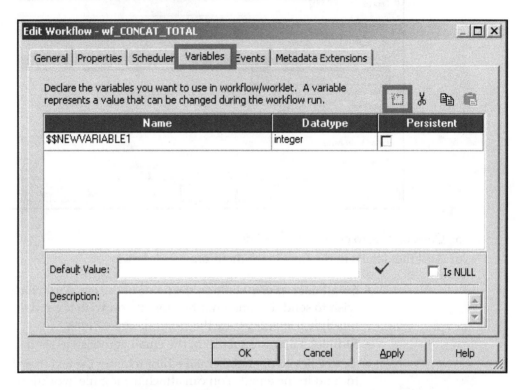

2. Click on the Add a new variable option to add a new variable to the workflow as shown in the previous screenshot.

A new variable is created as shown in the previous screenshot. The new variable created is $$NEWVARIABLE1. You can change the name of the variable and its data type.

# Creating an Assignment Task

To create an Assignment Task in Workflow Manager, follow these steps:

1. In Workflow Manager, go to **Task** | **Create**.

2. From the list of tasks, select Assignment task, and specify the name of the Assignment task, `amt_TASK_NAME`. For our reference, we are using `amt_ASSIGN_VALUE` as the assignment task name. Click on **Done**:

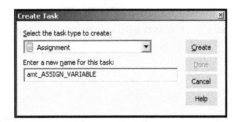

- The task appears in Workflow Manager. Use the Link task to connect the Start task to the assignment task:

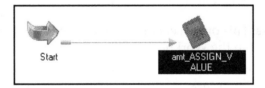

3. Double-click on the assignment task to open the task in the edit view. Go to **Expressions | Add a new Expression**:

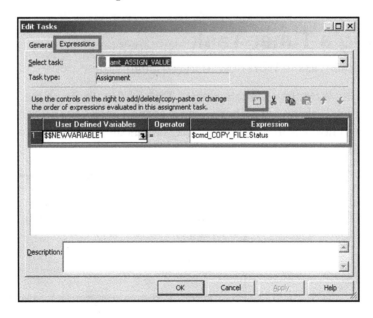

- Select the user-defined variable you added at the Workflow level. We have added $$NEWVARIABLE1.

4. Assign the value that you wish to assign to the variable. We have assigned the status of Command task **cmd_COPY_FILE** from the **Expressions** tab in the assignment task, as shown in the previous screenshot. Click on **OK**.

# Timer task

Timer task is used to add time gap between the execution of two tasks. In other words, you can specify the time in the timer task to wait before the process triggers the next task in the workflow. Also, another option in the timer task allows you to start the next task after a particular time gap in the workflow.

The timer task has two types of settings:

- **Absolute Time:** This option enables you to specify the time when you want the next task to start in the Workflow.
- **Relative Time:** This option enables you to start the next task by comparing the start time of the timer task. If you mention the relative time as 10 minutes, Informatica Power Center will wait for 10 minutes at the timer task before it triggers the next task in the workflow.

# Creating a Timer Task

To create a Timer Task in Workflow Manager, follow these steps:

1. In the Workflow Manager, go to **Tasks | Create**. From the list of tasks, select Timer Task, and specify the name of the Timer task, tm_TASK_NAME. For our reference, we are using tm_TIME_GAP as the Timer Task name. Click on **Create** and then on **Done**:

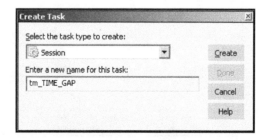

2. The Timer task appears in Workflow Manager. Use the Link Task to connect the Start task to the Timer task:

3. Double-click on the timer task to open the task in the edit view. Click on **Timer**. Based on your requirement, select the Relative or Absolute time option. Click on **OK**:

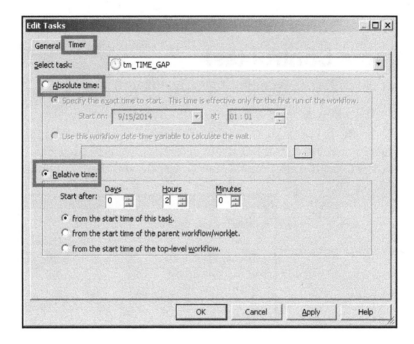

For reference, we have selected **Relative time** as shown in this screenshot. Based on the selection, our timer task will start the execution two hours after the end of the previous task.

# Control task

Control Task is used to control the execution of the Workflow. You can stop, abort, or fail the parent workflow or top-level workflow by defining the appropriate condition in the Control task.

The Control task acts as a green signal or a red signal. If you use a Control task in a branch in workflow and if everything is moving smoothly, that is, if there is no issue with the process, the Control task will not even be triggered. It will act invisible. But if the process catches up with the issue, the Control task will take the control, and based on the option you select in the properties, it will STOP, ABORT, or FAIL the workflow or top-level workflow.

## Creating a Control task

To create a Control Task in Workflow Manager, follow these steps:

1. In Workflow Manager, go to **Task** | **Create**.
2. From the list of tasks, select Control task, and specify the name of the control task, `cntl_TASK_NAME`. For our reference, we are using `cntl_ABORT_WORKFLOW` as the Control Task name. Click on **Create** and then on **Done**:

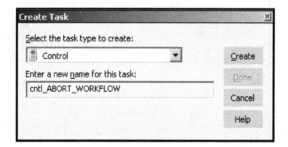

The Control task appears in Workflow Manager. Use the Link task to connect the Start task to the control task:

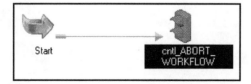

3. Double-click on the Control task to open the task in the edit view. Click on **Properties**:

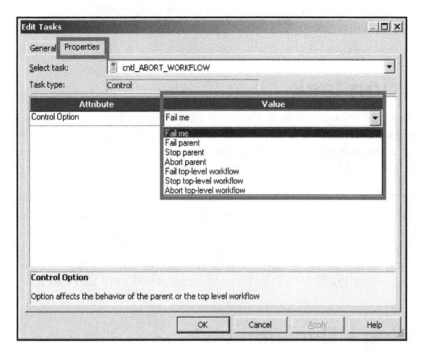

- Select a particular option from the drop-down list as per your requirement. Various options are present in the Control task properties:
- **Fail me:** If you select this option, the Control task will show the **FAILED** status in the Workflow Monitor if the task is triggered.
- **Fail parent:** If you select this option, the workflow will fail and you will see the status as **FAILED** in the Workflow Monitor.
- **Stop parent:** If you select this option, the workflow will stop and you will see the status as **STOPPED** in the Workflow Monitor.
- **Abort parent:** If you select this option, the workflow will abort and you will see the status as **ABORTED** in the Workflow Monitor.
- **Fail top-level workflow:** If you select this option, the top-level workflow will fail and you will see the status as **FAILED** in the Workflow Monitor.

- **Stop top-level workflow:** If you select this option, the top-level workflow will stop and you will see the status as **STOPPED** in the Workflow Monitor.
- **Abort top-level workflow:** If you select this option, the top-level workflow will abort and you will see the status as **ABORTED** in the Workflow Monitor.

# Decision task

You can control the execution of the Workflow by defining the condition in the decision task. Decision task allows you to specify the condition using which you can control the execution of branches in a Workflow. In other words, you can check the condition of multiple tasks and, based on that, decide whether you wish to trigger the next task or not.

Consider the workflow shown in the next screenshot. As you can see, the session task should be triggered only if the status of all the three tasks is successful. We can define the condition in the three link tasks, but the problem in that case will be that the session task will be triggered even if one command task is successful. This issue can be resolved using the decision task. You can define the condition in the decision task that will make the session task execute only if all the three command tasks are successful.

## Creating a Decision task

To create a Decision task in Workflow Manager, follow these steps:

1. In Workflow Manager, go to **Tasks | Create**.
2. From the list of tasks, select Decision task, and specify the name of the Decision task, dec_TASK_NAME. For our reference, we are using dec_CONDITION as the Decision task name. Click on **Create** and then on **Done**:

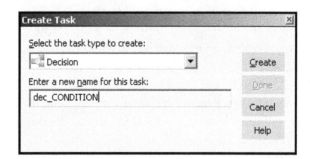

- The Decision task appears in Workflow Manager. Use the Link task to connect the Start task to the Decision task. In our case, we are implementing a scenario where the Session task s_m_max should be triggered only after successful execution of the Email task em_FAILURE_NOTIFICATION and the Session task s_m_CONCAT_TOTAL, as shown in the following screenshot:

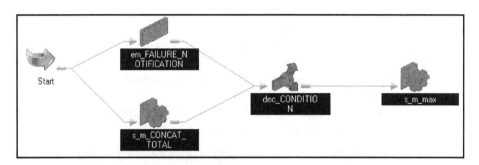

3. Double-click on the Decision task to open the task in the edit view. Click on **Properties**, and mention the condition under **Value**. As per our requirement, we have defined the condition as $em_FAILURE_NOTIFICATION.Status = SUCCEEDED AND $s_m_CONCAT_TOTAL.Status = SUCCEEDED. Click on **OK**:

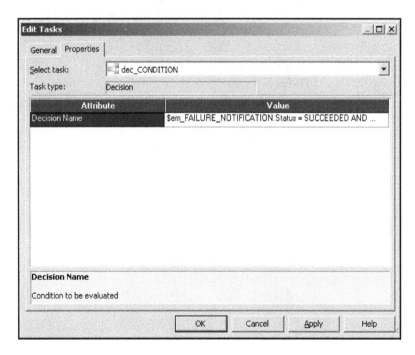

# Event tasks - Event Wait and Event Raise

Event is simply a functionality that you wish to implement in Workflow. Informatica Power Center has some system-defined events, and you can define user-defined events also.

There are two types of events:

- **Event Wait task:** This is the task that waits for a particular event to occur. You can define the event for which the Event Wait task should wait. Once triggered, the Event Wait task will wait for an infinite duration of time for the specified event. As soon the event occurs, the event wait succeeds and triggers the next task in the workflow.
  - In the event wait task, you can define system-defined event (pre-defined event) or user-defined event.
- **Event Raise task:** As against event wait, an event raise task triggers a particular event in the workflow.
  - You can define only user-defined events in the event raise task.
  - Informatica PowerCenter events can be of two types:

- **Predefined Event:** This is also referred to as system-defined event. It is generally called the File Watch event. You can use this task to wait for a specified file at a specific location. Once the file arrives at the path mentioned, the event wait or file watcher triggers the rest of the task in the Workflow.
- **User Defined Event:** You can create an event of your own based on the requirement. The event raise task is nothing but a sequence of tasks in the workflow. To use a user-defined task, first define the event under workflow.

Before you can use user-defined events under the Event tasks, you need to create the event at the workflow level. Perform the following steps to add the event to workflow:

1. Open the workflow in the Workflow Manager to which you wish to add the user-defined event, and go to **Workflow** | **Edit** | **Events**:

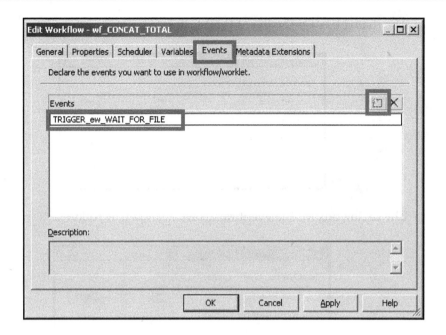

2. Add a new event as shown in the previous screenshot. Click on **OK**.

# Creating an Event (Wait/Raise) task

To create an Event Wait or Event Raise Task in Workflow Manager, follow these steps:

1. In the Workflow Manager, go to **Task** | **Create**.
2. From the list of tasks, select Event Wait or Event Raise task, and specify the name of the task, ew_TASK_NAME or er_TASK_NAME. For our reference, we are using ew_WAIT_FOR_FILE as the Event Wait task name and er_TRIGGER_TASK as the event raise task name. Click on **Create** and then on **Done**.

- The dialog box for the Event Wait task is shown as follows:

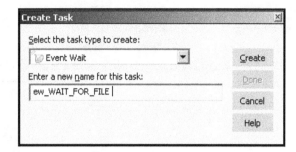

- The dialog box for the event raise task is shown as follows:

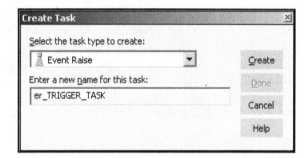

3. The Event (Wait/Raise) task appears in the Workflow Manager. Use the Link task to connect the Start task with the event tasks:

Note that you can use the event wait and event raise tasks individually also. We have used both the tasks together for reference purposes.

4. Double-click on the Event Raise task, and click on **Properties**. Add a new user-defined event as shown in the following screenshot:

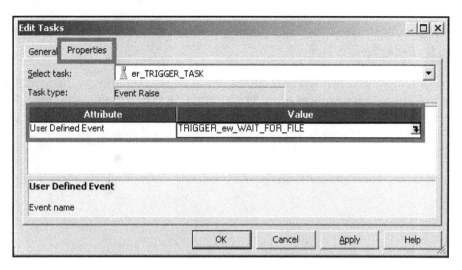

5. Double-click on the Event Wait task to open the task in the edit view. If you wish to use a pre-defined task, specify the path and file name in the option. If you wish to use a user-defined name, click on the add new event option. Click on **OK**:

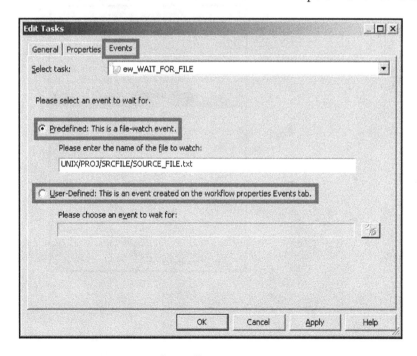

For our reference, we have added a pre-defined event called the file-watch event. We have added UNIX/PROJ/SRCFILES/SOURCE_FILE.txt as the Event Wait file.

# Link task

Link task is used to control the execution of the workflow. You can have multiple branches in the workflow that can be triggered using the link task. By now, you must have understood that we use the Link task to connect two tasks and also to connect the start task with other tasks in a workflow. You can define the condition in the Link task using which you can control the flow of the workflow.

You can define various conditions based on the tasks from which you are connecting the link.

## Creating a link task

To create a Link task to connect two tasks, follow these steps:

1. In the Workflow Manager, go to **Task** | **Link task**:

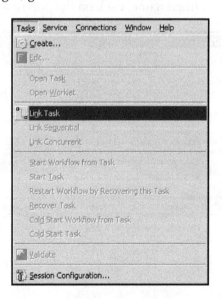

2. Drag the link between the tasks you wish to have linked.

# Worklets - Groups of tasks

A group of tasks that can be reused in multiple Workflows is called worklet. Worklets are similar to mapplets in Mapping Designer. As you know from the previous chapter, you use mapplets in place of multiple transformations; similarly, you can use worklets in place of multiple tasks. When you wish to reuse the functionality implemented using multiple tasks, worklet is your answer. Since reusing a reusable tasks itself is a rare occurrence as you do not frequently reuse the logic of individual tasks, that makes using a worklet a rarer occurrence in Informatica. Worklet can surely save your time if you can reuse some existing functionality. Similar to workflow, worklet should also start with a start task.

## Creating a Worklet

To create a Worklet, perform the following steps:

1. In the Worklet Manager, go to **Worklets** | **Create**:

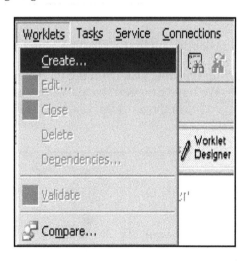

2. Specify the name of the Worklet. For our reference, we are using `wlt_WORKLET` as the Worklet name. Click on **Done**:

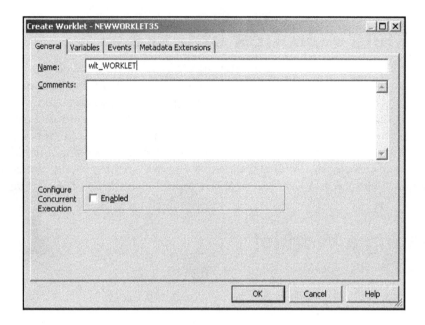

The start task appears in the Worklet Manager.

3. Drag the existing reusable task from the navigator under Sessions or Tasks to your Worklet. We have dragged the existing reusable session `s_m_CONCAT_TOTAL`to the worklet. Use the Link task to connect the start task to the session task:

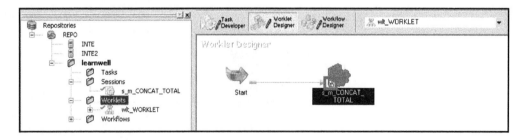

- The small green icon at the bottom of the session task, indicated in the previous screenshot, represents a reusable task.
- The Worklet gets added in the navigator under worklets.

With this, you have learned how to work on worklets in the Workflow Manager screen.

# Summary

In this chapter, we talked about the various aspects of the Workflow Manager Screen. We saw the detailed properties of the session task. Also, you learned about the various tasks present in the Workflow Manager and how to create the tasks and use them in the workflow.

Apart from that, you learned how to work on worklets, which are groups of tasks that allow us to reuse the existing functionality implemented.

In the next chapter, we will talk about the advanced features of the Workflow Manager Screen such as Schedulers, which help us in running the Workflows at a particular interval. You will learn about File lists, which provide us with a simpler way of merging the data from multiple files. Also, you will learn about parameters files using which we can easily pass the values of variables and parameters.

# 9

# Advanced Features of Workflow Manager Screen

In the previous chapter, you learned about the various tasks in the Informatica PowerCenter Workflow Manager screen and about their properties in detail.

In this chapter, you will learn about the various advanced aspects of Workflow Manager screen such as Schedulers, File list, Parameter files, and Incremental Aggregation.

## Schedulers

Scheduling is one of the most important aspects of any technology we use. We need to schedule the process so that the process executes at the specified interval regularly. Using the schedule, you can define the frequency at which you wish to execute the workflow. Based on the frequency you define, the workflow will automatically be triggered. Informatica Power Center comes with an internal scheduler. To create a schedule, perform the following steps:

1. Open the Workflow in the Workflow Manager for which you wish to define scheduler, and go to **Workflows | Schedulers**:

2. In the new window, you can add a Scheduler. Click on **New**:

2. In the new window specify the name of the scheduler as per your requirement, and click on **Schedule**:

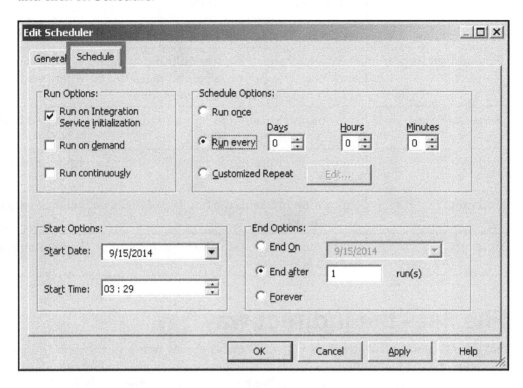

Various options present on the schedule screen are described as follows:

| Option | Description |
| --- | --- |
| **Run on Integration Service Initialization** | When you check this option, the workflow will be triggered as per your defined schedule. When you check this option, various options under the schedule option get enabled, and you can specify the time and frequency at which you wish to execute the workflow. |
| **Run on demand** | When you check this option, you can run the workflow manually. |
| **Run continuously** | When you check this option, the workflow will keep on running continuously from the time you define as start time. |
| **Run once** | This option indicates that the workflow will run only once at the scheduled time. |

| Run every | When you check this option, you can schedule to run the workflow at a particular interval. If you wish to run the workflow every day, mention 1 under Days, and define the Start date and End date. |
| --- | --- |
| Customized Repeat | You can customize the schedule at which you wish to run your workflow. This option is helpful in a scenario where you may only need to run your workflow on Mondays. |
| Start Date/Start Time | This option indicates the date and time from which you wish to schedule your workflow. |
| End On | This option indicates the date till which you wish to schedule your workflow. |
| End after | This option indicates the number of times you wish to let the workflow run. |
| Forever | If you check this option, the schedule will keep on running forever with no end date. |

# File list - the indirect way

File list is a concept that provides you with an easier way to merge the data and load it into the target. As the name suggests, the name is specifically related to Flat files. This is an indirect way of passing the source file. We have seen earlier that we define the source path and Source file name under the **Mapping** tab in the session task. There is another property in the session task called Source file type, where you can select the **Direct** or **Indirect** option as shown in the following screenshot:

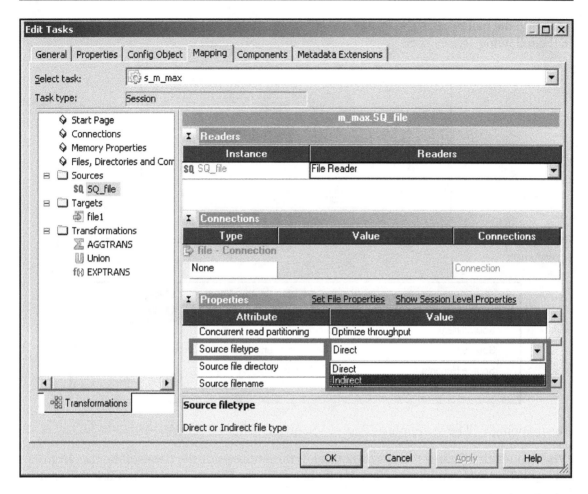

When we select Source filetype as Direct, Informatica directly goes to the defined Source file directory path and extracts the data from the file name defined in the Source filename option. When you select Source filetype as Indirect, Informatica reads the data from the file mentioned indirectly. Let's take an example to understand the concept.

Consider you have been provided with three source files with the same structure but different data. The names of the Source files are C:/FILE1.txt, D:/FILE2.txt, and E:/FILE3.txt. The requirement is to merge the data into a target file. You can achieve the requirement using Union transformation. The Indirect file type concept helps achieve the same requirement in an easier way. Remember, to implement the File list concept, the files you are willing to merge should have exactly the same data type. To implement the File list, we will create another file with a name, say FILE_LIST.txt.

Then add the names of all the three files with the path in the `FILE_LIST.txt` file as shown in the following screenshot:

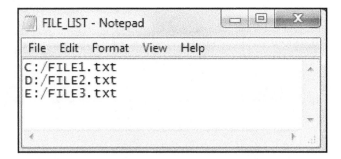

Define the properties in the session task for Indirect file type as shown in the following screenshot:

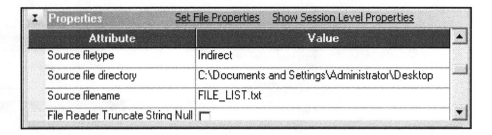

The mapping will be as simple as Source - Source Qualifier - Target.

When you define Source filetype as *Indirect*, Informatica reads the name of the files from FILE_LIST.txt and extracts the data one by one from the files mentioned in FILE_LIST.txt. This way the data will be appended in the target.

# Incremental Aggregation

This concept is related to aggregator transformation. When you have data that is increasing incrementally and the existing data remains constant, you can utilize the Incremental Aggregation functionality to achieve the output faster and enhance performance. When you select the Incremental Aggregation option in Session properties, Informatica saves the result of the last run in cache and replaces the value in the next run and hence enhances the performance. To understand the concept, let's take an example.

Consider you have a file with the salary of employees and you wish to get the SUM of the salaries of all the employees. Considering we have three employees in JAN month, six employees in FEB month, and nine employees in MARCH month as shown in the following screenshot:

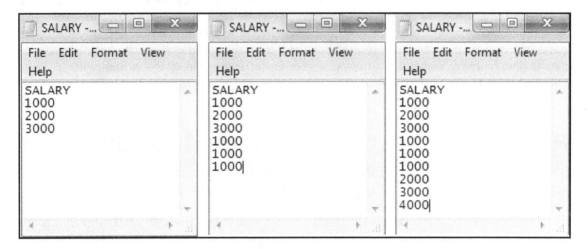

As you can notice, the data is increasing in the file. The First file with data of employees present in JAN month, second file with data of employees in FEB month, and third file for data in March. To get the SUM of salaries of all the employees, we will use aggregator transformation. Since the number of records is increasing, the time taken for calculation will also increase. Also, note that the previous data is not changing, only new data is added in the file. To save the time, we use the concept of Incremental Aggregation. The option is present in the session task as shown in the screenshot of the **Properties** tab in the *Tabs of a session task* section of Chapter 8, *Learning Various Tasks in Workflow Manager Screen*.

When you run the file for JAN month, aggregator transformation will calculate the value of three records and give the corresponding output, that is, 6,000 in our case. When you do not check the Incremental Aggregation option, Informatica again calculates the six records in the file for FEB month and gives the result, that is, 9,000 in our case. If you use the Incremental Aggregation option, the aggregator cache will save the value of the last run, that is, 6,000. When you run the same process for FEB month, Informatica replaces the first three records of the file with the value stored in cache and adds new records to get the result. This results in faster calculation as the number of records to calculate has reduced.

The basic criterion for using Incremental Aggregation is that the data from the previous run should remain the same.

If the records from the previous run change, the result will be incorrect as Informatica will not consider the changed value and will replace the value with the value stored in cache. To handle this, make sure to check the *Reinitialize aggregate cache* box. When you check this option, Informatica reinitializes the aggregate cache value and stores the new value. It is important to note that you need to uncheck the Reinitialize aggregate cache option if your data is not changing, else it will always keep on reinitializing the cache, which will indirectly hamper the performance.

# Parameter file - parameters and variables

It is always a best practice in coding that you should never hard code the values. The same applies to Informatica as well. It is always better to pass the values using parameters or variables in place of hard coding them. When you define parameters or variables in the code, you need to pass the values to those parameters and variables. A parameter file serves that purpose. Any value that you hard code can be passed through the Parameter file. You can define the Parameter file at the session level and workflow level.

You must have noticed that the system defined the variable *$PMSourceFileDir\* or *$PMTargetFileDir\*. Similar to that, we can define User Define variables. You can define the variable at both the mapping level and workflow level.

If the value passed remains constant across the session run, it is called **parameter**, and if the value changes across the session run, it is called **variable**.

Let's take an example to understand the Parameter file. You are aware that Informatica will have three different repositories to cater to the need of three regions. Let's say we have three repositories REPO_DEV, REPO_TEST, REPO_PROD serving the development, testing, and production regions respectively. Also, corresponding to three regions, we have three oracle databases--ORACLE_DEV, ORACLE_TEST, and ORACLE_PROD respectively. When you start the coding in the development region under REPO_DEV, you will hardcode the database connection value to ORACLE_DEV. Your code is working successfully, and when you want to deploy the code to test the region, you will need to replace the database connection value to ORACLE_TEST manually. Changing the code after testing is not allowed.

The same case applies when you wish to deploy the code from test to production. The solution comes as a Parameter file. Parameter files serve the purpose of passing the value based on the region in which you are running the code. We are defining the Parameter file for passing the value for the source database connection (*$DBCONNECTION1*), target file name (*$TGTFILENAME*), e-mail recipient (*$EMAILUSER*), and a mapping-level variable for the location (*$$LOCATION*). We are using the example of session-level variable, workflow-level variable, and mapping-level variable so you understand clearly how it works.

# Defining session-level variables

The variables that are defined under session task are called session-level variables. There are various values that can be passed via variables, such as source, target data base connection value, source/target file name, source/target file path, session log file name/path, and so on. session task does most of the work in Workflow Manager screen and, hence, has been assigned special privilege. To pass the value through a variable, simply replace the hard-coded value with a variable of your choice.

As shown in the following screenshot, we are using $DBCONNECTION1 as the database connection variable:

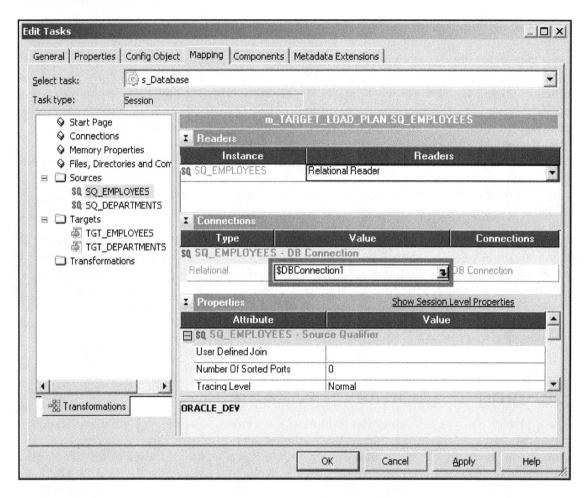

Similarly, assign the value to the target file name (*$TGTFILENAME*). Since we define the target file name under the session task, it will be referred to as session-level variable.

# Defining workflow-level variables

The variables that are defined under various tasks are called workflow-level variables. Note that you can define the session-level variables under workflow also in the Parameter file. In our case, we are passing an e-mail user value as the variable. To assign the value, simply replace the hardcoded value by the variable in the e-mail task as shown in the following screenshot:

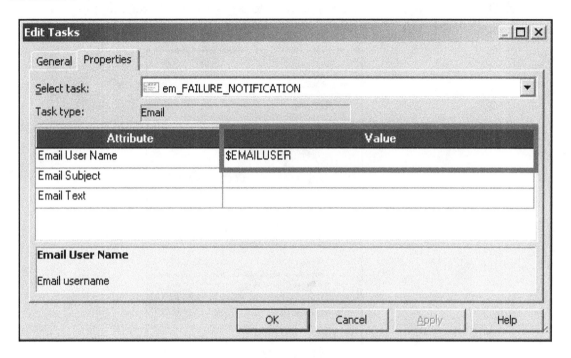

# Defining mapping-level variables

As mentioned earlier, you can define the variable for the hardcoded values in mapping inside transformations also. You need to define parameters or variables under mapping before you can use them in transformations, else the mapping will become invalid. To add the values, perform the following steps:

1. Open the mapping for which you wish to add variables in the Mapping Designer, go to **Mappings | Parameters and Variables**:

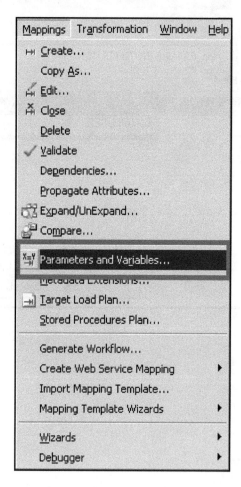

2.  In the next screen, click on **Add a new variable to this table**. Define the variable, and select the type as Parameter and Variable based on your requirement. Click on **OK**:

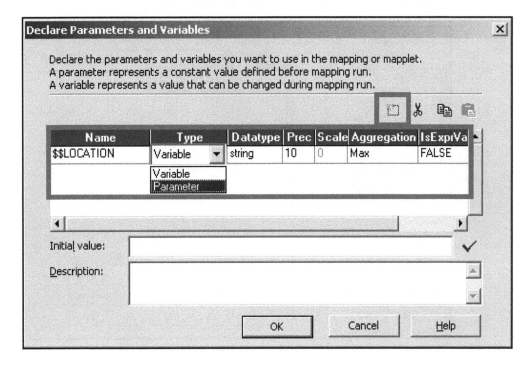

As you can notice, mapping-level variables are always defined as $$.

3. Open the transformation to which you wish to assign the variable or parameter. We are using filter transformation to pass the value:

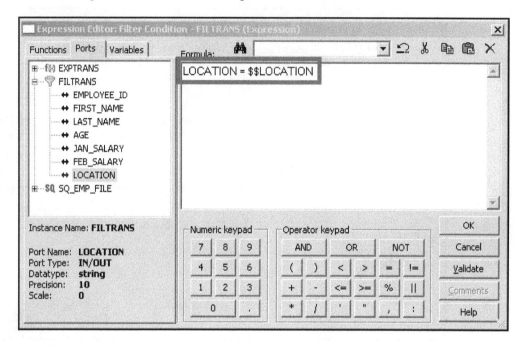

As you can notice, we have assigned $$LOCATION to the filter condition.

With this, we are done with defining the variables or parameters. Next, we will see how to pass the values to these using a parameter file.

# Creating a parameter file

A Parameter file is nothing but a simple `.txt` file that contains the values of the variable to be passed A sample Parameter file for the variable defined in the previous steps is shown as follows:

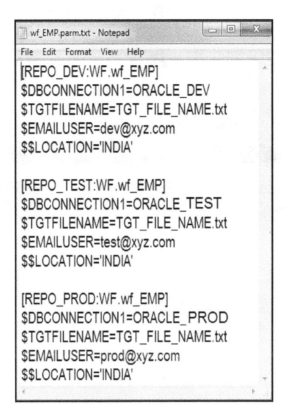

As you can see, the Parameter file contains the values of the variables to be replaced in the three regions. Informatica matches the Repository name against the name of Repository defined in the Parameter file and replaces the values of the variables internally before it runs the workflow. `wf_EMP` is the name of workflow for which you defined the Parameter file. So, suppose you are running in the production region, Informatica will match the Repository name REPO_PROD against the same name in the Parameter file, replace the variables with the value internally, and execute the workflow with the replaced values.

# Mentioning the Parameter file at the workflow level

To define the Parameter file at the workflow level, open Workflow Manager, go to **Workflow | Edit | Properties.** Specify the path and name of the parameter file for the attribute as indicated in the following screenshot:

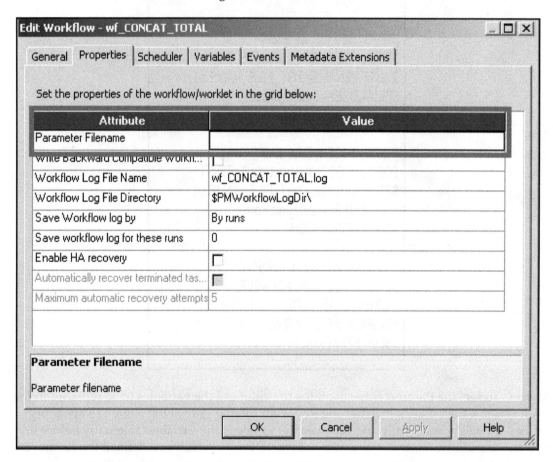

# Mentioning the Parameter file at the session level

To define the Parameter file at the session level, open the session in the Workflow Manager, double-click on the session task, and click on **Properties.** Specify the path and name of the Parameter file for the attribute as indicated in the following screenshot:

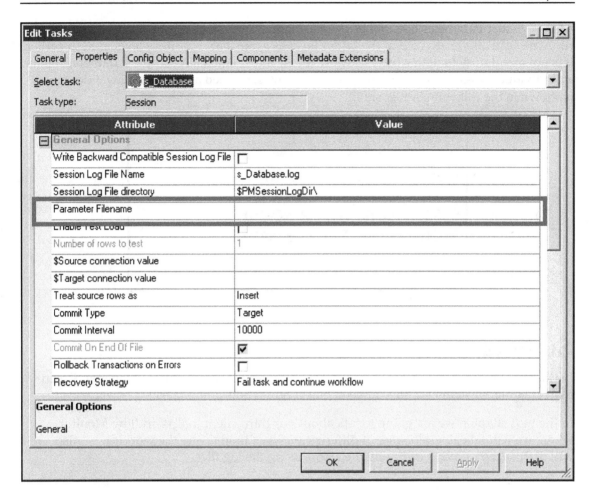

You have learned how to use parameters and variables, create a parameter file, and define the Parameter file. Another importance of parameter file is that if the value of any variable is changing, you need not modify the code; simply change the value in the Parameter file, and the changed value will take effect the next time you run the code.

Also, note that Parameter files can be used to replace the values for the individual session run. They can also be defined at the folder level as against at repository level as seen earlier. It is not mandatory to define the workflow for all three regions. A sample Parameter file for an individual session run (s_m_EMP_PASS_THROUGH) defined at the folder level (learnwell) is shown in the following screenshot:

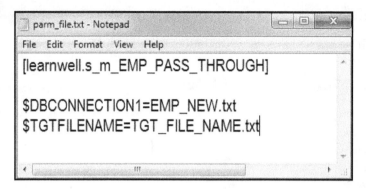

# Summary

In this chapter, we discussed the various advanced aspects of Workflow Manager Screen like Schedulers, Parameter files, Incremental Aggregation, and File lists.

In the next chapter, we are going to talk about our third client tool-Workflow Monitor-where we will talk about looking at different views of monitoring the workflows. Also, we will discuss the logs and rectifying the errors using the log files.

# 10

# Working with Workflow Monitor - Monitoring the code

In the previous chapter, we discussed the advanced topics of Workflow Manager Screen. When we jump into this chapter, we have an understanding of the various aspects of Informatica PowerCenter Designer and Workflow Manager Screen. This chapter will make your understanding about the Informatica PowerCenter Workflow Monitor Screen clear. At this stage, you must be very clear about the basic usage of the Designer and Workflow Manager Screen. We use the Workflow Monitor Screen to check the status of the Workflow that we executed in the Workflow Manager Screen. Apart from checking the status, the monitor screen serves various purposes such as checking the statistics and understanding run time details.

When you run the Workflow, Workflow Monitor continuously receives information from integration Services and other processes to display the information on the Screen. The Workflow Monitor Screen shows the status of the workflow and the tasks being executed.

# Using the Workflow Monitor

The Workflow Monitor Screen, as mentioned earlier, displays the status of the running workflow and tasks. It has two views to show the status -- the Gantt Chart view and the Task view. You can select the view you wish to see. The Workflow Monitor screen can be seen in the following screenshot:

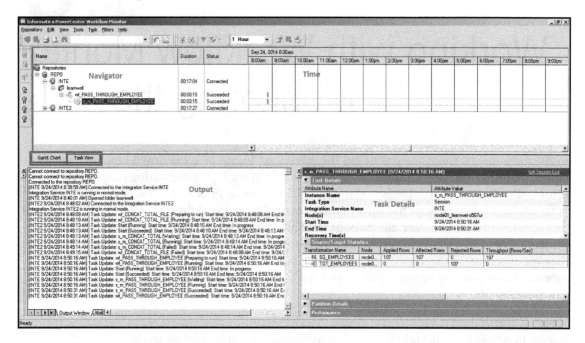

The screen is divided into the following sections:

- **Navigator:** This section of the screen displays various repositories, integration service, and the workflow names running at the instant. This section shows all the objects that have been executed at least once.
- **Output:** This section displays various system-level information details received from integration eervice and repository.
- **Time:** This section displays the timings of the execution of various workflows.
- **Gantt Chart View:** This view shows the information of various workflow runs in chronological order.

- **Task View:** This view shows the information of various workflow runs in a report form.
- **Task Details:** This section shows the details of the task. Also, it shows the source-to-target statistics and Performance and Partition details if selected.

We'll now move on to connecting the Workflow Manager screen.

# Connecting the Workflow Manager Screen

When you open the Workflow Monitor Screen, you need to connect to repository and integration service to view the workflow and task status. You can get the workflow Manager Screen in various ways:

- Under All Programs, go to **Informatica 9.5.1 | Client | PowerCenter Client | PowerCenter Workflow Monitor**.
- From Designer or Workflow Manager Screen, click on the icon representing the Workflow Monitor (M).

Once you open the Workflow Monitor Screen, perform the following steps to connect and view the workflow and task status:

1. Open the Workflow Monitor Screen.
2. Right-click on the repository you wish to connect (if you have multiple repositories available), and connect to it using username and password. In our case, the repository is REPO.
3. Once you connect to the repository, the next step is to connect to integration service. This is done by right-clicking on the integration service you created. In our case, the integration service is INTE.
4. Select the Workflow you wish to check the status of. You can see the status of the workflow is executed at least once.
5. Select the Gantt Chart or Task view under which you wish to see the status of the workflows and tasks.

Let's start with opening the previous workflow runs.

# Opening previous workflow runs

Apart from checking the status of the currently executing Workflow, you can also check the status of the existing Workflow runs in both the Gantt Chart and Task view.

In the Navigator of the Workflow Monitor, select the workflow for which you wish to see the previous runs. right-click on the workflow, and click on **Open Latest 20 Run** as shown in the following screenshot:

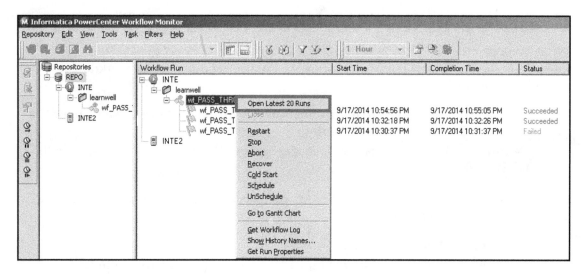

The list of the latest 20 runs of the Workflow will appear if available.

# Running or recovering workflow or task

As mentioned earlier, the Workflow Monitor Screen displays the workflow that is executed at least once. You can run or recover the workflow from the Workflow Monitor Screen. To run or recover the workflow or task, right-click the workflow/task in the Navigator, and select **Restart/Recover**:

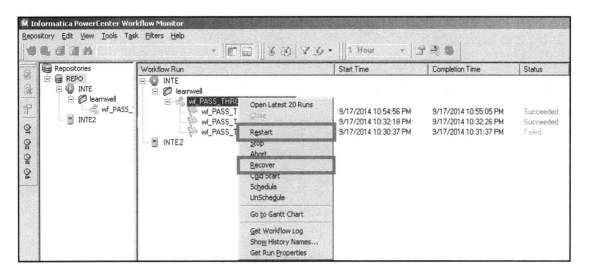

We now move on to stopping or aborting the workflow or task.

# Stopping or aborting the workflow or task

You can stop or recover the workflow from the Workflow Monitor Screen.

When you stop the process, integration service stops processing the scheduled tasks and all other processes of that workflow. But it continues processing the currently running task. The process will stop once the current task execution is finished.

When you abort the task, it kills the DTM, and hence, all the other processes get terminated. DTM in Informatica PowerCenter is called data transformation manager. This DTM does the work of managing and arranging all the perquisites for running a session such as checking the cache memory, checking buffer memory, and checking table deadlock. Also, it helps in generating the session log, executing pre-session and post-session SQL, and so on. To stop/abort the workflow or task, right-click on the workflow/task in the Navigator, and select **Stop/Abort**:

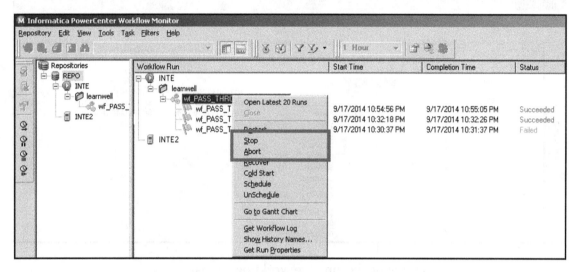

Let's start with checking the status of the workflow and tasks.

# Status of the workflow and tasks

Various statuses possible for the workflow and tasks are shown here:

| Status | Status for Workflow/Task | Description |
|---|---|---|
| Succeeded | Both | The process is completed successfully |
| Failed | Both | The process failed due to some error |
| Running | Both | The process is executing currently |
| Preparing to Run | Workflow only | The process is waiting for integration service to run the workflow |

| Scheduled | Workflow only | The workflow is scheduled to run in the future |
| Stopped | Both | The workflow has been stopped manually |
| Stopping | Both | The integration service is in process of stopping the workflow after manual selection |
| Aborted | Both | The workflow has been aborted manually |
| Aborting | Both | The integration service is in process of aborting the workflow after manual selection |
| Disabled | Both | You have manually selected to disable the Workflow or task |
| Suspended | Workflow only | The workflow will show a suspended status because of the failure of the task; this status is available only if you selected Suspend on error. |
| Suspending | Workflow only | The integration service is suspending the workflow |
| Terminated | Both | Integration service is terminated due to some unexpected reasons |
| Terminating | Both | Integration service is stopping or aborting or terminating the workflow |
| Waiting | Both | Integration service is waiting for the resources required to execute the Workflow |

Next, we move on to viewing the session and workflow log.

# Viewing session log and workflow log

You can view the Session and Workflow log from the Workflow Monitor Screen. When you run the Workflow, the workflow log and session log file are saved in the form of a file at the location you define in the session properties. You can maintain the history of the log files by adding a timestamp or by saving by session run.

To get the workflow log for the workflow, right-click on the workflow in the Navigator, and select **Get Workflow log**:

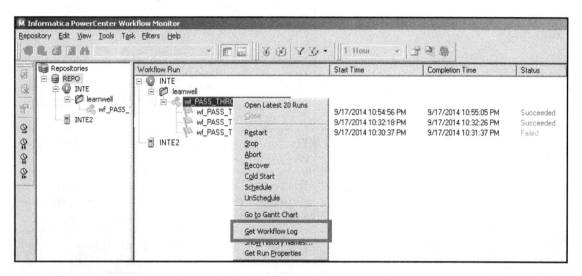

To get the session log for the Workflow, right-click on the session task in the Navigator, and select **Get Session log**:

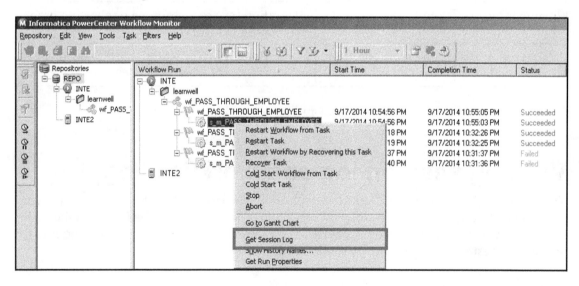

Let's now start working with the workflow log.

# Working with the workflow log

When you select to generate the workflow log, another screen opens that shows the details related to the workflow run. Informatica PowerCenter writes all the details related to the execution of the workflow in the log. Using the workflow log, you can check all the system-related information that was used in executing the workflow along with the error messages, if any. The following screenshot shows the workflow log:

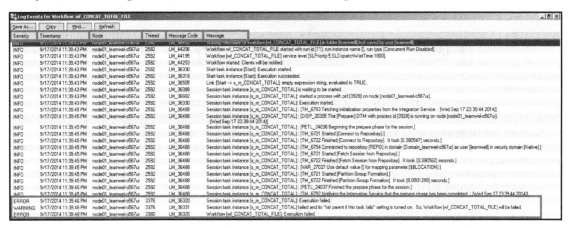

The following table describes the various options of the workflow log:

| Option | Description |
|---|---|
| Severity | It shows the status of the particular event that took place while executing the workflow.<br>INFO indicates general system-level information.<br>ERROR indicates the error that has occurred due to which the Workflow failed.<br>WARNING indicates the process that was not executed as per expectation. The workflow may not fail because of the warning. |
| Timestamp | This indicates the exact timing of the particular step that the workflow was running. |
| Node | This indicates the name of the node under which the workflow is executed. |
| Thread | This indicates the thread each step is using to execute. You can see the different threads in the session log. |

| Message Code | This indicates the system-defined message code. Usually, in Informatica PowerCenter, we do not refer to message codes. |
|---|---|
| Message | This shows the detailed message indicating the steps that occurred during the workflow execution. |

We will now work with the session log.

# Working with the session Log

Similar to the workflow log, the session log also indicates the detailed level of information that gives you a complete understanding of the process that occurred while the workflow was running. The session log in Informatica gives the exact reason of the error that has occurred, using which you can debug the issue and correct the code. For example, in the following screenshot, the session log is indicating the error as **The system cannot find the file specified**. This directly indicates that the file you wish to access does not exist. Check the details in the session task, correct the path. and your workflow will succeed.

| Severity | Timestamp | Node | Thread | Message Co... | Message |
|---|---|---|---|---|---|
| INFO | 9/17/2014 11:39:45 PM | node01_learn | DIRECTOR | TM_6683 | Repository Name: [REPO] |
| INFO | 9/17/2014 11:39:45 PM | node01_learn | DIRECTOR | TM_6684 | Server Name: [INTE2] |
| INFO | 9/17/2014 11:39:45 PM | node01_learn | DIRECTOR | TM_6686 | Folder: [learnwell] |
| INFO | 9/17/2014 11:39:45 PM | node01_learn | DIRECTOR | TM_6685 | Workflow: [wf_CONCAT_TOTAL_FILE] Run Instance Name: [] Run Id: [11] |
| INFO | 9/17/2014 11:39:45 PM | node01_learn | DIRECTOR | TM_6101 | Mapping name: m_CONCAT_TOTAL [version CheckedOut]. |
| INFO | 9/17/2014 11:39:45 PM | node01_learn | DIRECTOR | TM_8964 | Date format for the Session is [MM/DD/YYYY HH24:MI:SS.US] |
| INFO | 9/17/2014 11:39:45 PM | node01_learn | DIRECTOR | TM_6703 | Session [s_m_CONCAT_TOTAL] is run by 32-bit Integration Service [node01_learnwel-o557ur], version [9.5.1 HotFix2], build [0621]. |
| INFO | 9/17/2014 11:39:45 PM | node01_learn | MANAGER | PETL_24058 | Running Partition Group [1]. |
| INFO | 9/17/2014 11:39:45 PM | node01_learn | MANAGER | PETL_24000 | Parallel Pipeline Engine initializing. |
| INFO | 9/17/2014 11:39:45 PM | node01_learn | MANAGER | PETL_24001 | Parallel Pipeline Engine running. |
| INFO | 9/17/2014 11:39:45 PM | node01_learn | MANAGER | PETL_24003 | Initializing session run. |
| INFO | 9/17/2014 11:39:45 PM | node01_learn | MAPPING | CMN_1569 | Server Mode: [ASCII] |
| INFO | 9/17/2014 11:39:45 PM | node01_learn | MAPPING | CMN_1570 | Server Code page: [MS Windows Latin 1 (ANSI), superset of Latin1] |
| INFO | 9/17/2014 11:39:45 PM | node01_learn | MAPPING | TM_6151 | The session sort order is [Binary]. |
| INFO | 9/17/2014 11:39:45 PM | node01_learn | MAPPING | TM_6156 | Using low precision processing. |
| INFO | 9/17/2014 11:39:45 PM | node01_learn | MAPPING | TM_6180 | Deadlock retry logic will not be implemented. |
| INFO | 9/17/2014 11:39:45 PM | node01_learn | MAPPING | TM_6187 | Session target-based commit interval is [10000]. |
| INFO | 9/17/2014 11:39:45 PM | node01_learn | MAPPING | TM_6307 | DTM error log disabled. |
| INFO | 9/17/2014 11:39:45 PM | node01_learn | MAPPING | TE_7022 | TShmWriter: Initialized |
| INFO | 9/17/2014 11:39:45 PM | node01_learn | MAPPING | TM_6007 | DTM initialized successfully for session [s_m_CONCAT_TOTAL] |
| INFO | 9/17/2014 11:39:45 PM | node01_learn | DIRECTOR | PETL_24033 | All DTM Connection Info: [<NONE>]. |
| INFO | 9/17/2014 11:39:45 PM | node01_learn | MANAGER | PETL_24004 | PETL_24004 Starting pre-session tasks. : (Wed Sep 17 23:39:45 2014) |
| INFO | 9/17/2014 11:39:45 PM | node01_learn | MANAGER | PETL_24027 | PETL_24027 Pre-session task completed successfully. : (Wed Sep 17 23:39:45 2014) |
| INFO | 9/17/2014 11:39:45 PM | node01_learn | DIRECTOR | PETL_24006 | Starting data movement. |
| INFO | 9/17/2014 11:39:45 PM | node01_learn | MAPPING | TM_6660 | Total Buffer Pool size is 1219648 bytes and Block size is 65536 bytes. |
| INFO | 9/17/2014 11:39:45 PM | node01_learn | READER_1_1_1 | DBG_21437 | Reader: Source is a file-based source. |
| INFO | 9/17/2014 11:39:45 PM | node01_learn | READER_1_1_1 | FR_3118 | source [SQ_EMP_FILE] code page: [MS Windows Latin 1 (ANSI), superset of Latin1] |
| INFO | 9/17/2014 11:39:45 PM | node01_learn | READER_1_1_1 | FR_3071 | Maximum Line sequential buffer length is 1026 |
| ERROR | 9/17/2014 11:39:45 PM | node01_learn | READER_1_1_1 | FR_3000 | Error opening file [C:\Informatica\9.5.1\server\infa_shared\SrcFiles\EMP_FILE.txt]. Operating system error message [The system cannot find the file specified.] |
| ERROR | 9/17/2014 11:39:45 PM | node01_learn | READER_1_1_1 | BLKR_16002 | ERROR: Initialization failed. |
| INFO | 9/17/2014 11:39:45 PM | node01_learn | MANAGER | PETL_24031 | ***** RUN INFO FOR TGT LOAD ORDER GROUP [1], CONCURRENT SET [1] *****<br>Thread [READER_1_1_1] created for [the read stage] of partition point [SQ_EMP_FILE] has completed. The total run time was insufficient for any meaningful statistics. |
| INFO | 9/17/2014 11:39:45 PM | node01_learn | MANAGER | PETL_24005 | PETL_24005 Starting post-session tasks. : (Wed Sep 17 23:39:45 2014) |

Let's start with viewing the workflow run properties.

# Viewing workflow run properties

Informatica Power Center Workflow Monitor indicates the workflow-level properties. To open the workflow run properties, right-click on the workflow, and select **Get Run Properties** as shown in the following screenshot:

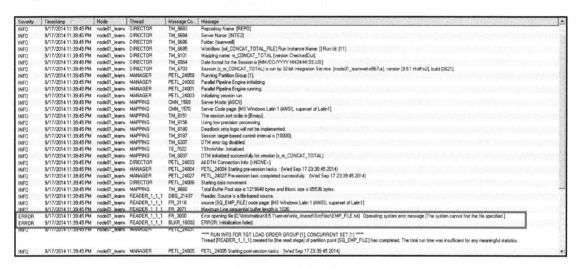

The Workflow-level properties section will appear at the right bottom of the Monitor screen as shown in the following screenshot:

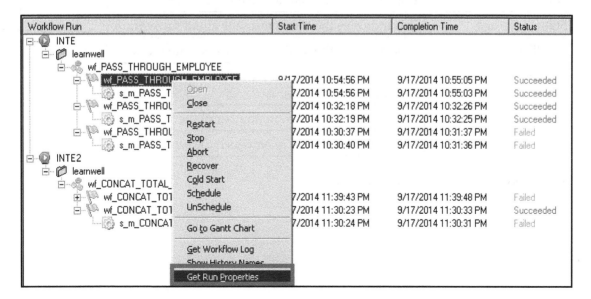

The various options under workflow run properties are as follows:

| Properties | Description |
| --- | --- |
| Task Name | This indicates the name of the workflow. |
| Workflow Run ID | This indicates the ID for the workflow run. |
| OS Profile | This indicates the name of the Operating System profile assigned to the workflow. Usually, it is empty. |
| Task Type | This indicates the type of task. The value can be workflow, session, and so on. In this case, it is workflow because we are looking at the workflow run properties. |
| Integration Service Name | This indicates the name of the integration services used to running the workflow. |
| User Name | This indicates the name of the user services running the workflow. |
| Start Time | This indicates the start time of the workflow. |
| End Time | This indicates the end time of the workflow. |
| Recovery Time(s) | This indicates the number of times the workflow has been recovered. |
| Status | This indicates the status of the workflow. |
| Status Message | This indicates the status message about the workflow. |
| Run Type | This indicates the method used to execute the workflow. |
| Deleted | This indicates whether the workflow is deleted. The value can be Yes/No. |
| Version Number | This indicates the version number of the workflow. |
| Execution Node(s) | This indicates the nodes on which the workflow is running. |

We will now be viewing session run properties.

# Viewing session run properties

Similar to workflow run properties, Informatica PowerCenter Workflow Monitor shows the session-level run properties. To open the session run properties, right-click on the session, and select **Get Run Properties**:

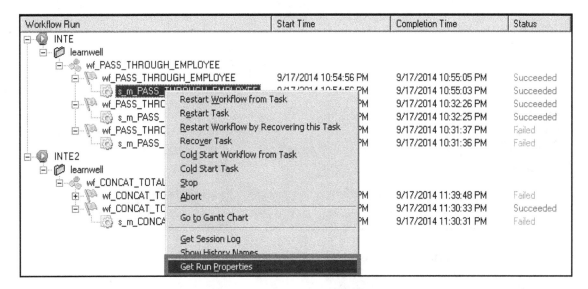

The session-level run properties section will appear at the right bottom of Monitor screen.

# Task detail properties

The task details under the session run properties are shown as follows:

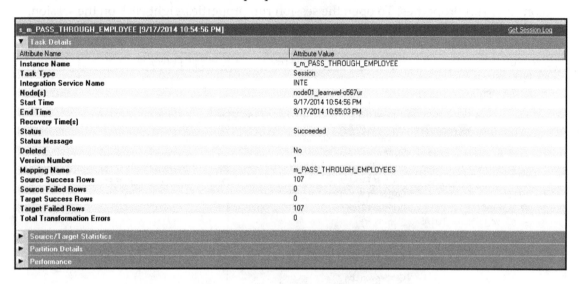

The various options under Task Details of session run properties are mentioned here:

| Properties | Description |
| --- | --- |
| Instance Name | This indicates the name of the session. |
| Task Type | This indicates the type of task. In this case, it is session. |
| Integration Service Name | This indicates the name of the integration services used for running the session. |
| Node(s) | This indicates the nodes on which the session is running. |
| Start Time | This indicates the start time of the session. |
| End Time | This indicates the end time of the session. |
| Recovery Time(s) | This indicates the number of times the session has been recovered. |
| Status | This indicates the status of the session task. |
| Status Message | This indicates the status message about the session task. |
| Deleted | This indicates whether the session is deleted. The value can be Yes/No. |

| Version Number | This indicates the version number of the session task. |
|---|---|
| Mapping Name | This indicates the name of the mapping associated with the session task. |
| Source Success Rows | This indicates the number of records successfully extracted using the session task. |
| Source Failed Rows | This indicates the number of records failed while extracting the data using the session task. |
| Target Success Rows | This indicates the number of records successfully loaded into the target using the session task. |
| Target Failed Rows | This indicates the number of records failed to load into the target using the session task. |
| Total Transformation Errors | This indicates the number of transformation errors occurred while executing the session task. |

# Source/target statistics properties

Source/target-level task details under session run properties are shown here:

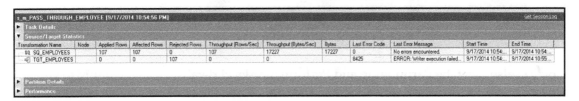

The various options under source/target statistics of session run properties are mentioned here:

| Properties | Description |
|---|---|
| Transformation Name | This indicates the name of the Source Qualifier or target instance name in the mapping. |
| Node | This indicates the nodes on which a particular transformation is running. |
| Applied Rows | This indicates the number of records successfully extracted from the source for processing or successfully loaded into the target after processing. |

| Affected Rows | This indicates the number of records successfully extracted from the source or successfully loaded into the target. |
|---|---|
| Rejected Rows | This indicates the number of records rejected while extracting from the source or the number of records rejected while loading into the target. |
| Throughput(Rows/Sec) | This indicates the rate at which the data is extracted from the source or the rate at which the data is loaded into the target. |
| Throughput(Bytes/Sec) | This indicates the rate at which the data is extracted from the source per second or the rate at which data is loaded into the target per second. |
| Bytes | This indicates the total number of bytes transferredwhile extracting and loading the data. |
| Last Error Code | This indicates the latest error code that occurred while extracting or loading into the target. |
| Last Error Message | This indicates the latest error message that occurred while extracting or loading into the target. |
| Start Time | This indicates the start time of the extraction of data and the start time of the loading into the target. |
| End Time | This indicates the end time of the extraction of data and the end time of the loading into the target. |

You can also view the Partitioning and Performance-level details if you configure to get those.

# Common Errors

When you execute the session and workflow, there are certain common error that you will face. Some of the common errors are as follows:

- **Source File Not found:** This indicates that the source file is not available at the specified location. Make sure you have placed the file in the correct folder.
- **Unable to generate Session log:** This may be due to some invalid session task or may show if you don't specify the lookup file name and path in the session task.

- **Table or view not found:** This indicates that the database table in which you are willing to load the data is not available. Make sure you have created the table before you load the data in the table.
- **Communication link failure:** This indicates that there are network issues affecting the integration service or repository.
- **Failed to allocate memory:** This indicates that the memory required for executing the process is not available.
- **Duplicate Primary/Foreign key:** This indicates that you are trying to load the duplicate data in the primary key in the table.

> For more details on common errors, you can refer to the link:
> `http://docs.oracle.com/cd/E12102_01/books/AnyInstAdm784/AnyInstA`
> `dmTroubleshooting3.html`

# Summary

In this chapter, we talked about the various aspects of Workflow Monitor Screen. We started with the discussion of the various sections of the Workflow Monitor Screen. We also saw the steps to connect to the Workflow Monitor, and you learned how to check the status of the workflow and tasks. We discussed how to restart and recover the workflow and task directly from the Monitor Screen. Also, we talked about the process to stop/abort the workflow. We saw how to check the workflow and session log. At the end, we saw the workflow-level and session level run properties.

In the next chapter, we are going to talk about the different types of transformations available in Informatica PowerCenter Designer Screen.

# 11

# The Deployment Phase - Using Repository Manager

In the previous chapter, we discussed the different functionalities of the PowerCenter Designer, Workflow Manager, and Workflow Monitor screen. At this stage, we have all the knowledge of the various components of the Informatica PowerCenter tool. We are left with the last client tool, that is PowerCenter Repository Manager. Repository Manager is not used for coding but used for certain administration related work and the deployment of power center components such as mapping, workflow, and so on. In this chapter, you will learn how to create and configure the domain and repository that we created in the Informatica Administrator console. Also, you will learn about the migration or deployment process we follow to migrate the code in Informatica PowerCenter.

## Using the Repository Manager

The following screenshot shows the Informatica PowerCenter Repository Manager screen:

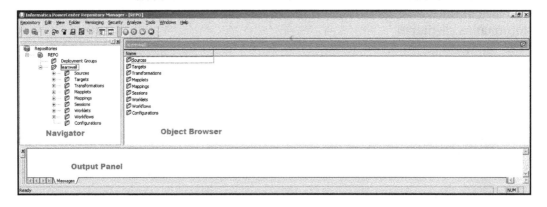

As you can notice, the screen is divided into sections that we discussed when we talked about Designer and Workflow Manager Screen.

The Navigator of Repository Manager consists of all the components such as sources, targets, mappings, workflows, and so on as seen in the previous screenshot. It contains all the components of Designer and Workflow Manager.

As mentioned previously, Repository Manager serves two purposes: one is the Client Server Configuration, and the and other is Deployment or Migration.

We already covered Client Configuration in Chapter 1, *Downloading and Extracting Informatica PowerCenter software* when we learned how to install and configure the server.

# Take me to the next stage - Deployment or Migration

One of the most important phases of any software project is deployment or some migration. Repository Manager provides a convenient way to migrate the code from one environment to another. As you are aware, we have three different environments for migration. Usually, we refer to them as DEV for development environment, TEST for testing environment, and PROD for production. DEV is the environment where you actually develop the code. You perform the unit testing, and then you migrate the code to TEST environment where the testing team performs the testing on the code to evaluate whether everything is running as per requirements. Once tested, the code is migrated to PROD where it actually goes live. When we wish to migrate the code, we need to make sure all the components along with their properties are migrated properly. We need to migrate all the sources, targets, mappings, workflows, and session tasks used in the code. Transformations and tasks get migrated along with mappings and workflows. So, you need not migrate them separately. Also, if your code uses parameter files or Unix shell scripts, you need to migrate them though the parameter file, and Unix scripts are migrated separately and not migrated from the Informatica client tool.

To migrate the sources, targets, and mappings, you can use PowerCenter Designer, and to migrate the session tasks and workflows, you can use PowerCenter Workflow Manager. Repository Manager can migrate all the components in one go for you.

Informatica PowerCenter provides three ways to migrate the code from one environment to another: Export/Import, Copy/paste, and Drag/Drop.

Let's talk about all the options.

# Export/Import

You can perform the Export/Import functionality from PowerCenter Designer or Workflow Manager Screen. Whenever you export the components, Informatica creates the .XML file for those components. Similarly, you can import the components if those are available as .XML files. Any export/import operation will happen in the .XML format. You can view the file in the XML editor and, in fact, change the file before you import the file. The code will be imported with the changes you made in the file. Ideally, you should not change the exported file for consistency issues across different environments.

To complete the migration, you export the components from one repository and import to another repository. A similar approach can be used to migrate code from one folder to another in the same repository.

## Migrating from Designer

Before we proceed, note that we can migrate only those components that are present in the PowerCenter Designer screen. To migrate the components, perform the following steps:

1. Open Designer, and from Navigator, select the component you wish to migrate. Go to **Repository | Export Objects**. We selected a mapping **m_UNION** for reference in this book as shown in the following screenshot. When you export a mapping, corresponding sources, targets, and transformations get exported. Similarly. when you export a workflow from Workflow Manager, all the tasks present in the workflow get exported. So, you need not separately export all the components.

We are exporting the components from the `learnwell` folder:

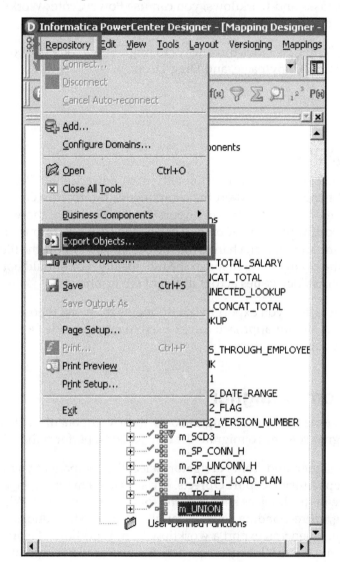

2. A new pop-up window will ask you to browse the location to save the `.XML` file. Specify the location, and click on **OK**.

Informatica will start the export process, and once done, you will get the description of the process. It will show the details of the components exported. Also, if it encountered any error, those will be mentioned. Refer to the following screenshot as a sample:

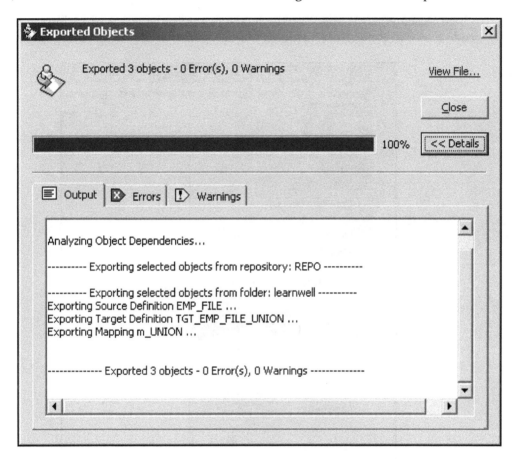

With this, the export process is complete, and you will be able to see the component at the specified location.

Once you are done with the export process, you are all set to import the file to get the components in another Repository or folder. We will be importing the mapping in the `learn` folder. Perform the following steps to import mappings:

1. Open Designer, and connect to the repository or folder you wish to import the code to. Go to **Repository | Import Objects** as shown in the following screenshot:

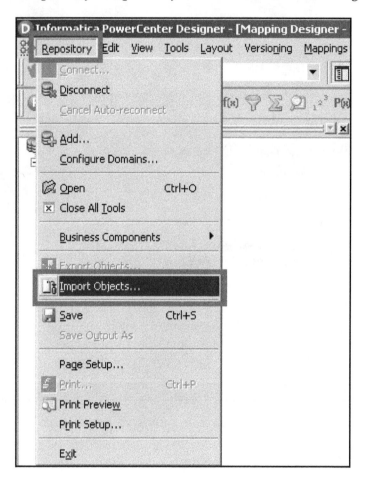

2. A new window will pop up asking you to browse the .XML file that you saved while exporting the code. Select the location where you wish to save the file, and click **Next**:

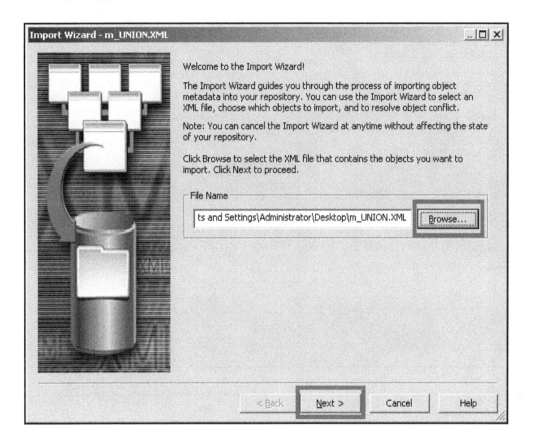

3. In the next step, you need to add the components to the new repository by clicking on **Add** as shown in the following screenshot. Click on **Next**:

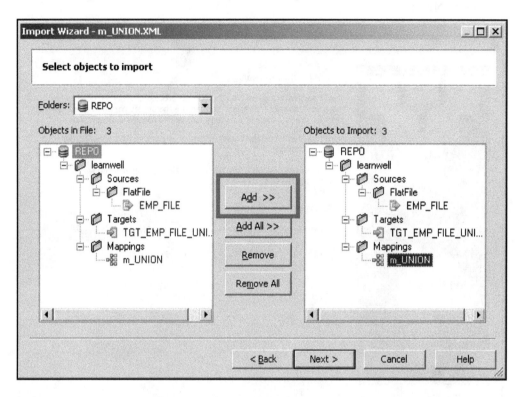

4. In the next window, you will be able to see whether there are any conflicts with the new code being migrated. If there are any conflicts, check the conflicts, else click on **Import** to allow the import process to finish:

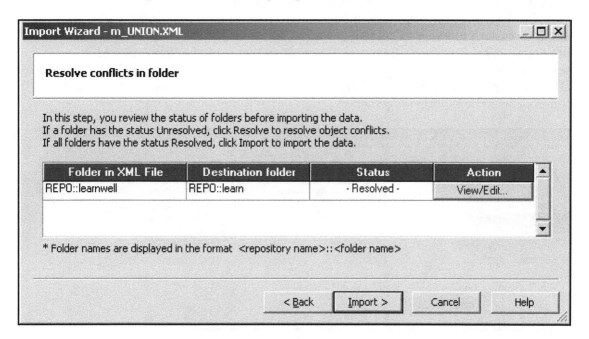

With this, the export and import process is complete for the Designer components. Similar to this, perform the migration for Workflow Manager components. When you migrate components from Designer and Workflow Manager, you get two .XML files: one for Designer mapping and another for Workflow Manager Workflow. You will need to import the .XML file for mapping before you import the .XML file for the workflow since the mappings are associated in the session task. So, if your mapping is not available, importing the workflow with the session task will be invalid.

# Migrating from Repository Manager

When you migrate the code from Repository Manger, you need not separately migrate mapping and workflow. Repository Manager lets you migrate complete components at once. So, the advantage of migrating the code from Repository Manager is that it saves time and is an easier process. You get only one .XML file instead of two files as seen in the previous section. To export all the components together from the Repository Manager, select the workflow related to your code in the Navigator, and go to **Repository | Export Objects** as shown in the following screenshot. Selecting the workflow will allow all the components to be exported together.

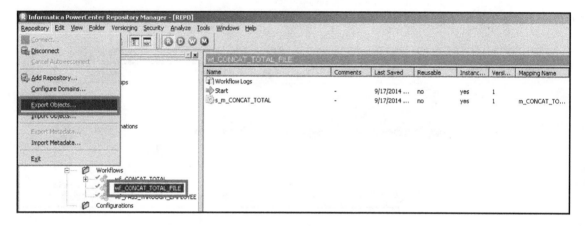

Follow the process similar to that mentioned in the preceding section to complete the migration. You will get a file at the specified location with all the code components migrated in one go.

Use the same file to import the component. When you import the file, Informatica puts the mapping-related components under Designer and the workflow-related components under Workflow Manager.

# Copy/Paste

Another way to achieve the migration functionality is to copy/paste or drag/drop the components. This is another way in which you can achieve the migration.

To copy the code, select the required component in the Navigator from the repository or Folder, and go to **Edit | Copy** in the toolbar. The components get copied as shown in the following screenshot:

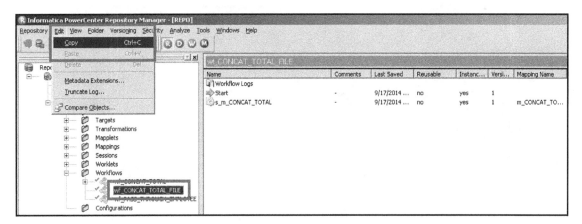

Open the Repository or folder where you wish to paste, and click on **Edit | Paste** (the screenshot is similar to the previous one, just the paste option will be highlighted). Informatica will paste the code, and this is another way you can achieve the migration process.

# Drag/Drop

Before we talk about this feature, let's take a look at the difference between the Connect and Open options. You must have noticed the Connect and Open option when you connect to your folder under repository in the Navigator as shown in the following screenshot.

The difference between Connect and Open is that Connect only connects you to the Repository so that you can view the components present in the folder, but Open allows you to actually use those components in the Workspace. When you click on **Connect**, you do not get the Workspace. But when you click on **Open**, Informatica performs the connect operation and also makes workspace available in your folder, so any coding done in the workspace will be done inside the folder opened. The folder that is open is shown at the top left corner of the screen as shown in the following screenshot:

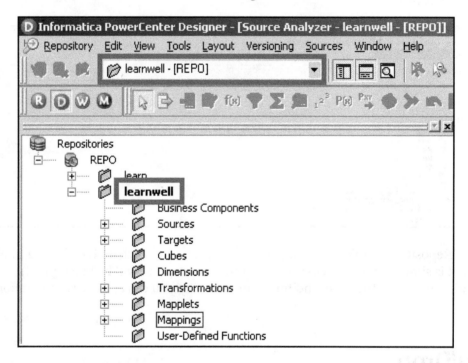

To migrate the code using the Drag and Drop feature, perform the following steps:

1. Connect to the repository or folder from where you wish to migrate the code. We have connected to the `learnwell` folder.

2. Open the Repository or folder where you wish to migrate the code. Click on **Open** to get the workspace assigned to the folder. We opened the `learn` folder.

3. Drag the required component from the connected folder to the opened folder. We are dragging from `learnwell` to the `learn` folder.

4. A pop-up window will ask you to confirm whether you wish to copy the code. Click on **OK**.

With this simple method, your code will get copied from one folder to another. As mentioned earlier, you can drag and drop the components across repositories also. We are done with the migration of the code. This is the beauty of the Informatica tool, the simplicity in the processing.

We saw various options from migration, but the best one recommended is using the export/import feature. When you use the copy/paste or drag/drop feature, there are chances that some of the properties in the code may get missed. There are not known instances where the code missed the properties. Hence, it's always recommended that you use the export/import functionality using the Repository Manager to complete the migration.

# Summary

In this chapter, you learned the very important aspect of Informatica, that is migration. We saw the various ways in which we can achieve the migration. We also saw the configuration part of the client tools with the server components.

In the next chapter, we will discuss another very important aspect of Informatica tool--the performance tuning.

# 12
# Optimization - Performance Tuning

Standing at the last chapter, you must be very clear with all the components and features of the Informatica tool. As with any other technology related to data, we need to understand the performance tuning of Informatica as well. It is necessary to follow the best practices to achieve the best performance out of your code. Similar to SQL tuning, which is done to enhance the performance of SQL query, we do performance tuning on Informatica. If you follow the best practices of Informatica, your code will be automatically tuned. There are many best practices that are recommended by Informatica-many of which we have already discussed in previous chapters. We will be talking about those best practices under this chapter as well to understand how to use them in order to achieve better performance.

When we talk about performance tuning, you need to find out the issues in your code called bottlenecks. The regular process is to first find out the bottlenecks and then eliminate them to enhance the performance.

We will discuss various components that need to be tuned to enhance the process. In the next section, we will talk about identifying bottlenecks at various components. We will also talk about eliminating the bottlenecks.

## Bottlenecks

As mentioned, we can have bottlenecks at various stages of the Informatica PowerCenter code. Don't be in a rush to find all the bottlenecks and eliminate them together. Try to find the first bottleneck, resolve it, and then jump to another.

# Finding the target bottleneck

Always consider checking the bottlenecks at the target side first. There can be various reasons for bottlenecks at the target. First, we need to know how to find the target bottleneck.

# Using thread statistics

Thread statistics are a part of the session log. When you run the workflow, the session log generates the thread statistics, which can provide you with information about the bottlenecks present in Source, Target, or Transformation. Thread statistics give information about the total runtime, idle time, and busy percentage of Source, Target, and Transformation.

Thread statistics consist of Reader thread, Writer thread, and Transformation thread. Reader thread gives information related to the total runtime, idle time, and busy percentage of the sources in the mapping. Writer thread gives information about the total runtime, idle time, and busy percentage of targets in the mapping. Similarly, Transformation thread gives information related to transformations in the mapping, as indicated in the following sample thread statistics:

***** RUN INFO FOR TGT LOAD ORDER GROUP [1] *****

Thread [ READER_1_1_1 ] created for [ the read stage ] of partition point [ SQ_EMPLOYEES ] has completed.

Total Run Time = [ 100.11 ] Secs

Total Idle Time = [ 90.101 ] Secs

Busy Percentage = [ 10.888141628 ]

Thread [ TRANSFORMATION_1_1_1 ] created for [ the transformation stage ] of partition point [ SQ_EMPLOYEES ] has completed.

Total Run Time = [ 123.11 ] Secs

Total Idle Time = [ 100.23 ] Secs

Busy Percentage = [ 18.585005278 ]

Thread [ WRITER_1_1_1 ] created for [ the target stage ] of partition point [ TGT_EMPLOYEES ] has completed.

Total Run Time = [ 130.11 ] Secs

Total Idle Time = [ 1.23 ] Secs

Busy Percentage = [ 99.054646069 ]

Writer thread is busy for 99 percent as compared to Reader and Transformation. We can say that, in this case, the Target is the bottleneck. Similarly, you can identify if the source or transformation has bottlenecks.

## Configuring the sample target load

It is a simple understanding that loading data in the target table will take more time as compared to loading data in the target file. Consider that you are loading data in the target table in your mapping, configuring a sample run, and trying to load the same data in a test target file. Check the difference in the runtime of both the processes. If there is a significant difference, you can easily say that the database target table has the bottleneck.

## Eliminating the target bottleneck

There are various ways in which you can optimize the target loading.

## Minimizing target table deadlocks

There can be a scenario when Informatica is trying to load data in a table that is already being used by another system. When Informatica encounters the deadlock, it hampers the processing by slowing the loading process. To avoid this, make sure that the target table is not being used by other processes at the same time.

## Dropping indexes and constraints

Loading data in the table takes more time because there are multiple indexes and constraints created on the table. Each time a new record is loaded in the table, it is first checked for indexes and constraints. This hampers the performance. To avoid this, you can use pre-SQL and post-SQL commands in the Session task. Using pre-SQL commands, you can remove the indexes, and using post-SQL, you can apply the indexes. When you define pre-SQL and post-SQL, Informatica applies those commands before and after the data is loaded in the table.

Removing the indexes and constraints is not always recommended, but it definitely improves the performance. You can opt for this option if the data that you are loading is not very critical.

## Increasing the checkpoint interval

When you run the workflow, the integration service keeps on creating checkpoints at predefined intervals. The checkpoints are used for recovery purposes. Reducing the checkpoint interval will help enhance the performance by storing less checkpoints and storing less data related to checkpoints.

If you reduce the checkpoint interval, even though the performance will increase, it will hamper the recovery time if the system fails with some error.

## Using an external loader

Informatica PowerCenter supports the usage of multiple external loaders (IBM DB2, Oracle, Teradata, and Sybase IQ), which can help in loading data in the target table faster. To add the external loader, open Workflow Manager, and click on **Connection | Loader**, as shown in the following screenshot:

In the next screen, select the loader based on your requirement:

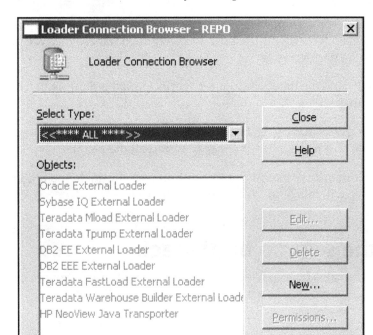

This will help in enhancing the performance by loading the data at a faster pace in the target.

## Increasing the network packet size

Every table has a capacity, referred to as Network Packet size, with which it can accept data. If you increase the packet size, the table can accept greater volumes of data.

These properties can be enhanced by a database administrator. Consult your database admin team.

# Using bulk load

By configuring the session properties to use the bulk load, your performance can be significantly enhanced. When you use bulk loading, the database logs are not created; this, in turn, enhances the performance.

However, if you disable the database log, recovery cannot be done as there is no log of the events on the database.

As you can notice, performance can be achieved by compromising on some other factors. You need to decide and make a fine balance between all the factors.

These were the various ways in which you can find and eliminate the target bottleneck. In the next section, we will talk about the source bottleneck.

# Finding the source bottleneck

The performance can also be impacted at the source side. Various factors can hamper the performance at the source side as we have discussed at the target side.

## Using thread statistics

As discussed under the *Finding the target bottleneck* section, use thread statistics to find the source bottleneck. Refer to that section to use thread statistics.

## Test mapping

Using a passthrough mapping can help you identify if the bottleneck is at the source side. Configure a test mapping to have only source, source qualifier, and target. Consider that you have a mapping with one source, one target, and ten transformations; the time taken to process the data through mapping is 60 seconds. This means that combining the source, target, and transformation is taking 60 seconds. Create another mapping by eliminating all the transformations and run the process and check the time. Suppose that now the time taken to complete the process is 50 seconds. As compared to the combined time of target and transformation, which is 10 seconds, 50 seconds is relatively high, which can indicate we have a source bottleneck.

## Using filter transformation

You can use a filter transformation to check whether the source has a bottleneck. Put a filter transformation in front of the Source Qualifier and set the condition to False; that is, don't allow any record to pass through the filter ahead in the mapping. Using this method, you can compare the runtime of the process with and without the filter condition. This way, you can identify if the source has a bottleneck.

## Checking the database query

This is another simple method to find the source bottleneck if you are extracting the data from the table. When you use the source qualifier to read the data from the database table, the integration service writes a query to extract the data. Copy the query and run the same query at the database level in SQL developer or a similar tool. Compare the time taken by the query to execute at both places, which can give you an idea if the source has a bottleneck.

# Eliminating the source bottleneck

There are various ways in which you can optimize the source. They are discussed as follows.

## Increasing the network packet size

As discussed under the *Eliminating the target bottleneck* section, increasing the network packet size of the table will allow greater volumes of data to pass the network at the particular instance.

These properties can be enhanced by the database administrator. Consult your database admin team to increase the network packet size.

## Optimizing the database query

When you read the data from the database table, the integration service generates a query to extract the data from the table. You can fine-tune the query to extract only the required data. If you extract all the data and then add filter or other transformations, it will hamper the performance. You can tune the query to extract only the required data, which will save time and help in performance enhancement. This is called SQL override.

These were the various ways in which you can find and eliminate the source bottleneck. In the next section, we will talk about the mapping and transformation bottleneck.

# Finding the mapping bottleneck

If you don't have a source or target bottleneck, you can have mapping or transformation bottlenecks.

## Using thread statistics

As discussed under the *Finding the target bottleneck* section, use thread statistics to find the transformation bottleneck. Refer to that section to use thread statistics.

## Using filter transformation

You can use a filter transformation to check whether transformation or mapping has a bottleneck. Put a filter transformation before the target and set the condition to False; that is, don't allow any record to pass to the target. Using this method, you can compare the runtime of the process with and without the filter condition. This way, you can identify if the transformations have bottlenecks.

# Eliminating the mapping bottleneck

There are various ways in which you can optimize the transformations and mapping.

## Using single pass mapping

Consider a scenario where you have multiple targets to load from the same source; in such a scenario, avoid creating multiple mapping. You can save significant time by loading multiple targets in the same mapping. Use a single source and pass the data to different pipelines and then to multiple targets. This way, you can save the time of reading the same data multiple times in multiple mappings.

# Avoiding data type conversions

Avoid changing the data types across the transformations in the mapping. When you change the data type, the integration service takes time for the processing. It is always recommended that you should not change data types wherever not required.

# Unchecking unnecessary ports

Passing unnecessary data through the mapping will hamper the performance. It is recommended that if you do not need certain data, disable the output port of the column so that you don't pass the data.

# Processing numeric data

The integration service processes numeric data faster compared to other data. Try to process as much numeric data as possible.

# Using operators instead of functions

The integration service processes operators faster compared to functions. For example, consider using | | (pipe) in place of the CONCAT function to concatenate the data.

# Using Decode in place of multiple IIF

If your logic contains multiple **Informatica Inbuilt function** (**IIF**) functions, try replacing them using DECODE. The decode function is faster compared to multiple IIFs.

# Tracing level

The tracing level defines how much detailed information you wish to write to the session log. When you run the process, the integration service writes the information about the run in the session log. Setting a proper tracing level will help in improving the performance.

# Using variable ports

If you are performing the same operation multiple times in a transformation, consider calculating the value in a variable port and use the variable port value multiple times in the transformation. Suppose you need to convert the first name and last name to uppercase, concatenate them, and need to cut part of the data. In place of using the UPPER function every time, use the variable port to convert data to uppercase and use the variable port to perform other operations. This way, you save time of performing the save operation multiple times.

# Optimizing filter transformation

You can use filter transformation as early as possible in the mapping to avoid processing unnecessary data. If you filter unwanted records early in the mapping, you can enhance the performance.

Similarly, using Router transformation in place of multiple filter transformations will have help save time.

# Optimizing Aggregator transformation

Always pass sorted data to Aggregator transformation to enhance the performance. When you pass the sorted data, the integration service needs to save less data in the cache, which helps in enhancement of performance.

You can also improve performance of Aggregator transformation by doing group by numeric columns. For example, consider grouping the data on department ID in place of location. It is possible to do this only as per your business requirement.

Use incremental aggregation whenever possible in the session properties to enhance the performance. When you use incremental aggregation, the performance is improved as aggregator transformation now needs to calculate lesser records.

# Optimizing joiner transformation

It is recommended to assign the table with lesser number of records as master while using joiner transformation. A table with lesser number of duplicates should be used as the master table.

It is also recommended to perform joining in the source qualifier using SQL override as performing joins on the database is sometimes faster compared to performing in Informatica.

Additionally, pass the sorted data to joiner transformation to enhance the performance as this utilizes less disk space compared to unsorted data.

# Optimizing lookup transformation

Lookup transformations are one of the complex transformations in Informatica PowerCenter. Optimizing lookups will significantly help in improving the performance.

When you use lookup transformation in the mapping, use the concurrent cache. When you use concurrent cache, the integration service caches the lookup table data before it starts processing the data from the source; otherwise, lookup performs cache on row-wise basis, which utilizes more time. So it is recommended that you enable caching when you use lookup.

If your mapping contains multiple lookups that look up on the same lookup table, it is suggested you share the cache in order to avoid performing caching multiple times.

You can reduce the processing time if you use lookup SQL override properly in the lookup transformation. If you are using lookup to look up on the database table, you can use the lookup SQL override to reduce the amount of data that you look up. This also helps in saving the cache space.

If you are using more than one lookup condition in lookup transformation, it is recommended that you place the conditions in an optimized order; that is, place the equal to (=) condition first, then less than (<), greater than (>), less than or equal to (<=), greater than or equal to (>=), and at last, Not equal to (!=). This enhances the performance.

These were the various ways in which you can find and eliminate the mapping and transformations bottlenecks. In the next section, we will talk about the session bottleneck.

# Eliminating the session bottleneck

If you do not have source, target, and mapping bottlenecks, you can check for session properties for bottlenecks.

## Optimizing the commit interval

Commit interval is the number of records after which the integration service commits the data into the target. Selecting an appropriate commit interval will help in enhancing the performance. If you select a low value as the commit interval, it will make the integration service commit data more number of times, which will hamper the performance.

## Buffer memory

When you run the workflow, the integration service needs to allocate blocks of memory to hold the data at various stages of processing, including cache if required. Make sure that you have sufficient buffer memory available for the processing; otherwise, the integration service fails the process because of lack of memory.

## Performance data

Session properties allow you to store the performance-related details in the repository. If you select to save the performance details, the integration service writes the log to the repository. This will consume processing time. Make sure that you are not checking the option if you do not require to save the performance details.

# Eliminating the system bottleneck

The last step in performance enhancement you can try is to find the bottlenecks in the system. Eliminating the system bottleneck may not be in your control; you can contact your admin team to improve the system capabilities to enhance the system performance.

You can add multiple CPUs to make the process run faster or make the session run in parallel.

You can check with the admin team if the network is working properly at the optimized speed to confirm if the processing is optimized.

Contact your admin team to add extra memory if the buffer memory or cache memory is not sufficient. Adding extra space may save processing time if your cache memory requirements are more.

Using these performance rules, you can make your process optimized. After taking care of all these rules, if you feel your system is not utilized fully, you can make use of partitioning.

# Working on partitioning

Before we discuss partitioning, make a note that partitioning is a high availability feature that you need to purchase separately from Informatica. If you enable high availability features, you can make use of the partitioning functionality.

By default, a mapping containing source, target, and transformations has a single partition. A single partition means that a single record can flow from the source to target at a time. By adding multiple partitions, you logically divide the mapping into multiple sections-each section can pass a record at a time. So if you make three partitions in the mapping, three records can pass through the mapping, making your runtime reduced by one third. When you add a partition at any stage of the mapping, the integration service adds partitions at other stages of the mapping. You need to make sure that you have sufficient memory space and system capacity to handle the processing of multiple records at a time.

If you have 1,000 records to process and you created four partitions, the integration service will process four records at a time and the total time required to process 1,000 records will be reduced to a fourth.

To enable partitions, you need to set the partitioning properties in the Session task.

# Partitioning properties

To enable partitioning, you need to define the following attributes.

# Partition points

You can define the partition points in a pipeline. By default, the integration service sets partitions at various transformations. You can define the partition at any stage in the mapping.

# Number of partitions

Based on your system capability, you can increase or decrease the partitions. When you add a partition at any stage of the pipeline, the integration service adds the same number of partitions at other stages of the mapping. The number of partitions in a mapping should be equal to the number of database connections at the source and target side. When you create partitions, the integration service processes the data concurrently. Suppose you create three partitions; the integration service reads three records from the source, passes three records to transformations, and concurrently loads three records to the target.

# Partition types

Informatica supports multiple types of partitions to distribute the data. Partition types control how you wish to divide the data among the partitions that you created in the mapping. If you have high availability features, you can define the type of partitions at different stages of the mapping. You can define the type of partitioning in Session properties. Different types of partitions are mentioned as follows:

- **Pass-through:** In the pass-through type, the integration service does not distribute the data among partitions. The data in the particular partition stays in the partition after passing through the partition point.
- **Round-robin:** In round-robin partitioning, the integration service distributes the data evenly among the partitions. This makes equal amounts of data pass through each partition.
- **Key range:** In key range partitioning, the integration service distributes the data on the basis of ports or set or ports defined. You also define the range of value for each port. When the source and target are partitioned by key range, select this type of partitioning.
- **Database partition:** This type of partitioning is possible with Oracle or DB2 database. When you select database partitioning, the integration service reads the partitioning information from the nodes in the database.
- **Hash auto-keys:** In hash auto-key partitioning, the integration service divides the data based on the partition key using the hash function. All the grouped and sorted ports in transformations are used as partition keys. This type of partition can be used in Rank, Sorter, and Aggregator transformations.
- **Hash user keys:** Similar to hash auto-keys, the integration service in this partitioning uses the hash function to partition the data. You need to manually define the number of ports for the partition key.

# Pushdown optimization

Pushdown optimization is a concept using which you can push the transformation logic at the source or target database side. When you have the database table as the source, you can make use of SQL override to remove the logic written in the transformation. When you use SQL override, session performance is enhanced as processing the data at the database level is faster compared to processing the data in Informatica. You cannot remove all the transformations from the mapping. The part of transformation logic that can be pushed at source or target level is referred to as pushdown optimization.

Consider that you have a mapping with a sequence indicated as follows:

Source - Source Qualifier - Filter - Sorter - Aggregator - Expression - Lookup - Rank - Target

In filter transformation, we are filtering the data on a particular location. In sorter transformation, the data is sorted on a particular department ID. In aggregator, we are grouping the data on department ID. In expression transformation, the unconnected lookup transformation is called using the :LKP function, and finally, rank is used to get the top salaried employee in the target.

We can remove the filter transformation, sorter transformation, and aggregator transformation by adding the WHERE clause, ORDER BY clause, and GROUP BY clause, respectively, in the SQL override in the source qualifier transformation. We cannot remove expression transformation as we cannot write the :LKP function in SQL override.

So our mapping becomes simple after using SQL override indicated as follows:

Source - Source Qualifier - Expression - Lookup - Rank - Target

Pushdown optimization will help in saving the processing time by extracting lesser numbers of records of data from the source and also by processing lesser number of records in the transformations.

# Summary

In this chapter, we talked about various techniques using which you can enhance the performance. We talked about source, target, and transformation bottlenecks. Even after optimizing your source, target, and mapping, your performance is not up to date, then take a look at your session and system bottlenecks. We also slooked at various ways of optimizing the components of the PowerCenter tool. Later, we discussed partitioning and pushdown optimization, using which you can enhance the performance.

With this, we have completed all the concepts of the Informatica PowerCenter tool. In this book, you have learned concepts that are useful for beginner- and intermediate-level experience in the Informatica tool. We have also touched on a lot of advance-level concepts in this book. With some more practice and theory exposure, you will be able to clear the first level in the Informatica Power Center certification.

# Index

## P

parameter file
  about 344, 345
  creating 351
  defining, at session level 352, 354
  defining, at workflow level 352
parameters
  about 344
  using 205, 206, 207
parent workflow 296
partitioning
  about 399
  enabling 399
  properties 399
partitions
  database partition 400
  hash auto-keys 400
  hash user keys 400
  key range 400
  pass-through 400
  round-robin 400
  types 400
persistent cache 182
ports, in transformation 123, 124
ports, Lookup transformation
  input port 165
  lookup port 165
  output port 165
  return port 165
predefined event 328
prerequisites, Informatica PowerCenter
  database 16
  operating system 16
  system requisites 16
pushdown optimization 401

## Q

Queue Connection 290

## R

Rank Index option 140
rank transformation
  about 137, 138
  Group by Ranking feature 140

Rank Index option 140
Relational Connection 290
relational database tables
  working with 78, 79
relational tables
  data, previewing in 109
Repository Manager
  client authentication 62, 63, 64, 65, 68
  code, migrating from 382
  using 373, 374
repository services 41
repository
  about 41
  creating 44, 45, 46, 48, 49
reusable transformation 196
router transformation 136

## S

SCD1 mapping
  transformations 222
SCD1
  about 213
  implementing 217, 218, 219, 220, 221, 222
SCD2 (date range)
  implementing 242, 243, 244, 245, 246, 247,
  248
  transformations 250, 251
SCD2 (flag)
  implementing, by maintaining history 232, 233,
  234, 235, 236, 237, 238, 239
SCD2 mapping
  transformations 230, 240
SCD2
  date range 215
  FLAG 214
  implementing 224, 225, 226, 227, 228, 229,
  230
  version number 214
SCD3
  about 215, 216
  implementing 252, 253, 254, 255, 256, 257
  transformations 259
SCD
  type 1 dimension mapping (SCD1) 211
  type 2 dimension/effective date range mapping